HERMANN & VALENTINY AND PARTNERS

JETZT | NOW
HERMANN & VALENTINY AND PARTNERS

Von | by Liesbeth Waechter-Böhm
Vorwort von | foreword by Massimiliano Fuksas

Birkhäuser – Publishers for Architecture | Verlag für Architektur
Basel · Boston · Berlin

JETZT | NOW
HERMANN & VALENTINY AND PARTNERS

Diese Publikation wurde unterstützt von:
KALLCO Projekt, A-1050 Wien
GESIBA Gemeinn. Siedlungs- und Bau-AG, A-1010 Wien

A CIP catalogue record for this book is available from the Library of Congress, Washington D.C., USA.

Deutsche Bibliothek Cataloging-in-Publication Data
Hermann & Valentiny and Partners : now - jetzt / Liesbeth Waechter-Böhm. [Transl. from German into English: Roderick O'Donovan]. - Basel ; Boston ; Berlin : Birkhäuser, 2001
ISBN 3-7643-6337-1

This work is subject to copyright. All rights are reserved, whether the whole or part of the material is concerned, specifically the rights of translation, reprinting, re-use of illustrations, recitation, broadcasting, reproduction on microfilms or in other ways, and storage in data bases. For any kind of use, permission of the copyright owner must be obtained.

© 2001 Birkhäuser – Publishers for Architecture, P.O. Box 133, CH-4010 Basel, Switzerland.
http://www.birkhauser.ch
Member of the BertelsmannSpringer Publishing Group
Printed on acid-free paper produced from chlorine-free pulp. TCF ∞

Translation from German into English Roderick O'Donovan, Vienna
Graphic Design A|H Haller, Vienna
Printed by Grasl Druck und Neue Medien, Bad Vöslau, Austria

ISBN 3-7643-6337-1

9 8 7 6 5 4 3 2 1

INHALT | CONTENTS

8	Hubert Hermann & François Valentiny Massimiliano Fuksas
11	Jetzt	Now Liesbeth Waechter-Böhm

BAUTEN UND PROJEKTE | BUILDINGS AND PROJECTS

26	Architekturbüro Remerschen-Luxemburg Architects' office Remerschen-Luxembourg
32	Architekturbüro Wien-Wieden Architects' office Vienna-Wieden
38	Stadtteilzentrum Halle-Neustadt, Deutschland Urban district centre in Halle-Neustadt, Germany
54	Philharmonie auf dem Kirchberg, Luxemburg-Stadt The Philharmonic building on the Kirchberg, Luxembourg-City
58	Musiktheater in Linz, Oberösterreich Music theatre Linz, Upper Austria
62	Weingut an der Mosel, Luxemburg Winery on the Moselle, Luxembourg
68 69	Perfektastrasse	Steinergasse	Telefonweg Wohnbau in der Perfektastraße, Wien-Liesing Housing development on Perfektastrasse, Vienna-Liesing
77	Wohnbau in der Steinergasse, Wien-Liesing Housing development on Steinergasse, Vienna-Liesing
82	Reihenhäuser am Telefonweg, Wien-Donaustadt Terrace houses on Telefonweg, Vienna-Donaustadt
88	Bankgebäude auf dem Kirchberg, Luxemburg-Stadt Bank building on the Kirchberg, Luxembourg-City
92	Einfamilienhaus in Klosterneuburg, Niederösterreich Single family house in Klosterneuburg, Lower Austria
100	Einfamilienhaus in Wien Single family house in Vienna
106	Umbau eines Einfamilienhauses in Großau, Niederösterreich Redesign of a single family house in Grossau, Lower Austria
110	Gasometer in Wien-Simmering Gasometer in Vienna-Simmering
114	Büro-, Geschäfts- und Gewerbebauten Modecenterstraße, Wien-Simmering Office, retail and commercial buildings, Modecenterstrasse, Vienna-Simmering
118	Gemeindezentrum in Bech-Kleinmacher, Luxemburg Town council building in Bech-Kleinmacher, Luxembourg
124	Umbau und Aufstockung Gemeindehaus in Dalheim, Luxemburg Redesign and addition of a storey to the council building in Dalheim, Luxembourg
130	Museumsum- und Zubau in Luxemburg-Stadt Reorganisation of and extension to a museum in Luxembourg-City
132	Geschäft in Wien-Innenstadt Shop in Vienna's Inner City
136	Galerie Rackey in Bad Honnef, Deutschland Gallery Rackey in Bad Honnef, Germany
139	Galerie Clairefontaine und Wohnung in Luxemburg-Stadt Gallery Clairefontaine and apartment in Luxembourg-City
146	Kindertagesstätte in Bettemburg, Luxemburg Children's day care centre in Bettembourg, Luxembourg
156	Kaufhaus in Wien-Favoriten Department store in Vienna-Favoriten
160	Um- und Zubau eines Gymnasiums in Diekirch, Luxemburg Redesign of and extension to a secondary school in Diekirch, Luxembourg
170	Volksschule, Vorschule und Kindergarten in Schüttrange, Luxemburg Primary school, pre-school and nursery school in Schüttrange, Luxembourg
174	Einfamilienhaus in Sanem, Luxemburg Single family house in Sanem, Luxembourg
180	Einfamilienhaus in Remich, Luxemburg Single family house in Remich, Luxembourg
186	Einfamilienhaus in Wellenstein, Luxemburg Single family house in Wellenstein, Luxembourg
190	Schwimmbad in Bonnevoie, Luxemburg-Stadt Public swimming pool in Bonnevoie, Luxembourg-City
194 195	Kirchberg	Dudelange	Dessau-Ziebigk Wohnbauten auf dem Kirchberg, Luxemburg-Stadt Housing development on the Kirchberg, Luxembourg-City
200	Wohnbau in Dudelange, Luxemburg Housing development in Dudelange, Luxembourg
206	Wohnanlage in Dessau-Ziebigk, Deutschland Housing development in Dessau-Ziebigk, Germany
212	Wohnen und Arbeiten am Höchstädtplatz in Wien-Brigittenau Living and Working on Höchstädtplatz in Vienna-Brigittenau
216	Neuorganisation des Bahnhofsareals Esch/Alzette, Luxemburg Reorganisation of the area around Esch-sur-Alzette railway station, Luxembourg
220	Seniorenresidenz und Hotel in Köln, Deutschland Senior citizens home and hotel in Cologne, Germany

230	Bauten	Buildings
231	Projekte	Projects Wettbewerbe	Competitions
233	Veröffentlichungen	Publications
236	Bücher	Books Ausstellungen	Exhibitions Vorträge	Lectures / Seminare	Seminars
237	Biografien	Biographies
238	Mitarbeiter/innen	Assistants
239	Fotonachweis	Photo credits

HUBERT HERMANN & FRANÇOIS VALENTINY

Hermann & Valentiny sind Repräsentanten einer Generation, die die Schwierigkeiten und „Befürchtungen" aller ideologischen Bindungen hinter sich gelassen hat. Ende der siebziger Jahre hatte sich diese Generation aus Mangel an verständigen privaten und öffentlichen Auftraggebern einem Vorhaben verschrieben, in dem die Architektur, da sie zu keinem baulichen Ausdruck finden konnte, sich gänzlich auf sich selbst bezog. Es war die Zeit der „Idiosynkrasien" und der „Worte".

Die achtziger Jahre haben überraschend, aber entschieden dazu beigetragen, dass wieder Hoffnung geschöpft und in der Folge eine Reihe von Arbeiten realisiert werden konnte. Eine Unzahl von jungen Architekten konnte nun die Freude am „Bauen" genießen.

In den darauf folgenden Jahren wurden die vorerst sporadischen Bauaufträge immer zahlreicher; die Architekten erlangten technische Versiertheit, Sicherheit und ein Gespür für Qualität in den Details.

Nach den ersten Arbeiten, die mit ihrem Streben nach geometrisch komplexen Flächen und Fassaden noch stark von einer literarischen Bildung geprägt waren, gelangten Hermann & Valentiny Ende der neunziger Jahre zu Realisierungen von großer Intensität, deren „Botschaft" (die immer schon in ihren Arbeiten präsent ist) mit wachsender Kohärenz vermittelt wird. Der Entwurf entwickelt sich von innen nach außen und gewinnt an Bedeutung sowohl was die Dimensionen als auch das Volumen betrifft: vom Schnitt bis zur äußersten Haut, die das Gebäude von der Landschaft oder dem Kontext trennt.

Als ich ihr Büro in der wogenden Hügel- und Waldlandschaft Luxemburgs, quasi an der deutschen Grenze gelegen, besuchte, wurde mir die Beziehung zumindest eines der Partner, François Valentinys, zu seiner Heimat und der nicht-urbanen Kultur klar.

Zwischen Weinbergen, die einen köstlichen und aromatischen Weißwein hervorbringen, wirkt das Atelier fast wie eine natürliche Erweiterung des bestehenden Gebäudes. Die außergewöhnliche Sorgfalt, mit der hier das Tageslicht eingefangen, gebündelt und gestreut wird, ist denn auch für einen Großteil der Arbeiten des Gemeinschaftsbüros kennzeichnend.

Ihr kluger Einsatz des Materials und ihre Fähigkeit, auf die Veränderlichkeit des Lichtes zu reagieren, zeugt von beachtlicher Sensibilität, aber auch von außerordentlichem technischen Geschick. Die Details sind in letzter Zeit einfacher geworden und haben an Emphase verloren zu Gunsten der Gesamtarchitektur.

Die Arbeiten in Deutschland, Österreich und Luxemburg, wo beide studiert, gelehrt und über viele Jahre hinweg gebaut haben, bezeugen ihr beständiges Engagement als Architekten und Handwerker, die mit großem Vergnügen ihre reiche Kreativität weiterentwickeln.

Man kann ziemlich sicher sein, dass Hubert Hermann und François Valentiny in den kommenden Jahren durch weitere qualitätvolle Werke angenehm überraschen werden.

Massimiliano Fuksas

HUBERT HERMANN & FRANÇOIS VALENTINY

Hermann & Valentiny represent a generation that has left all ideological straitjackets and "angst" behind it. At the end of the seventies this generation, due to a lack of understanding private or public clients, devoted itself completely to the move towards an entirely self-contained architecture. This was the time of "idiosyncrasy" and "language".

However, this situation began to change quite unexpectedly but decisively in the eighties and architects could once more begin to hope and subsequently start to build. A large number of young architects thus came to experience the "joy of building".

In the following years sporadic commissions were replaced by series of buildings. Architects acquired technical competence, a sense of self-assurance and a feeling for high quality even in the details.

The first works by Hermann and Valentiny characterised by a search for geometrically complex surfaces and façades are strongly influenced by literary culture. At the end of the nineties they arrived at works of greater intensity which transmitted those messages (always present in their work) with greater conviction. Starting from the interior and extending outwards their projects acquire increasing significance, both in terms of dimension and extent, from the section to the last diaphragm separating the building from the landscape or the context.

When I visited their office in the hilly, wooded landscape of Luxembourg, at the border with Germany, the relationship of, at least, one of the partners, François Valentiny, to his native land and to a non-urban culture became more clear to me. Their studio, located among vineyards producing an excellent fragrant white wine, is an almost natural extension of the existing building. The extraordinary care with which daylight is gathered, captured and spread is a characteristic of much of the work coming from this office. The intelligent use of materials and of the way they react to the changing nature of light shows remarkable sensitivity and also extraordinary technical competence. More recently the details have become simpler and have dropped the emphatic connotations in order to better serve the architecture.

Buildings in Germany, Austria and Luxembourg, countries where both have studied, taught and built over the years, offer proof of their constant involvement as architects and craftsmen who continue to develop their rich creativity with great joy.

One can say with a high degree of certainty that, in the years to come, Hubert Hermann and François Valentiny will surprise us pleasantly with further works of high quality.

Massimiliano Fuksas

JETZT

Vorweg hypothetisch behauptet: Das Grundmuster der Entwicklung im Werk von H & V folgt einer Strategie der verlangsamten Dynamik. Projekte und Bauten – ein Moment des Innehaltens im ruhigen Prozess des Gedankenflusses. Der Atem des singulären Objekts als Energieträger für die Transformation von Lebensräumen. Thema: elektrische Aufladung, knisternde Funkenbildung im atmosphärischen Einerlei des Kontextes. Oasendenken an den Kreuzungspunkten alltäglicher (Nutzungs-)Bewegungen. Verknüpft mit dem Umfeld, aber komprimiert zum eigenen, eigenwilligen, eigenartigen Ort.

Rückblende: Am Anfang war der Aufbruch aus einer architektonischen Tradition. Kein Ausbruch wie bei anderen zeitgenössischen Architekten, sondern ein Aufbruch, der sich erst im Lauf von Jahren, fast Jahrzehnten zum Ausbruch gesteigert hat. Dabei immer: ein Ausbruch mit Vorbehalten, mit Einschränkungen. Erste private Momentaufnahme dazu: Der Luxemburger François Valentiny und der Österreicher Hubert Hermann – beide in der Donaumetropole ausgebildet – auf der Terrasse des Café Landtmann in Wien, den Blick auf die Ringstraße gerichtet. Darauf, wie die Prachtbauten entlang des Rings aufgefädelt sind, wie harte Platzfläche und weitläufige Parkkomposition die rhythmische Grundmelodie einer symphonisch angelegten, städtischen Kunstlandschaft bilden. Unvermeidliche erste Einsicht: Nichts geht mehr. Zweiter Gedanke: So geht es nicht mehr. Optimistische, dabei logische Konsequenz: eine Art alternative gedankliche Spurensicherung tradierter Qualitäten, materialisiert mit den Mitteln von heute.

Also eine vorsichtige Gegenbewegung zur Architektur des Zeitgeistes. H & V produzieren anders und anderes. Nicht die technoide Raumhülle, die neutral, anonym ihren lebendigen Inhalt umfasst (und nur durch diesen Inhalt zum Leben erwacht), die dabei Schnelligkeit suggeriert, temporeich eine Richtung anpeilt, eine Art Neue-Welt-Denken vor Augen (oder anders, vielleicht zutreffender formuliert: diese alte, heute schon fast wieder sentimenta-

NOW

Firstly a hypothetical assertion: the basic pattern of development in the work of H & V reflects a strategy based on dynamic motion at a reduced speed. Their projects and buildings are a moment of repose in the calm process of the flow of thought. The breath of the individual object is loaded with energy to transform the spaces in which we live. The theme: electric charging, a crackle of sparks in the atmospheric uniformity of the context, oases of thought at the crossing points of everyday (functional) movements. Linked with the surroundings but compressed to form a place that is individual, uniquely its own.

Flashback: the start was marked by the process of emerging from an architectural tradition, not quite the same process as that undergone by other contemporary architects, rather an emergence which only became such in the course of years, almost decades. And always an emergence with reservations, restraints. A first private snapshot: the Luxembourgeois and the Austrian – both trained as architects in Vienna – on the terrace in front of Café Landtmann in that city, their gaze fixed on the Ringstrasse, i.e. fixed on how the monumental buildings are strung along the Ring, on how hard paved areas and spacious parks form the main rhythmic theme of a symphonically composed artificial urban landscape. Inevitably their first conclusion was: nothing is possible any longer, their second thoughts: it can't go on like this. The optimistic and also logical conclusion: a kind of alternative intellectual search for traces of traditional qualities that can be given material form using contemporary means.

In other words, a cautious counter-movement to the architecture of the zeitgeist. H & V produce different things, in a different manner. Not the technological spatial shell which neutrally and anonymously encloses its living contents (and is in fact brought to life only by these), which suggests quickness, speedily adopts a direction, is focussed on a kind of new world way of thinking (or to put it differently and perhaps better: the same old utopian

le, utopistische Architekturvision aus den sechziger Jahren). Das ist nicht Sache von H & V. Ihre Arbeit: Resultat eines anderen Ansatzes. Im Fokus: eine Architektur, die sich – selbst noch im Schweben – auf eine sichere, gesicherte „Pattern-Language" (Alexander) bezieht (natürlich ohne sich mit den billigen, den abgedroschen-üblichen Lösungen gemein zu machen). Resultat: Bauten und Räume, denen der formale Ausdruck ihrer Entstehungszeit zwar eingeschrieben ist, die sich jenseits davon aber ganz fundamentalistisch entlang „überzeitlicher" – archetypischer, struktureller – Qualitäten bewegen.

Zweite private Momentaufnahme: François Valentiny als Kind in Remerschen. Eine intakte dörfliche Umgebung, in der später dann auch das erste Architekturbüro H & V entsteht. Auf dem Weg in den nächsten größeren Ort – der Blick über die Mosel, auf das andere Ufer. Dort steht – auf festem Grund – ein Schiff. Es steht dort bis heute. Es wächst im Wechsel der Jahreszeiten beinahe zu, dann wird es wieder deutlicher sichtbar. Unverändert, seit Jahrzehnten. Daran festgemacht – der Traum des Künstler-Architekten: einmal eine Skulptur, ein gewissermaßen zweckfreies Objekt, in die intakte Landschaft zu stellen.

architectural vision from the sixties that today seems almost sentimental). This is not H & V's thing. Their work is the result of a different approach. In focus: an architecture which, although itself still unsettled, refers to a safe, secured "pattern language" (Alexander) (but which, naturally, has nothing in common with cheap, commonplace and hackneyed solutions). The result: buildings and spaces in which the formal expression of their time is clearly inscribed but which, independent of this, emanate qualities that are "beyond time", are archetypal and structural.

Second private snapshot: François Valentiny as a child in Remerschen, an intact village environment in which, much later, H & V's first architect's office was to be established. On the way to the next larger town there is a view of the Moselle and the riverbank opposite. There, on dry ground, stood a ship. It still stands there today: during the change of the seasons it is almost covered by vegetation and then becomes more clearly visible. Unchanged for decades. The dream of the artist-architect anchored itself there: a dream of one day placing a sculpture, an object in a sense without a function, in an intact landscape.

Daraus entwickelt: eine architektonische Strategie, die die Außenmauern, die Fassaden der Bauten durchdringt. Ein flächendeckender Vorstoß ins Umfeld. Kunst kommt von künstlich, heißt es. Dagegen das Architektur-Gerüst von H & V: wuchernde Natur. Sie gehört nicht nur zum Wortschatz des Teams, sie ist grundlegender Bestandteil aller gedachten, gebauten Texte von H & V. Dabei immer wieder Mehrfachcodierungen. Ein Rankgerüst am Wohnbau als zweite (grüne) Haut, Sichtschutz, Abdeckungsmembran, Schattenspender – und Traggerüst für eine Schicht über die eigentliche Wohnschicht hinaus; für das Zusatzangebot, das den guten Wohnbau vom schlechten unterscheidet. Ein grünes Traggerüst für Frei(t)räume – und für die Anliegen der Architekten, die sich nicht zwangsläufig mit jenen der Bauträger decken. So sind sie verbrieft, nicht einfach streichbar (auch nicht aus Kostengründen). Wenn das grüne Gerüst mehr als Natur trägt, wenn es sich konstruktiv rechtfertigt, dann, so will es die heutige Praxis des Bauens, ist alles erlaubt. Also auch: strategisches Denken als Grundlage und Antriebsmotor der architektonischen Planung.

Dritte private Momentaufnahme: auf der Luxemburger Seite ein alter Stadel, auf der Wiener, ein Holzhaufen im Garten von Hubert

From this dream there developed an architectural strategy which penetrates the external walls and façades of the buildings. A sally on all fronts into the surroundings. Art, it is said, comes from artificial. In contrast H & V's architectural framework: luxuriant nature which is not only part of the team's vocabulary but an essential element in all texts imagined and built by H & V. The coding is repeatedly multiple: a trellis on a housing block as a second (leafy) skin, a visual screen, a covering membrane, a sun-shade and a load-bearing frame for a layer placed outside the actual living layer, to provide that additional quality which distinguishes a good housing project from a poor one. A green framework for open spaces and dreams and for the architects' concerns – not inevitably the same as those of the client/builder. These concerns thus have vested rights and cannot be simply eliminated (not even for budgetary reasons). If the green frame carries more than nature, if it is justifiable in structural terms then, according to current building practice, everything is permissible. Strategical thinking as a basis and motor for architectural planning.

Third private snapshot: on the Luxembourg side an old barn, on the Viennese side a pile of wood in Hubert Hermann's garden.

Hermann. Aufprall, unvermitteltes Zusammentreffen, auch zärtliche Berührung. Holz und Gras; Beton, Ziegel und wiederum Holz. Material brute. Zeitschichten als Oberfläche. Und andere, eindeutiger inhaltliche Schichten: die minimalistische Hütte, mehr Andeutung als Bau, die Hubert Hermann von einer Afrika-Reise als bleibenden Eindruck mitbringt. Nomadische Architektur. Das Gegenteil einer Architektur der dauerhaften Perfektion. Bruchstücke, die den Kreativschlamm des eigenen architektonischen Denkens zum Gären bringen.

Ein uferloser, bodenloser und überaus fruchtbarer Sumpf voller Keime, aus denen die Ideen langsam und irgendwie zart, entwicklungs- und schutzbedürftig sprießen. Daraus wird nie auf die Schnelle die große, pompöse, trendige Geste werden. Aber heute kann man sowohl in Deutschland als auch in Luxemburg und Österreich überprüfen, dass überlebensfähige, robuste Pflanzen daraus geworden sind, Prototypen einer Architekturauffassung, die verallgemeinerbare Lösungen parat hält.

Es gibt Standardthemen. Die Materialität eines Bauwerks zum Beispiel. Die hat sich sehr konsequent über zwei Jahrzehnte hinweg entwickelt. Vom Putzschnitt zum Streckmetall und zum fein strukturierten Beton. Der Putzschnitt stand am Anfang und wurde aufgegeben. Aus pragmatischen Gründen: weil heutiger Putz den

A collision, an unarranged meeting, but also a gentle caress. Wood and grass, concrete, brick and, again, wood. "Material brute", layers of time as the surface. Other layers, less ambiguous in terms of content: the minimalist hut, more a suggestion than a building, which Hubert Hermann brought back from Africa as a lasting impression. Nomadic architecture, the opposite to an architecture of long-lasting perfection. Fragments which cause the creative residue of one's own architectural thought to ferment.

A swamp: endless, bottomless and extremely fruitful. A swamp full of buds from which ideas slowly and delicately sprout, in need of protection and development. A major, pompous, trendy gesture can never hastily grow from beginnings such as these. Today one can confirm for oneself in Germany, Luxembourg and Austria that robust plants capable of survival have developed from these seedlings, prototypes of an understanding of architecture that has on hand solutions suitable for general application.

There are standard themes: the choice of materials used in their buildings is one example. This has developed consistently over a period of two decades from plaster sections to expanded metal and finely structured concrete. Plaster was used initially and then abandoned for pragmatic reasons: because modern plaster no longer permits a system of plaster sections appropriate to the

materialgerechten Putzschnitt gar nicht mehr erlaubt. Auch aus anderen: erstens, ist seine Handwerklichkeit überholt (der Styropor-Nachbau wird zwangsläufig zur Kulisse); zweitens, ist eine Fassadenstrukturierung, die sich nur in der Fläche abspielt, einfach doch zu flach. Andererseits: Es war die „Meinung" von Materialien gefragt, in einem solchen gedanklichen Kosmos kann es nicht nur um die technoide Meinungslosigkeit bloßer Glashäute gehen. Daher zum Beispiel der strukturierte, speziell geschalte Beton (oder auch Betonfertigteile, in denen diese Strukturierung enthalten ist). Daher das Streckmetall als durchlässige Hülle, in der sich der Prozess des Alterns aufschreibt. Von daher auch die immer deutlicher artikulierte Neigung zum Material brute.

Eine Architektur gegen den willkürlich festgeschriebenen Punkt der absoluten Perfektion. H & V denken in Zeiträumen. Metall, das sich verfärbt; Beton, auf dem Algen wachsen; Putz, in dem sich Sprünge bilden. Anständige Alterung, Geschichte, die Charakter hat. Aber nicht: die absolute architektonische Kreation, für die jede Veränderung auch eine Vergewaltigung bedeutet. Architektur für Menschen, für die Zeit, für den Rhythmus der Welt.

Bauten wie Sushis: innen gekocht, außen roh. Das Bild stimmt. Innen, drinnen Räume, Volumina, die auf der sicheren, der bewiesenen, der vielfach erprobten Seite der gebauten Architektur

material. But also for other reasons: firstly the handcraft aspect of this technique is outdated (the imitation using polystyrene profiles inevitably has the decorative quality of a backdrop), secondly a structuring of the façade that is restricted to the surface is simply too flat. On the other hand: the materials were required to demonstrate an "opinion": in an intellectual cosmos of this kind the technoid indifference of a glass skin can ever be the central theme. Hence, for example, the structured, specially shuttered concrete (or also pre-cast concrete elements in which the structure is integrated), hence too expanded metal as a perforated shell in which the ageing process is inscribed. This too is where their tendency towards "Material brute", increasingly clearly articulated, is derived from.

An architecture opposed to any wilfully determined point of absolute perfection. H & V think in terms of periods of time. Metal that discolours, concrete on which algae grow, plaster that develops cracks: a dignified ageing history that has character rather than an absolute architectural creation for which each change is equivalent to rape. Architecture for people, for the time and rhythm of the world.

Buildings like Sushi, cooked inside, raw outside. The image is appropriate: the interior spaces and volumes are located on the

angesiedelt sind; außen dagegen die Spontaneität des Unvermittelten, des Nicht-Zubereiteten, die Ästhetik der Beeinspruchung einer glatten, auf Unveränderbarkeit (und eben: Meinungslosigkeit) ausgerichteten Materialwelt.

Es gibt andere Standardthemen. Ein ausgeprägtes Schichtendenken zum Beispiel. Da bildet die Streckmetall-Haut eine vereinheitlichende Hülle, hinter der etwas – und sei es ein Bau aus den sechziger oder siebziger Jahren – durchschimmert. Da ist die Anspielung einer Lochfassade als äußere, strukturierende Schicht vor der – wie gesagt: meinungslosen – Glashaut eines Bauwerks. Da ist der Lattenholz-Rost als Verbindungsglied zwischen hausinternem Außenraum und hauszugeordnetem Außenraum. Da ist aber auch das Dach als vereinheitlichende fünfte Fassade nach oben, eine Schutzschicht, unter der sich dann jeder beliebige architektonische Tatbestand, auch der Sonderfall abspielen kann.

Also immer wieder: das Thema der differenzierten Außenhautlösung. Schichten als Zeitschichten angelegt, oft als Nutzungsschichten zugespitzt. Die Erschließungsschicht vor der Wohnbaufassade haben andere auch. Die vorgesetzte Lochfassade als einpassendes Moment in den gebauten Kontext vor der Glashaut schon weniger. Und das architektonisch bewusst durchgeplante Gerüst über einer (auch alten, übernommenen) Substanz ganz wenige. Dieser kalkulierte Zusammenprall von Gegensätzen bildet dabei eine Einheit: Er ist pragmatische Anforderung aus der Nutzerperspektive und zugleich umgesetzte architektonische Verantwortung im großen städtebaulichen Kontext. Dieses Schichtendenken spitzt sich aber auch auf das Kleine zu: Das Einfamilienhaus aus

sure, proven, tried and tested side of architecture whereas the exterior reveals the spontaneity of something not transmitted, not prepared, the aesthetic of an objection lodged against a smooth world of materials that aims at remaining unchanged (and is consequently indifferent).

There are also other standard themes: for example a strongly developed way of thinking in layers. A layer of expanded metal creates a unifying shell behind which something else, perhaps a building from the sixties or seventies, shimmers through. The use of a punched hole façade as an outer, structured layer in front of (as we already said) the indifferent glass skin of a building. The grid of timber battens as a linking element between the house's own internal outdoor space and the external space ascribed to the house. There is also the roof as a unifying, upward-facing fifth façade, a protective layer beneath which any architectural situation, even an one-off case can be created.

Another reoccurring item: the differentiated solution of the external skin. Layers applied as layers of time, often developed to form functional layers. The circulation layer in front of the apartment block façade is also found in the work of other architects, the punched hole façade placed in front of a glass skin is less common, but the deliberately planned architectural frame over an old (adopted) substance is even more rare. This calculated collision of opposites then forms a unity. Seen from the viewpoint of the user it is a pragmatic requirement but is, at the same time, an application of architectural responsibility in the major urban context. This way of thinking in layers also focusses on small-scale projects.

den sechziger Jahren, später unsäglich transformiert, wird als fragwürdige Substanz zunächst einmal akzeptiert. Aber es erfährt eine plötzliche, ungeahnte Metamorphose; Schichten als intimer Erlebnisraum formuliert, bereichern den auch noch so bescheidenen Neubau. Und im heutigen sozialen Wohnbau sind solche architektonischen Schichten die Qualitätsschiene schlechthin: Was auf diese Weise an Mehrwert entstehen kann, macht den entscheidenden Unterschied aus. Hier will man wohnen, dort nicht.

Noch ein Standardthema: die Farbigkeit. Es ist müßig, von der Weiße der Moderne zu reden. H & V sind farbiger. Und jetzt ausnahmsweise ganz absolut postuliert – in der Beziehung sind sie wirklich besser. Was wäre die Dachlandschaft des Stadtteilzentrums in Halle ohne seine Farbigkeit (natürlich auch ohne seine Materialität)? Die „meinungslose" Technizität der Glasaufbauten gewinnt durch die schillernde Vielsprachigkeit der changierenden, fast schwarzen Klinkeraufbauten und die melonengelb gestrichenen „Verletzungen" der verputzten Aufbauten; insgesamt entsteht auf diesem einen Dach – Streckmetall und Beton kommen als Material hinzu – ein ganzes Stadtbild. Und wenn man sich die geparkten Autos wegdenkt, dann ist es wahrhaftig eine de-Chirico-Stadt.

The single-family house from the sixties, later transformed in an appalling way, is initially accepted as a rather questionable substance but undergoes a sudden, unexpected metamorphosis. Layers formulated as an intimate space for experience enrich the modest new building. In contemporary social housing architectural layers of this kind represent quality, the additional value that can result from their use generally means the decisive difference between a good apartment block and a poor one.

A further standard theme is colour. It is pointless to refer to the white of classic modernism. H & V are more colourful and here, exceptionally, we make an absolute assertion: in this regard they are better. What would the roofscape of the urban district centre in Halle be without its colours (or, of course, without its materials)? The glass rooftop elements which have an "uncommitted" technical quality profit from the gleaming, multilingual quality of the shimmering, almost black engineering brick elements and the "injuries" painted melon yellow. All in all on this roof, where expanded metal and concrete are also used, an entire urban image is created and, if one imagines the cars removed, it is truly an image of a de Chirico town.

Farbe: Sie kann natürlich schwarz sein. Aber ist Schwarz in der gebauten Architektur wirklich schwarz? Nein, das ist es nicht. Schwarz kann alle Farben spielen. Es hängt von der Umgebung, es hängt aber vor allem vom Lichteinfall ab. Schwarz ist vielschichtig. Und aufregend. Bech-Kleinmacher ist nach wie vor ein Paradefall. Auch Rot kann solche Eigenschaften haben. Das Rot von H & V ist eigens gemischt und immer wieder ein Anschauungsbeispiel: Es nimmt, je nach den Außeneinflüssen, Schattierungen an, die unvorhersehbar sind. Und – noch einmal ein Brückenschlag zur Moderne: Es ist einfach der bessere Hintergrund für eine auch natürlich gewachsene Umgebung.

Ein entscheidender Punkt: H & V sind heute soweit, dass sie ihre Bauten nicht mehr ohne ein entsprechend gestaltetes Umfeld denken können. Die Betonung liegt allerdings leider noch immer auf dem Denken. Bauherren sehen die Notwendigkeit des komponierten Umfelds in einer desolaten Umgebung bis heute nicht ohne weiteres ein. Denn dieses Umfeld ist nicht direkt verwertbar. Über diesen Mechanismus wissen wir heute alle bis zum Überdruss Bescheid. Trotzdem geht es darum, es immer wieder und immer weiter zu versuchen. H & V beweisen in dieser Hinsicht fast schon obsessive Konsequenz. Das Biotop beim Wohnbau. Die gepflanzte Baumreihe. Wasser als integrierender Bestandteil von Außenraumgestaltungen. Hausbegrünung. Valentiny hat sein Schiff an der Mosel nie vergessen. Hermann hat in seinem Wiener Privathaus eine Terrasse, die von einem unglaublich dichten Gründach (Wein) überwachsen ist. Man getraut sich heute fast nicht, es auszusprechen, hinzuschreiben: Aber das architektonische Ziel von H & V liegt in der Harmonie.

Das hört sich merkwürdig und irgendwie veraltet an. Und es hat seine sur-, wenn nicht sogar subrealen Qualitäten. Bauten von H & V zeichnen sich grundsätzlich immer durch eine fast programmatische Plastizität aus. Sie sind geformtes Volumen, modellierter Körper. Aber da schlägt dann auch der Künstler in den beiden Architekten durch. Und bekanntlich malen sie ja beide und machen Skulpturen, Objekte. Mir fällt ad hoc kein Beispiel ein, wo der Bau-„Körper" unverletzt geblieben wäre, wo er nicht auch

Colour: it can, of course, be black but in built architecture is black truly black? No, it is not. Black can play all colours depending on the surroundings and, above all, the light. Black has many qualities and is exciting, Bech-Kleinmacher remains an excellent illustration of this fact. Red too can have such qualities. H & V's red is specially mixed and is time and time again an example of their approach. Depending on external influences it acquires unpredictable shades and (a further link to modernism) it is quite simply a better background for surroundings that have also developed naturally.

A decisive point: H & V have arrived at a point where they can no longer imagine their buildings without appropriately designed surroundings. Unfortunately the emphasis here still lies on the word "imagine". Even today clients do not see the necessity of composed surroundings in a desolate environment, as such surroundings have no immediate function. Today we all know more than enough about this mechanism. Nevertheless the thing is to make the attempt again and again. In this respect H & V demonstrate an almost obsessional consistency: the biotope in the housing project, the planted row of trees, water as an integrated element of the external design, greenery around the house. Valentiny has never forgotten his ship on the Moselle. In his own house in Vienna Hermann has a terrace overgrown by an incredibly densely planted roof garden (vines). One hardly dares say it or write it nowadays but the architectural goal of H & V is harmony.

This sounds curiously old-fashioned in a way and it has certain surreal if not sub-real qualities. Buildings by H & V are essentially characterised by an almost programmatic sculptural quality. They are formed volumes or modelled shapes. Here the artist in these two architects emerges. It is well-known that both these architects paint and make sculptures and objects. Ad hoc not a single example from their oeuvre occurs to me in which the "body" of the building is left uninjured, where it is not cut open, cut up, cut out, where they do not work into the volume producing an articulated, implicitly harmonious landscape of buildings. In the most extreme examples this cutting open, cutting up and cutting out, this creating

aufgeschnitten, zerschnitten, ausgeschnitten ist; wo nicht hineingearbeitet ist ins Volumen und eine (harmonisch? jedenfalls angedeutet!) gegliederte Baukörperlandschaft die Folge ist. In den schärfsten Beispielen wird dieses Auf-, Aus- und Zerschneiden, dieses Ausbuchten und Hereinholen zur Zerklüftung, getragen vom Willen zur Transparenz, zum Austausch. Landschaft drinnen, Landschaft draußen. Minimierte Barrieren, Übergang.

H & V als Künstler. Auch ein Thema, das sich durchzieht. Es wurde von Anfang an gemalt, es wurde von Anfang an modelliert. Dabei bemerkenswert: die Art, wie beide mit diesem Medium umgehen. Ganz schnell hingemalt, eine Gedächtnis-, Eindrucks- und Vorstellungsskizze, die Bilder; in sehr schnellem Material modelliert (Gips, Lehm) auch die allergrößten Skulpturen. Und trotzdem: Vorne, an der Rampe steht der Architekt, der sich sein potenzielles Inspirationsmaterial nach Belieben sucht. Er hält es in gemalten Skizzen fest. Aber es bleiben Skizzen. Der Konflikt des Architekten mit dem Künstler: Wenn diese Skizzen überarbeitet werden, wenn sie mit Zielrichtung „Bild" verewigt werden, dann werden sie auch irgendwie tot. Ein Scheitern? Aus der engen Perspektive des Kunstkontextes betrachtet, mag sein: ein Scheitern. Von den Skulpturen lässt sich das aber nicht ohne weiteres behaupten. In denen ist schon eine Qualität, die standhält (auch jedem Vergleich auf durchaus kunstspezifischer Ebene).

Harmonische Architektur. Das ist es, darum geht es H & V. Und längst sind sie an einem Punkt – soweit wie möglich entfernt von Zeittrends. Diese Art der Historisierung der eigenen Arbeit ist alles andere als leicht. Aber wenn man nicht blind durch die Welt geht, wenn man Fragen stellt und Antworten sucht, dann spitzt sich die Reflexion der jüngsten Architekturentwicklung automatisch zu. Und in der Architektur geht es längst nicht mehr um Züge, auf die man aufspringt, um sich hochglänzend-vierfärbig publiziert zu sehen. Das wissen wir doch alle inzwischen. In der Architektur fahren die Züge zwar rasant, aber in so verschiedene Richtungen ab, dass innerhalb weniger Jahre die schlimmsten Kollisionen passieren, weil irgendwann doch alles ungewollt in einem Punkt zusammentrifft. Einem Punkt, an dem es um die Annehmbarkeit, die Brauchbarkeit geht. Um die Frage der Akzeptanz. Und dann geht es sich oft nicht mehr aus.

H & V nehmen an dieser Debatte teil. Sie vertreten eine eigene Meinung, sie verkörpern einen eigenen Stellenwert. Man wird darüber nachdenken müssen.

of bulges and incorporation of the outside to produce fissures that is driven by the will to create transparency becomes an exchange. Landscape inside, landscape outside, barriers reduced to a minimum. Transition.

H & V as artists: also a reoccurring theme. From the very start they painted and made models, the remarkable thing is the way in which both use these media. Painted quickly, a sketch from the memory, an impression or idea, the images modelled in a quick-setting material (plaster, loam), used even for the very largest sculptures. Nevertheless at the front, on the ramp stands the architect who seeks his potentially inspirational material where he chooses. He records it in painted sketches. But it remains sketches. The conflict between architect and artist: if these sketches are reworked and made permanent as a "picture" then they are, in a way, dead. A failure? Seen from the narrow perspective of the art context this may well be the case. A failure. The same cannot be easily maintained of the sculptures: they have a quality that holds its ground (also against any comparison on an unspecified level).

Harmonious architecture, this is what H & V are about. Quite some time ago they arrived at a point as far distant as possible from current trends. Such a way of historicising ones own work is anything but easy. However, if one does not move blindly through this world, if one asks questions and looks for answers then the reflection on recent developments in architecture automatically come to a point. In architecture the issue is no longer band-wagons one jumps aboard in order to see ones work published in glossy periodicals. We all know this by now. In architecture the band-wagons move off rapidly, in many different directions. Within a few years, the worst possible collisions occur because at some time, unintentionally, all meet at the same point, at a point where the issue is reasonableness, usability, the question of acceptance – and then this is often no longer achievable.

H & V take part in this debate, represent their own opinion, embody their own values. Something we will have to reflect on.

BAUTEN UND PROJEKTE
BUILDINGS AND PROJECTS

ARCHITEKTURBÜRO REMERSCHEN-LUXEMBURG
ARCHITECTS' OFFICE REMERSCHEN-LUXEMBOURG

Die dritte Erweiterung eines Bürobaus, minutiös hineinkomponiert in eine durchgrünte Dorfstruktur.

Schon die Ausgangssituation ist speziell: ein wundervoller Garten, in den ein langes schmales Haus mit einem steilen Giebel gesetzt ist. An diesen Bestand angefügt und über eine gehörige Distanz mittels überdachtem Brückenbauwerk verbunden: die letzte Ausbaustufe.

Ein Bauwerk aus Stahl und Glas, roh, robust. Aber auch transparent. Eine rudimentäre Konstruktion. Das hat mit den spezifischen Voraussetzungen in Luxemburg zu tun. Holz ist hier kein etablierter, beliebig verfügbarer Werkstoff, das Know-how in Sachen Holzkonstruktion lässt ebenfalls zu wünschen übrig. Daher: besser – und auch ökonomischer – Stahl.

Der Zubau nimmt im Erdgeschoss die Funktionen Kochen / Essen auf (im Büro wird tatsächlich gemeinsam gekocht und gegessen) und, nur abgeschirmt durch eine Zeitschriftenwand, dahinter das Atelier von François Valentiny. Darüber: ein Besprechungsraum und Büro-Reservefläche.

Fast eine Idylle. Jedenfalls nichts, was herkömmlichen Arbeitssituationen entspricht. Angenehm jenseits davon. Ein Ort – gut für die alltägliche Befindlichkeit der Akteure, und daher auch gut für Architektur.

The third extension to an office building inserted with painstaking precision in the leafy structure of a village.

Even the starting point is special: a marvellous garden in which a long, narrow building with a steep gable is placed. The most recent phase was added to the existing building and connected by a roofed bridge structure spanning a considerable distance.

A building made of steel and glass: bare, robust, but also transparent. A rudimentary construction which has to do with the specific circumstances in Luxembourg. There wood is not an established, easily available material and the level of know-how in timber construction also leaves much to be desired, therefore steel is better – and more economical.

On the ground floor the extension incorporates the functions cooking and eating (in this office meals are both prepared and eaten together) screened only by a magazine wall behind which François Valentiny's office is located. Above: a meeting room and reserve office space.

Almost an idyll. Nothing here relates to a traditional work situation. It is pleasant outside of such parameters. A place that is good for the everyday mood of the protagonists and therefore good for architecture.

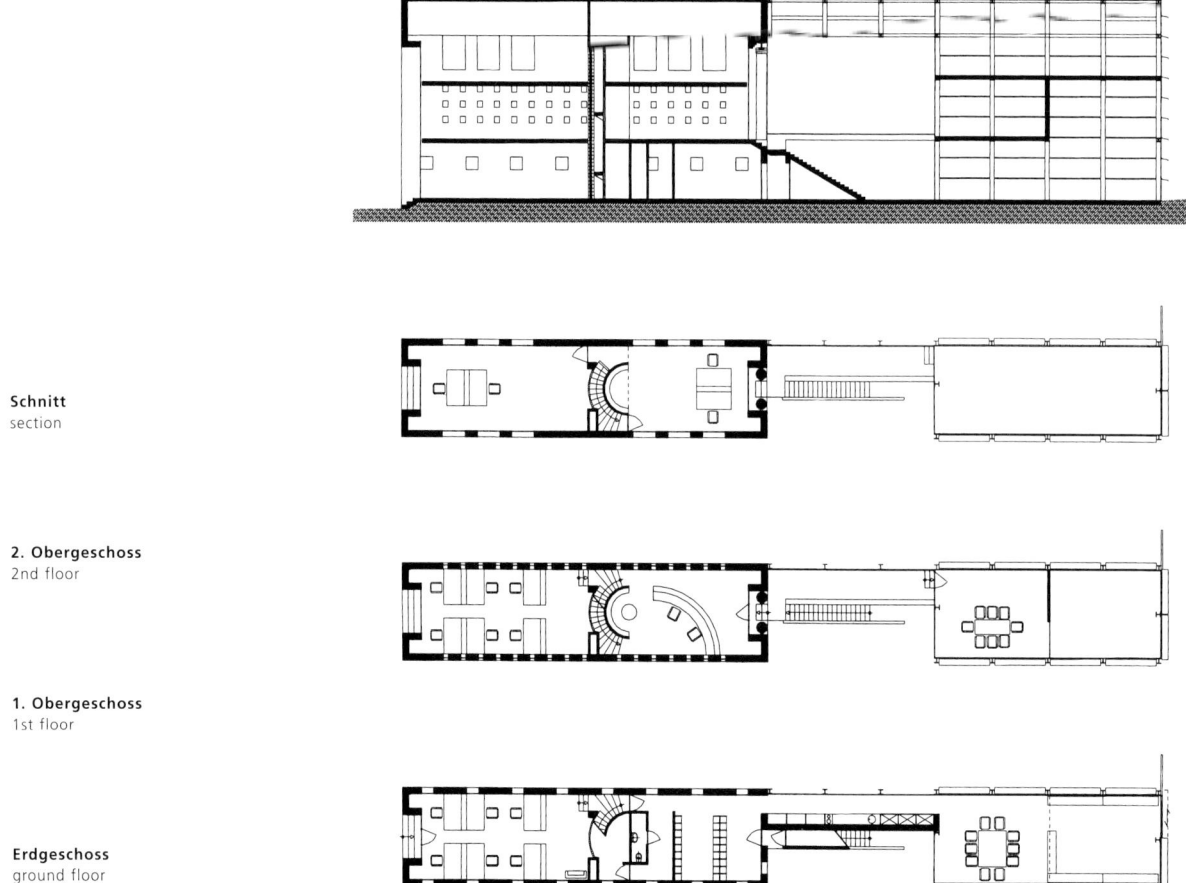

Schnitt
section

2. Obergeschoss
2nd floor

1. Obergeschoss
1st floor

Erdgeschoss
ground floor

Bauherr | client **François Valentiny**
Projektleiter | project manager **Bob Strotz**
Bruttofläche | total floor area **210 m²**
Planungsbeginn | start of planning **8/1997**
Baubeginn | start of construction **11/1997**
Fertigstellung | completion **2/1998**

ARCHITEKTURBÜRO WIEN-WIEDEN
ARCHITECTS' OFFICE VIENNA-WIEDEN

Ein Wiener Gründerzeithaus in relativ zentraler Lage. „Abgeräumt" (von den gründerzeitlichen Stukkaturen befreit), in den sechziger Jahren entkernt – die Mittelmauer wurde herausgenommen, ein Stahlbetonskelett hineingestellt – und aufgestockt. Also eine teilweise sehr problematische Bausubstanz, vor allem weil das Dachgeschoss mit der Gebäudestruktur darunter nichts zu tun hat und die äußere Erscheinung des Hauses nichts mit der gründerzeitlichen Bausubstanz in der Umgebung.

Voraussetzungen für die architektonische Intervention: die Bildung einer Hauseigentümer-Gemeinschaft, der neben H & V als Mehrheitseigentümer ein großes Ingenieurbüro angehört. Rahmenbedingungen: ein limitiertes Budget, das keine substantiellen Eingriffe gestattete.

Ausgangsidee: die Neudefinierung des Baukörpers durch eine Membran, einen „Schleier" aus Streckmetall, der in einem Stück über die (Loch-)Fassade und das Dach gezogen ist. Der Gedanke bedurfte dann aber einer Modifizierung. So wäre der Körper maximal semitransparent geworden, schwer verkraftbar also für die Menschen in den Büros, unzumutbar für die beiden penthouseartigen Wohnungen im Dachgeschoss. Die realisierte, verträglichere Lösung: horizontale Streckmetall-Elemente vor der Putzfassade, teilweise auch um 90 Grad gedreht und quer über die südseitige Straßenfassade geführt, zugleich schmale Sonnenlichtbrecher und sichtbares Zeichen. Und darunter ein farbiger Putzanstrich: tomatenrot.

A Viennese Gründerzeit building in a relatively central location. "Cleansed" (freed from Gründerzeit stucco decoration), the core removed in the sixties. The central load-bearing wall was taken out, a steel frame inserted and a storey added. In total a very difficult building substance above all because the top storey had nothing to do with the structure of the building below and the external appearance in no way related to the surrounding Gründerzeit buildings.

The precondition for the architectural intervention: the establishment of a new group of owners including, in addition to H & V, a large engineering office. The outline framework: a limited budget that allowed no major interventions.

The original idea: a new definition of the building by using a membrane, a "veil" of expanded metal drawn in one piece over the punched hole façade and the roof. This idea had to be modified as the building would have become, at best, semitransparent creating conditions very difficult for those working in the offices and unacceptable for the two penthouse-type apartments at roof level. The final solution was more amenable: horizontal expanded metal elements in front of the rendered façade, others turned through 90 degrees are placed across the south-facing street façade. They both provide protection from sunlight and function as a symbol. The render underneath them is coloured tomato red.

Das Büro selbst: eine offene Fabriksetage (früher war eine Taschenfabrik in diesem Haus). Der schwarze Gussasphalt auf dem Boden beibehalten, nur gereinigt und oberflächenbehandelt, daraufgestellt die Einbauten. Im schwarzen Rahmen, wie in einem Passepartout, die freigestellte Nasszelle, die Küche, der Besprechungsbereich dazwischen. Letzterer mit einer Profilit-Haut, die Tageslicht durchlässt. Und die Farben des H & V-Vokabulars: tomatenrot, melonengelb, pfefferminzgrün.

Eine offene Raumsituation, nicht einmal Hubert Hermann selbst hat ein eigenes Zimmer. Unhierarchisch, kommunikativ. Räumlicher Ausdruck für eine eingeschworene Arbeitsgemeinschaft.

The office itself is an open factory floor (there used to be a handbag factory in the building). The black poured asphalt flooring was retained, it was merely cleaned and the surface treated. In this black "picturemount" are the free-standing sanitary facilities and the kitchen with the conference area between them. The latter has a skin of industrial glazing which allows daylight to enter. The colours are familiar from H & V's vocabulary: tomato red, melon yellow, peppermint green.

An open spatial situation, not even Hubert Hermann has his own room. Non-hierarchical and communicative, the spatial expression of a committed working community.

Bauherr | client **Hubert Hermann**
Nutzfläche | net floor area **220 m²**
Bruttofläche | total floor area **240 m²**
Projektleiter | project manager **Reinhard Wimmer Jun.**
Planungsbeginn | start of planning **10/1998**
Baubeginn | start of construction **11/1998**
Fertigstellung | completion **2/1999**

STADTTEILZENTRUM HALLE-NEUSTADT, DEUTSCHLAND
URBAN DISTRICT CENTRE IN HALLE-NEUSTADT, GERMANY

Städtebaulicher Gesamtkontext

Halle-Neustadt ist eines der ganz seltenen Beispiele für eine größer angelegte, zeitgenössische städtebauliche Neuplanung, die auch tatsächlich umgesetzt wurde. H & V haben hier ein Drei-Sterne-Hotel in Verbindung mit einem Büro- und Geschäftskomplex und einer Passage realisiert, außerdem fünf Punkthäuser, jeweils neun Geschosse hoch. Der Bestand selbst, noch aus ostdeutschen Zeiten, wurde nicht angetastet. Vielmehr wurden die Fragmente dieser gar nicht so falschen Stadtplanung, die allerdings in der Ambition stecken geblieben ist, modifiziert und – gewissermaßen – vervollständigt.

Das neue Stadtteilzentrum liegt zwischen der Magistrale und einer Erschließungsstraße für die Plattenbauten. Es wurde auf der grünen Wiese realisiert. Auch die Punkthäuser, im Halbkreis um den Plattenbaubestand errichtet, stehen auf der ehemals grünen Wiese. Städtebauliches Kuriosum aus DDR-Zeiten, das erst durch die Neuplanung von H & V sinnvoll erscheint: eine zweigeschossige Passage mit Geschäften, die früher im Niemandsland geendet hat. Jetzt verbindet sie den von H & V geplanten Hotel-, Büro- und Geschäftskomplex mit dem neuen Stadtteilzentrum. Die Punkthäuser bilden die äußere Fassung dieser städtischen Entwicklung.

General urban context

Halle-Neustadt is one of the very rare examples of a large scale, contemporary urban design which actually got built. H & V designed a three-star hotel connected to an office and business complex and a shopping arcade and, in addition, five point blocks, each nine storeys high. The existing buildings which date from the days of East Germany were not touched. Indeed fragments of this urban design, which was not so wrong but never developed beyond the original ambitions, were modified and, in a sense, completed.

This new urban district centre lies between the main thoroughfare and an access road leading to the prefabricated blocks, it was built on a greenfield site. The point blocks, placed in a semicircle around the panel buildings, also stand on what was once a green field. There is an urban curiosity dating from the days of the GDR which first acquired a certain sense through H & V's planning: a two-storey shopping arcade which previously ended in no-mans land. It now connects the hotel, office and shopping complex designed by H & V with the new urban district centre. The point blocks form the outer setting for this urban development.

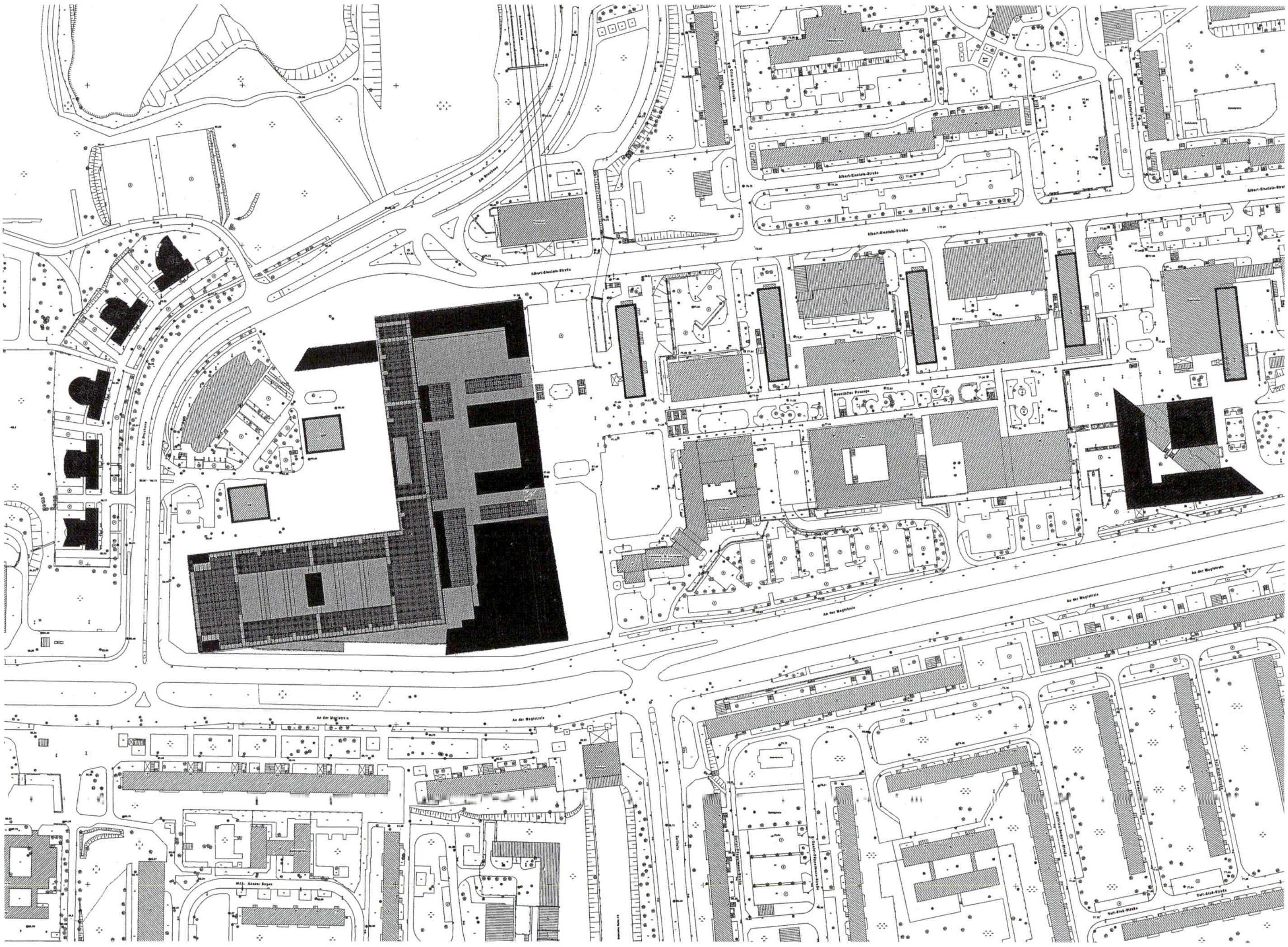

Stadtteilzentrum

Eine Brache an der Magistrale – der äußerst breiten Hauptstraße von Halle-Neustadt –, im Hintergrund 35-geschossige Plattenbauten. Aufgabe: ein eingeschossiges Einkaufszentrum mit Kinocenter, darüber Büroflächen. Das gesamte Projekt mehrfach verknüpft mit dem Umfeld und eingebettet in eine Platz- und Grüngestaltung.

In Relation zu den umgebenden Plattenbauten – ein ausgesprochen flaches Gebäude. Daher Hauptaugenmerk von H & V: einen Körper zu schaffen, einen nicht zu niedrigen – dreigeschossigen –, flächenmäßig ohnehin breit mit dem Boden verwachsenen Baukörper. Der Hauszuschnitt eine L-Form, deren Schenkellänge etwa 180 Meter beträgt. Richtung Stadt und zur Magistrale, dort, wo Hauptfunktionen untergebracht sind, eine dunkel schimmernde Klinkerfassade, die anthrazitfarbene Verfugung einige Millimeter zurückversetzt. Nebenfunktionen verschwinden hingegen hinter Beton und Streckmetall. An der Magistrale ist dieser Übergang besonders reizvoll. Da geht der Wechsel der Materialien fließend vor sich.

Urban district centre

An undeveloped site on a thoroughfare, the extremely wide main road from Halle-Neustadt; the backdrop is provided by 35-storey high, system-built housing blocks. The commission: a single-storey shopping centre plus a cinema complex with offices on the upper floors. The entire project connects at several points to its surroundings and is embedded in a design for open spaces and green areas.

In comparison with the nearby prefabricated panel blocks this building is particularly low and flat. Hence H & V's principal concern to create an element – not too low, three storeys high – broad in terms of surface area, that grows out of the ground. The building is L-shaped, the legs about 180 metres long. Towards the town and the thoroughfare i.e. where the main functions are located, is a dark shimmering brick façade with anthracite coloured pointing recessed a few millimetres. The service areas disappear behind concrete and expanded metal. Along the thoroughfare this transition is particularly attractive, the change from one material to another is flowing.

A A' B B' C D E F G H I K' L M N O P' Q R S T U V

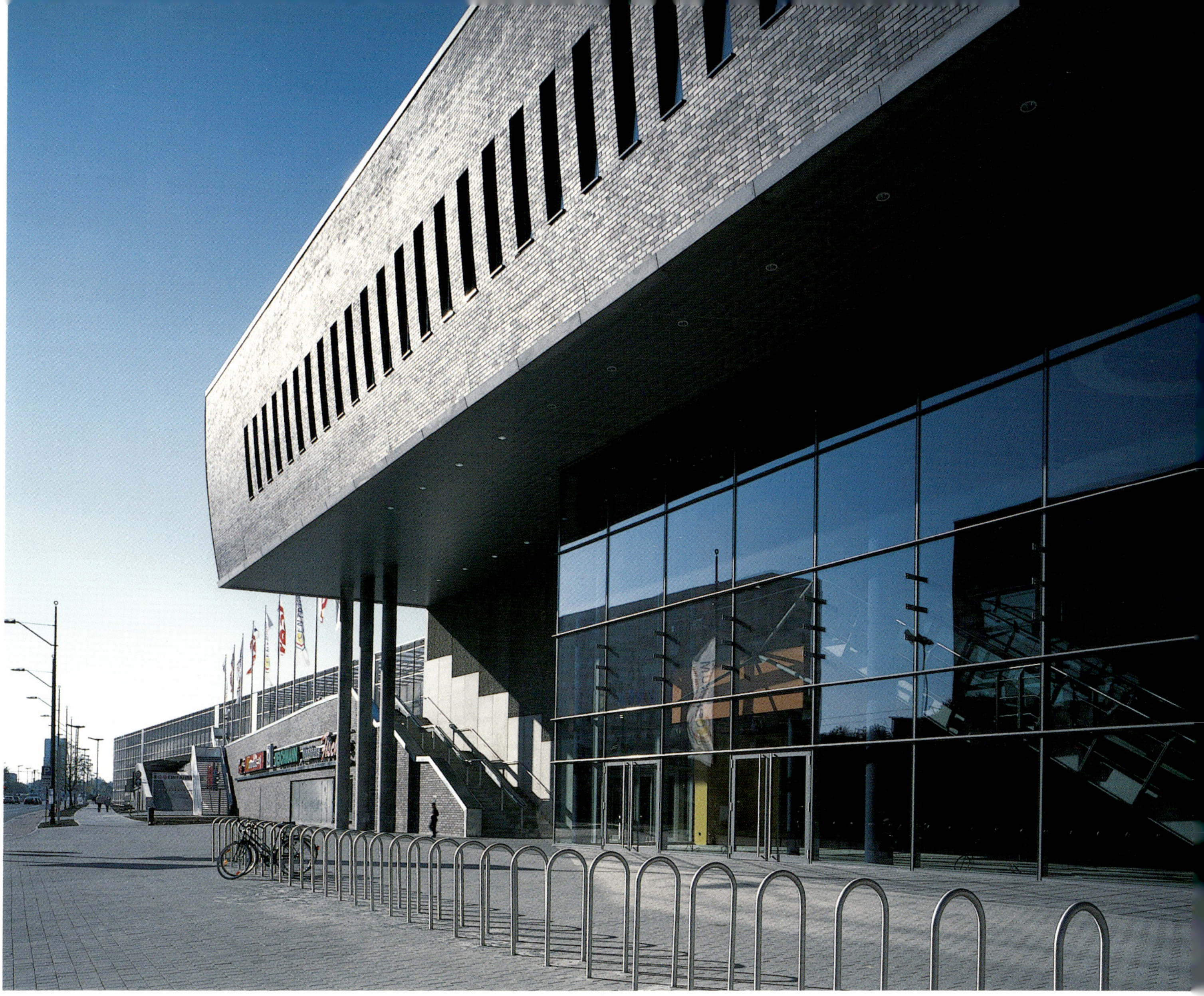

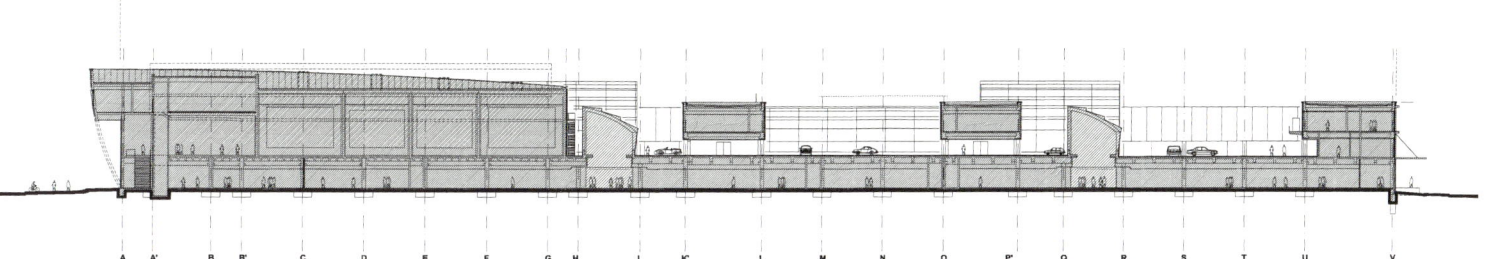

Zweigeschossig gläsern aufgerissen: der Zugang zum Kinocenter. Drinnen waren den Architekten die Hände allerdings gebunden – Kino-Innenarchitektur wird von Großkonzernen gemacht, Architekten haben da nichts zu bestellen (siehe Coop Himmelb(l)au in Dresden). Einzige architektonische Besonderheit: der Schiffbauch des Gebäudes, besonders schön an der Ecke formuliert, bildet sich in einem Kinosaal ab.

The approach to the cinema complex is a two-storey glass element. Internally the architects' hands were tied as cinema interiors are made by big business, architects have nothing to say (see Coop Himmelb(l)au in Dresden). The only architectural special feature is the ship's rump of the building, particularly well formulated at the corner, that is re-echoed in one of the cinemas.

Das Einkaufszentrum selbst ist entlang von Ladenstraßen und rund um zwei 21 Meter hohe, glasgedeckte Malls organisiert. Das Farb- und Materialspiel in Verbindung mit dem natürlichen Lichteinfall von oben lädt hier die Atmosphäre auf. An den Stirnwänden ein tomatenroter Anstrich, flaschengrüne Glasschürzen als ruhige, einheitliche Bahn über den Geschäften, noch darüber Terracotta. Man kommt ohne Wegweiser und Schilder aus: minimierte Hinweise im Fußboden-Muster erfüllen diese Aufgabe.

Ungewöhnlich für ein Einkaufszentrum: Es ist nicht nur nach innen zu den Ladenstraßen und Malls orientiert, es hat auch von außen zugängliche (vorwiegend gastronomische) Einrichtungen und Schaufenster. Und das Problem der Werbung an der Fassade, das üblicherweise jeden solchen Bau zunichte macht, ist hier intelligent gebändigt: Über der Geschäftszone kragen Vordächer aus, darüber ist der Fassade eine Streckmetallmembran vorgeblendet. Unter dem Vordach kann der Passant also bei jedem Wetter trockenen Fußes am Gebäude entlang gehen, die Membran darüber dient – eine zeitgenössische Interpretation der klassischen Fries-Thematik? – als Hintergrundfolie und Träger für die Werbung.

The shopping centre itself is organised along shopping streets and around two 21 metre high, glass-roofed malls. The play with materials and colours in conjunction with the daylight entering the building heightens the atmosphere. The end walls are painted tomato red, bottle-green glass panels form a calm, uniform band running above the shop fronts. Above that again there is terracotta. You can find your way around without signs or guides, minimal indications in the flooring fulfil this function.

Unusually for a shopping centre this project is not oriented exclusively inwards towards the streets and malls, it also has units (principally restaurants) and shop windows that face outwards. The problem of advertising on the façade, which generally ruins every such building, is here intelligently handled. Canopies project over the shop zone, the façade above is screened by an expanded metal membrane. Passers-by can walk along the building beneath the canopy, protected from inclement weather; the membrane above serves as a background foil and carrier for advertising – perhaps a modern day interpretation of the classic frieze?

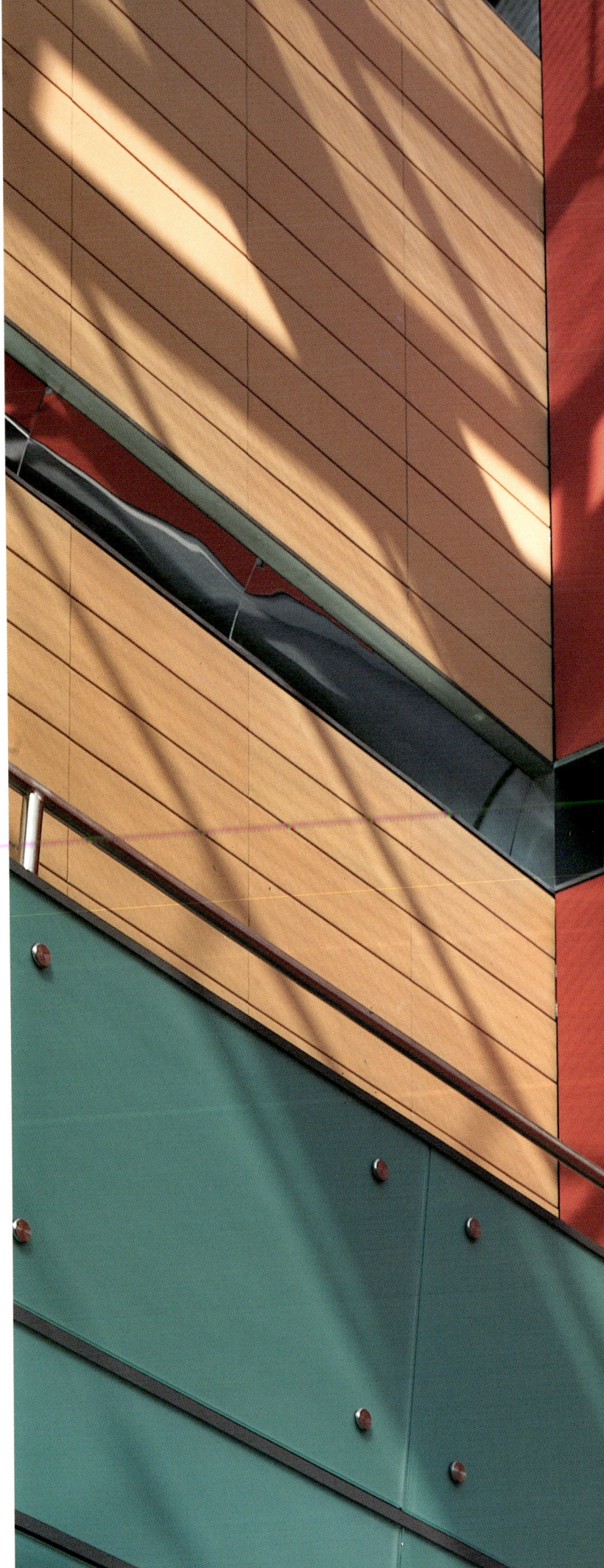

Bauherr | client **MENGLER Die Stadtgestalter – Darmstadt, BRD**
Planung | planning **Hermann & Valentiny & Partner**
in Zusammenarbeit mit | in collaboration with
**Gunnar Noack & Partner (Dresden),
Hauke Rietdorf (Mengler Darmstadt)**
Grundstücksgröße | size of site **37.597 m²**
Bruttofläche | total floor area **76.530 m²**
Wettbewerb | competition **6/1996**
Planungsbeginn | start of planning **4/1997**
Baubeginn | start of construction **4/1999**
Fertigstellung | completion **9/2000**

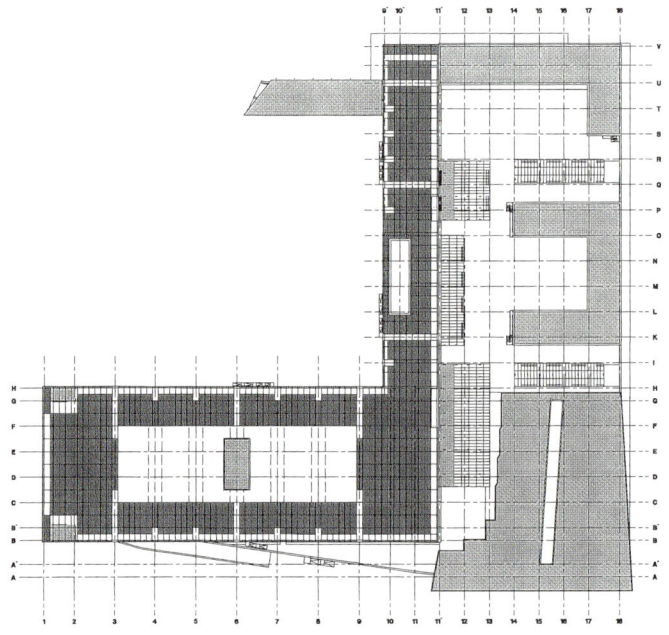

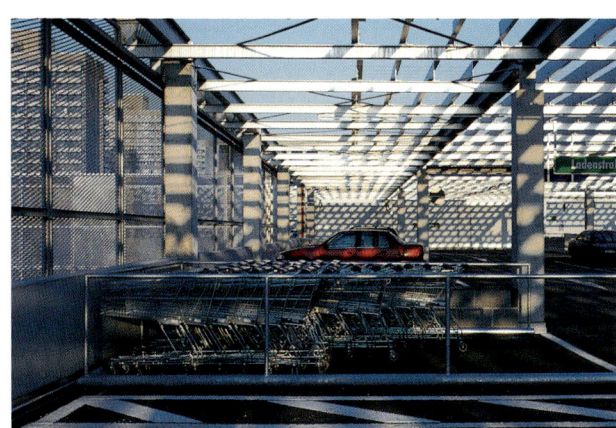

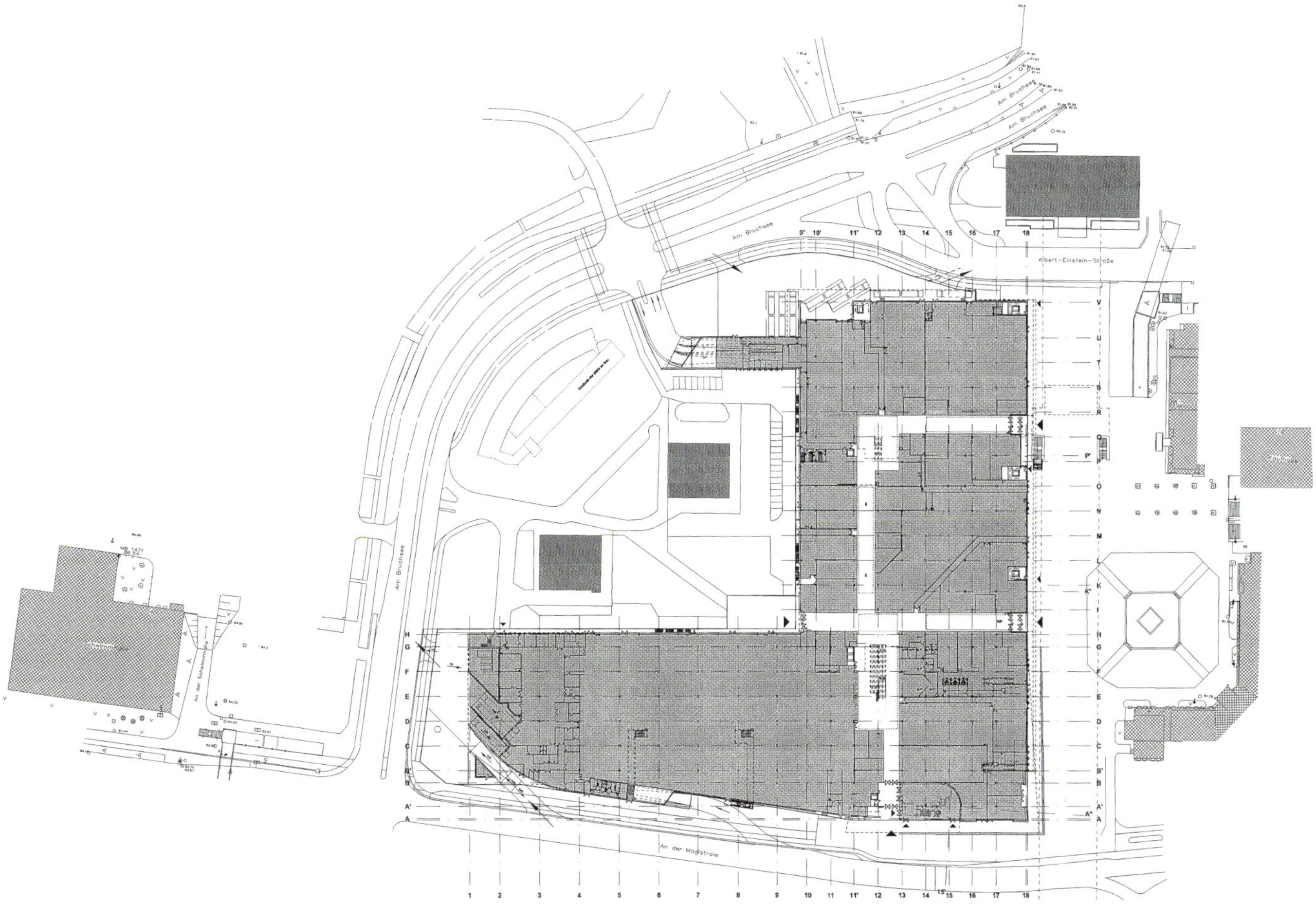

Ebenfalls Hauptbestandteil des Programms für dieses Stadtteilzentrum: 1000 Parkplätze. Sie sind hinter Streckmetall auf Parkdecks und unter der begrünten „Andeutung" einer Pergola auf dem Dach untergebracht. Wobei dem Dach – als fünfte Fassade, auf die alle Bewohner der umgebenden Plattenbauten schauen – besondere Bedeutung zukommt. Daher auch die atmosphärisch ungemein dichte de-Chirico-Szenerie über den Bauteilen mit den Hauptfunktionen. Eine Dachlandschaft als Stadtlandschaft: die gläsernen Malls als eigene Körper, geklinkerte Bauteile, teilweise „aufgeschnitten" und an den Schnittstellen melonengelb gestrichen, dazwischen: ein gepflastertes Platz- und Wegenetz. Es wird in der Regel voll geparkt sein, leider. Leer kippt es in die Irrealität, die aber ganz reale Festtagsnutzungen zulässt.

Infrastrukturell bietet der Bau mehr als die Summe aus Einkaufszentrum und Kinopalast. Vom Rechtsanwalt über das Ärztezentrum bis zum Pensionistenclub haben hier verschiedenste Einrichtungen Einzug gehalten, die für das städtische Umfeld interessant sind. Der budgetäre Aktionsrahmen war trotzdem sehr eng: Die Verglasung der Malls etwa, die muss man unter „Low Tech" subsumieren.

Another main element of the brief for this urban district centre was the 1000 car parking spaces. They are placed behind expanded metal on parking decks beneath the planted "suggestion" of a pergola on the roof. The roof is the fifth façade onto which all the residents of the surrounding system-built blocks look and thus acquires a special importance. Hence the incredibly intense atmosphere created by de Chirico-esque imagery used above of the elements that house the main functions. The roof top is here an urban landscape: the glass malls are independent elements, some of the brick parts are "sliced" open and the cut is painted melon yellow between these is a paved network of open spaces and paths. Generally this space is full of cars, when empty it becomes unreal and yet permits very real uses on public holidays.

In terms of infrastructure the building offers more than just the sum of shopping centre and cinema complex. From lawyers office to doctors surgery to a pensioners club, a variety of facilities important for the urban surroundings has been established here. The budgetary framework was very restrictive: one example is the glazing of the malls which one must describe as "low tech"!

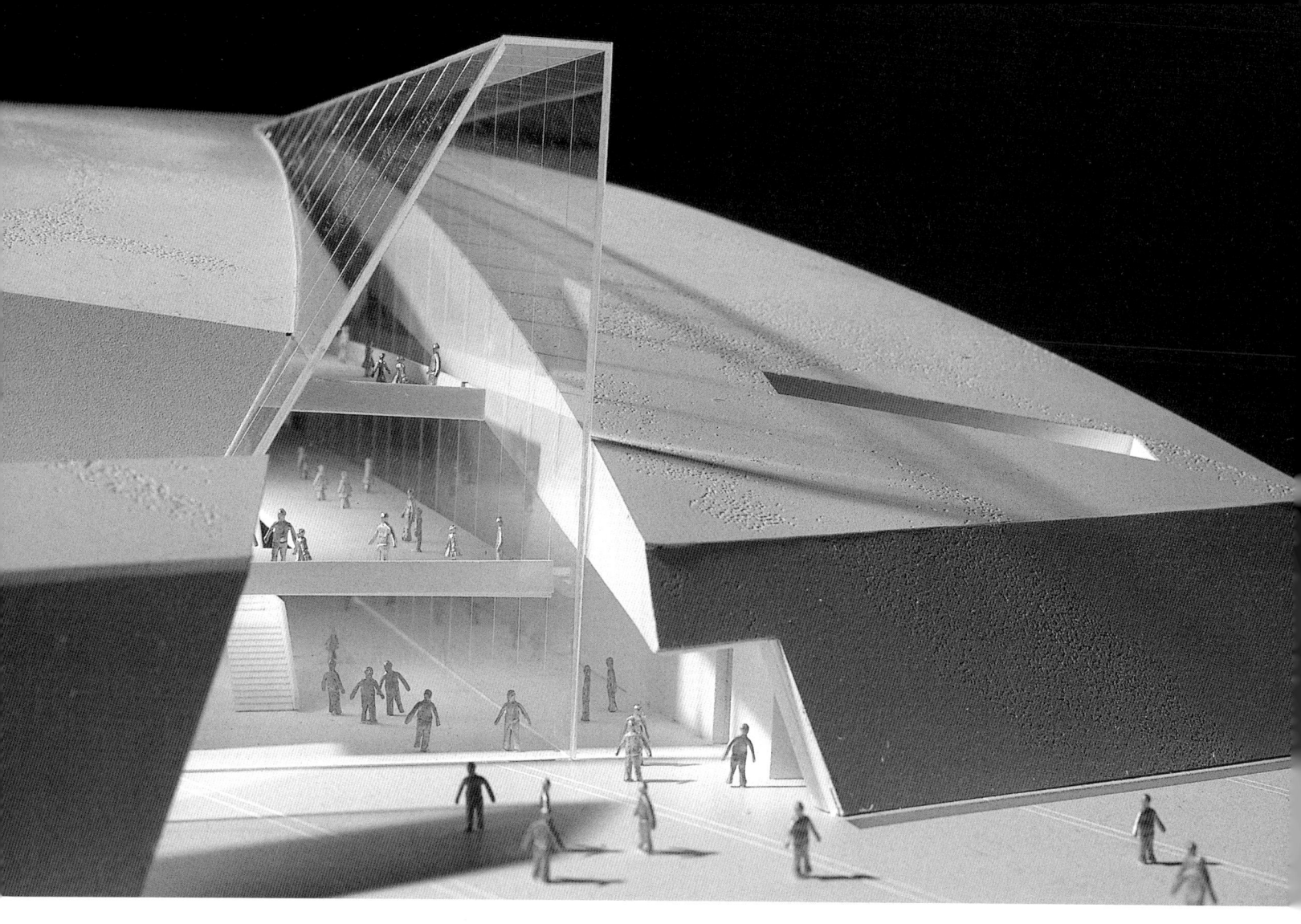

PHILHARMONIE AUF DEM KIRCHBERG, LUXEMBURG-STADT
THE PHILHARMONIC BUILDING ON THE KIRCHBERG, LUXEMBOURG-CITY

Ein geladener Wettbewerb. Schauplatz: neben dem einzigen Hochhaus, das es in Luxemburg gibt, am Ende der so genannten „roten Brücke" gelegen; gleich daneben ein Verwaltungsbau und im weiteren Umfeld die Bauten der europäischen Institutionen, außerdem das Museum von I. M. Pei. Vorgelagert ein Dreiecksplatz, von dem man auf eine Autobahn sieht, aber auch hinüber zur Altstadt.

Eine komplexe Situation. Primärer Entwurfsgedanke: ein Objekt, kein Gebäude im traditionellen Sinn, das aus der Erde heraus entwickelt ist; eine große Platte, die schräg aus dem Terrain wächst, von der Rückseite her betrachtet fehlt eigentlich eine Fassade. Diese äußerste Schicht: eine massive Hülle aus rotem Granit, genau wie die Pflasterung auf dem Platz vor dem Haus; Verkleidung, sichtbares Fassadenkleid der tragenden Betonstruktur. Darunter geschoben und von vorne betrachtet, ein paar Meter zurückgesetzt: eine (teilweise gläserne) Schachtel, die die Hauptfunktionen enthält. Sie tritt an der äußeren Haut in Form von „Verletzungen" in Erscheinung, von verglasten Einschnitten, die sowohl funktionell als auch durch die Sichtbeziehungen begründet sind.

Unmittelbarer Zugang zum großzügigen Eingangsbereich: von einem Boulevard. Hinter dem Eingangsbereich ein festliches Foyer. Es ist zwei Sälen vorgelagert: dem Kammerkonzertsaal und dem Großen Saal. Letzterer rechteckig, mit 2000 Sitzplätzen einschließlich Logen. Zugeschnitten – das war in der Ausschreibung verlangt – nach dem Vorbild des großen Wiener Musikvereinssaales. Dadurch sind optimale akustische Voraussetzungen garantiert. Vom Eingang linkerhand: die Proberäume. Unter allem eine zweite Ebene, ein vielfach vernetztes Betriebsniveau, das für alle Akteure des Konzertbetriebes einen kreuzungsfreien Zugang zu den Sälen gewährleistet und mit dem dritten Gebäudeteil, der Verwaltung, architektonisch verwoben ist.

Gestalterisches Aperçu in der Außenhaut: eingeätzt in die Draufsicht des Bauwerks, in die mächtige Granitplatte, ein riesiger Notenschlüssel, der durch die verglasten Einschnitte im Baukörper verletzt, verunklärt ist. Das Hochhaus daneben begründet diese Interpretation der Dachlandschaft als fünfte Fassade.

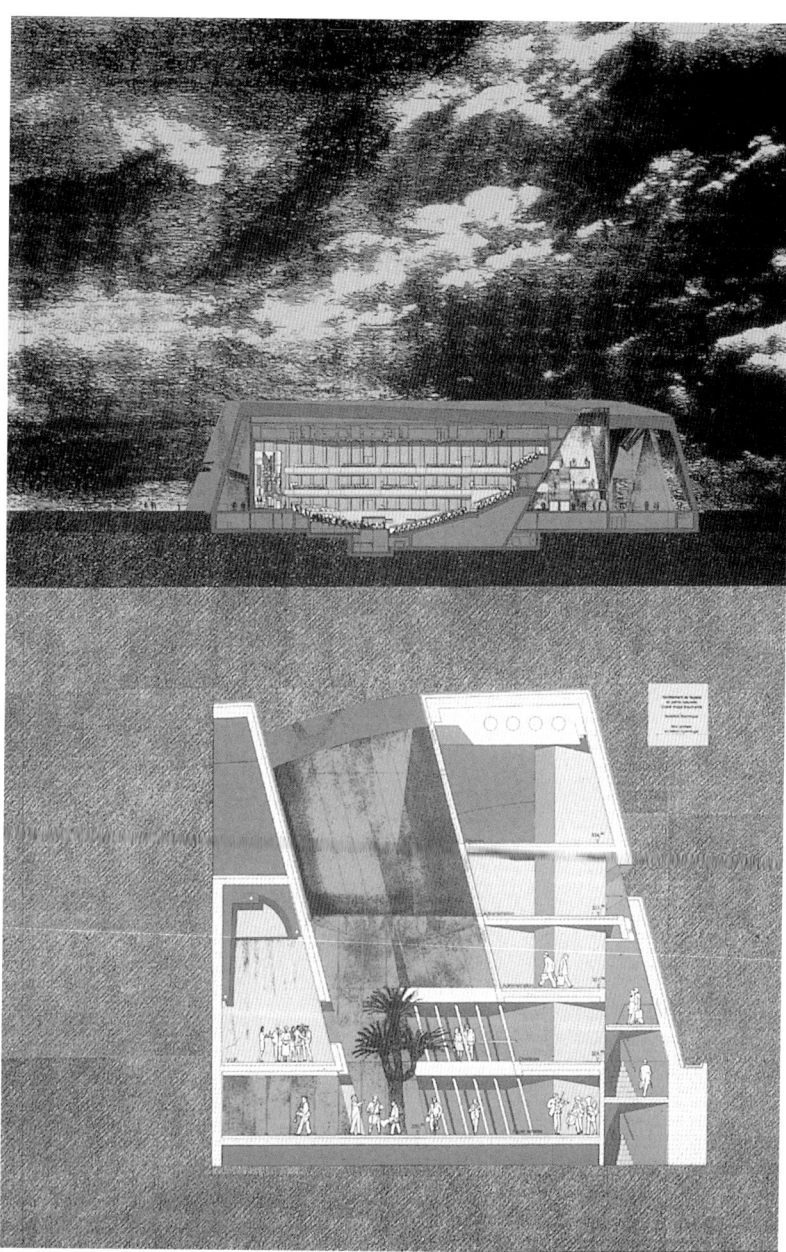

An invited entry competition. The location: beside Luxembourg's only high-rise building, at the end of the so-called "red bridge". Directly beside it is an administration building, the surroundings include the buildings of the European institutions and, in addition, I. M. Pei's museum. At the front is a triangular shaped open space from which one sees the motorway but can also look across to the old town.

A complex situation. The primary design idea: an object, not a building in the traditional sense, a building that develops out of the ground. A large slab which grows at an angle out of the site, in fact seen from the rear a façade is missing. This outermost layer is a massive shell of red granite, exactly like the paving in front of the building; it is the cladding, the visible façade clothing to the load-bearing concrete structure. Slid beneath it and, seen from in front, set back a few metres, is a (partly glazed) box which contains the primary functions. It is manifested in the external skin in the form of "injuries", glazed cuts that are justified both in terms of function and by the visual relationships they establish.

The direct approach to the generous entrance area is from a boulevard. A festive foyer lies behind the entrance space, it stands in front of two auditoriums: the chamber music hall and the major hall. The latter is rectangular with 2000 seats, including boxes. Its proportions match those of the Musikverein concert hall in Vienna – a requirement of the brief. This guarantees optimal acoustic conditions. To the left of the entrance are the rehearsal rooms. Beneath is a second level, an interconnected operational area that provides unhindered access for all the participants to both halls and is architecturally linked with the third part of the building, the administration.

A design aperçu in the external skin: in the view of the building from above, etched in the mighty granite slab, is a giant clef which, "injured" by the glazed incisions in the building, is somewhat blurred. The neighbouring high-rise building provides the justification for this interpretation of the roof as a fifth façade.

Partner **Architecture & Environnement SA**

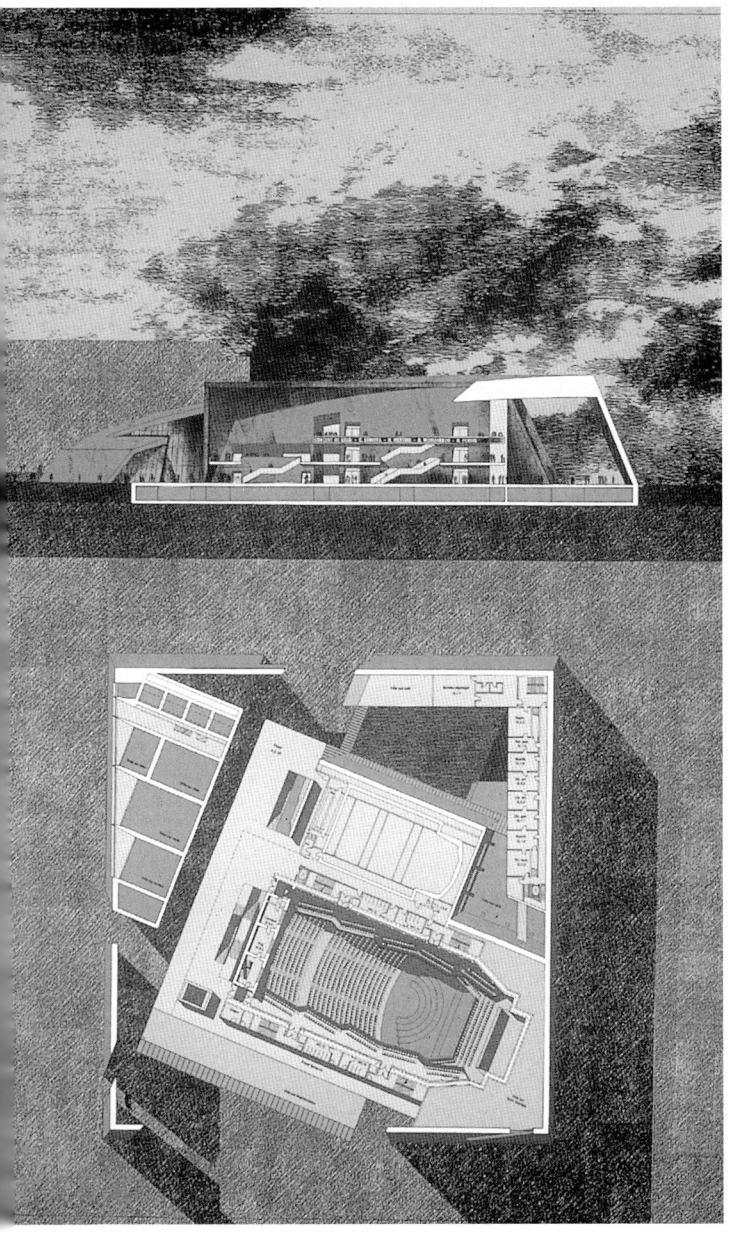
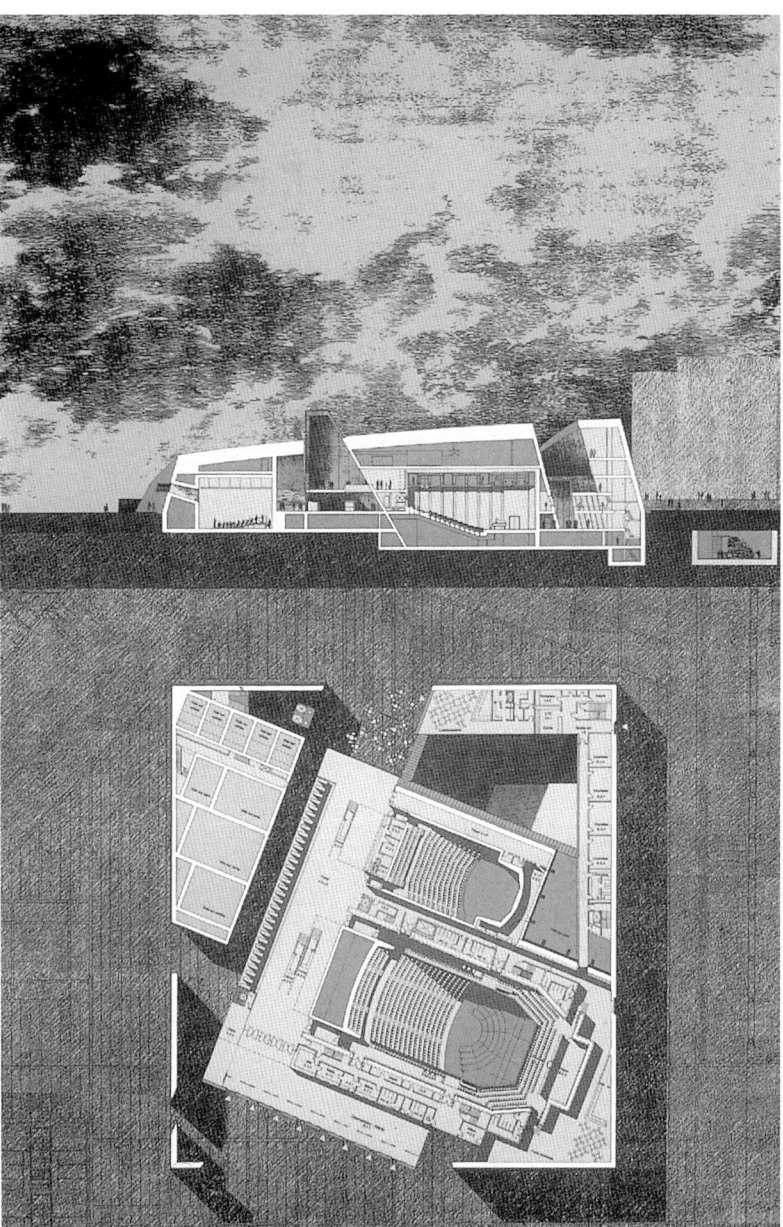

MUSIKTHEATER IN LINZ, OBERÖSTERREICH
MUSIC THEATRE LINZ, UPPER AUSTRIA

Ein Musiktheater ist eine Oper ist ein Musiktheater. In diesem Fall: in der oberösterreichischen Landeshauptstadt. Nur haben sich dort die Politiker nicht entschließen können, ihren eigenen Willen sichtbar zu demonstrieren. Daher der Gedanke: eine Oper im Berg, zwar unmittelbar an der Donau und direkt unter dem Schloss, aber als Bauvolumen nicht sichtbar, sondern tiefgründig versteckt. Hollein mit seinem (schon aus Platzgründen weitaus berechtigteren) Salzburger Mönchsberg-Museumsprojekt lasst grüßen.

Der andere Ansatz von H & V: ein Opernhaus an der Donau. Die aufregende Sichtbeziehung zum Fluss, aber ohne dass man die sechsspurige Straße im Vorfeld sieht. Das heißt: weit vorkragende Foyers – sogar die Fassade ist schräg nach außen gekippt –, Zuschauerraum und Bühne, auch alle anderen – besonders umfangreichen – Gebäudeteile hingegen in den Berg hinein.

A music theatre is an opera house is a music theatre. In this particular case in the state capital of Upper Austria. The politicians there could not decide to visibly demonstrate their own will hence the idea of an opera house in the mountain which, although directly on the Danube and directly below the castle, is an invisible building volume hidden in the ground. This calls to mind Hollein's Mönchsberg museum project in Salzburg (which, however, was far more easily justifiable due to the shortage of space there).

H & V's different starting point: an opera house on the Danube. The exciting visual relationship to the river while avoiding the view of the six lane road in the foreground. This means: widely projecting foyers – even the façade is tilted outwards at an angle – auditorium, stage and all other (particularly comprehensive) elements of the building inserted in the mountain.

Der städtebauliche Kontext: oben das überdimensionale Schloss, unten, entlang der Donau, niedrige Speichergebäude und die Verkehrsader der maßstabsprengenden Straße; im weiteren Umfeld: kleinteiligere Altstadt und jenseits des Flusses die neue Stadt. Folgerichtiges Planungsziel: die Oper als Stadttor, als definiertes Portal zur Stadt, dabei vielfach eingebunden in den örtlichen Kontext.

Alle Wege führen in diese Oper: mit dem Auto, von der Straße am Fluss kommend, entlang von Werkstattgebäuden, die den Maßstab der alten Speicher aufnehmen, hinein in die Garage und über ein Verteilergebäude hinauf in die Foyers; aber auch zu Fuß, von der Altstadt kommend, durch das Schloss hindurch und über einen offenen, spiralförmig angelegten Wandelgang, der in den Berg zylindrisch eingeschnitten ist; schließlich über einen mäandrierenden Weg entlang der Gebäudedächer, die als Terrassen formuliert sind.

Schweben über der Donau: daher Glas für die Foyerbereiche auf filigranen Galerien. Und ein Gewand aus Basalt für die der Stadt abgewandte Gebäudeseite und die Draufsicht. Wichtig für letztere: Sie ist leer, eine heilige Fläche fast, unberührbar; nur der Himmel spiegelt sich im Stein.

The urban context: above the monumental castle, below, along the Danube, low warehouses and the traffic artery of the road which explodes the scale. In the broader surroundings the small-scale patchwork of the old town and, on the far side of the river, the new town. The correctly established planning goal: the opera house as an urban gateway, a defined entrance to the city that is integrated in a variety of ways in the urban context.

All routes lead to this opera house: driving by car from the road along the river, past the workshop buildings which take up the scale of the old warehouses, into the garage and through a distributor building upwards into the foyers; but also by foot coming from the old town through the castle via an open spiral concourse cylindrically incised into the mountain; finally along a meandering route across the roofs of buildings that are formulated as terraces.

Hovering above the Danube: hence glass for the foyer areas on filigree galleries. A robe of basalt for the side of the building that is turned away from the city and for the roof seen from above. The important aspect of the latter: it is an empty, almost sacred area, untouchable, only the heavens are reflected in the stone.

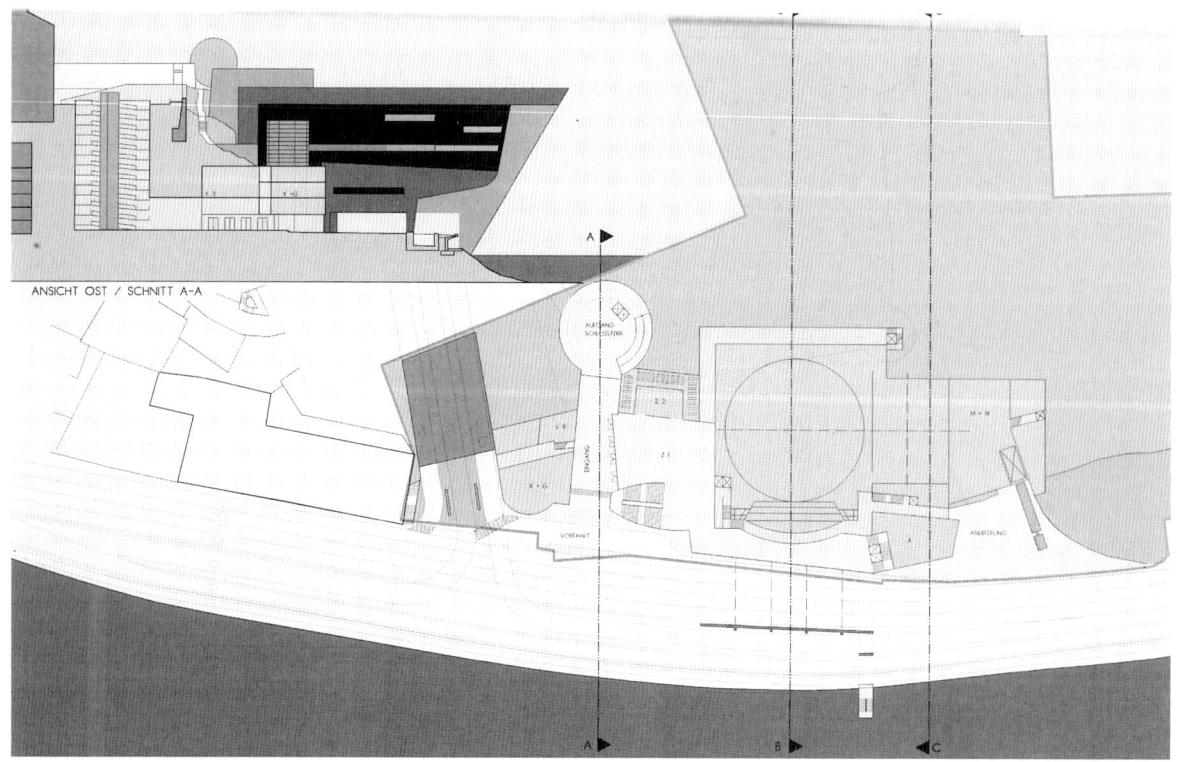

Ansicht Ost/ Schnitt A-A
east view/ section A-A

Eingangsniveau
entrance level

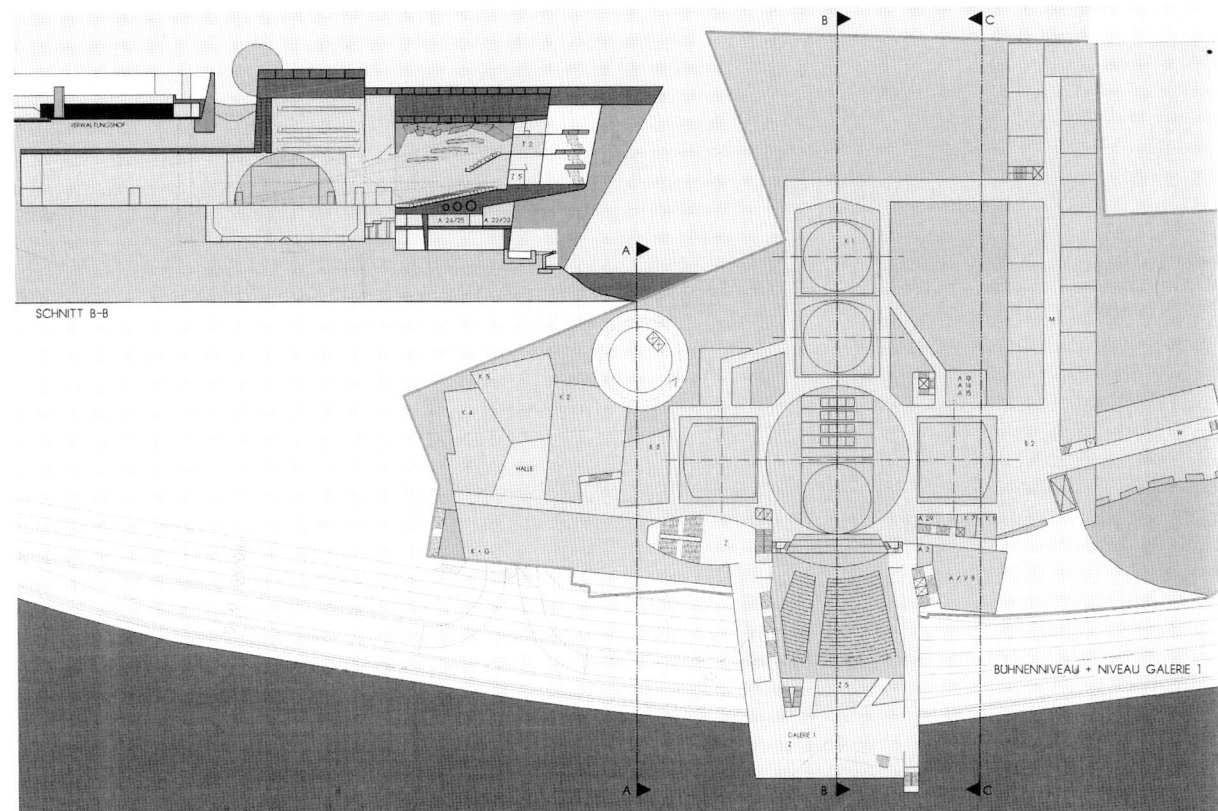

Schnitt B-B
section

**Bühnenniveau
Niveau Galerie 1**
stage level
level gallery 1

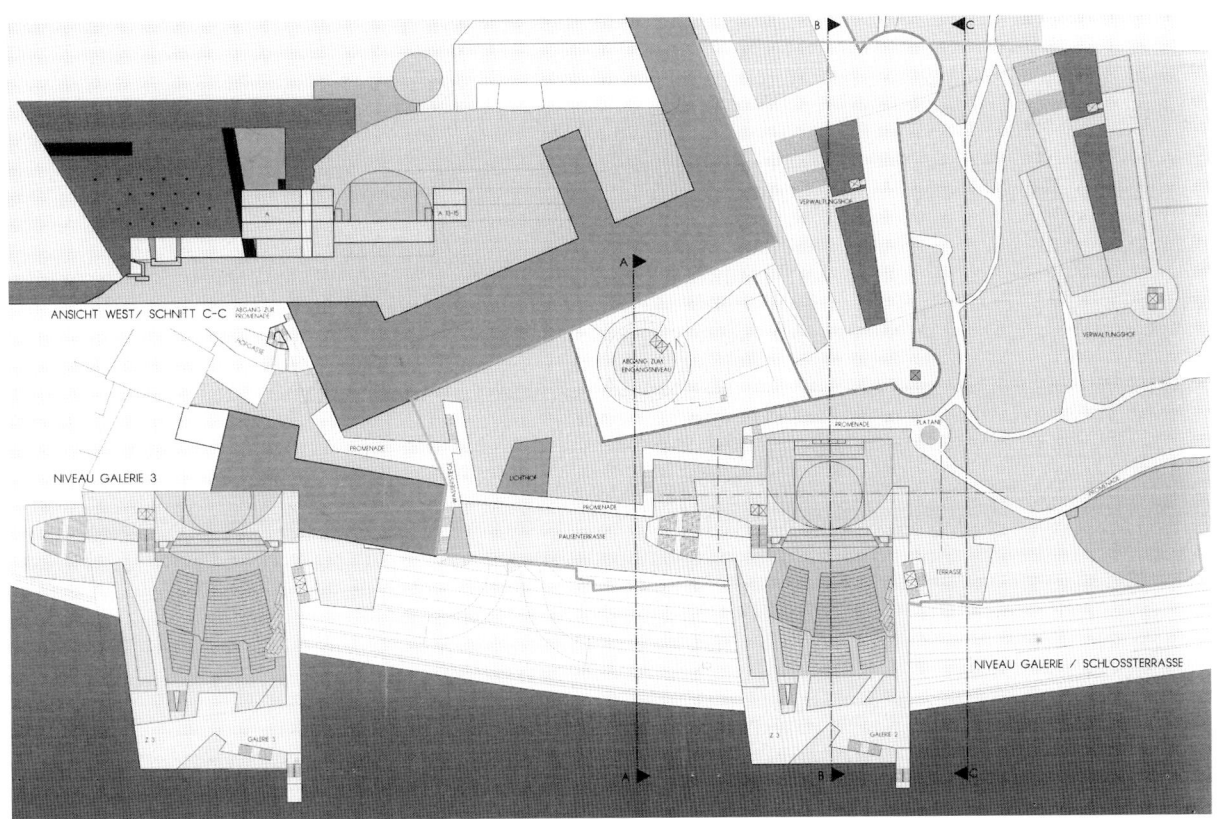

**Ansicht West/
Schnitt C-C**
west view /
section C-C

**Niveau Galerie/
Schlossterrasse**
level gallery/
castle terrace

WEINGUT AN DER MOSEL, LUXEMBURG
WINERY ON THE MOSELLE, LUXEMBOURG

Ein Hanggrundstück zwischen Weingärten, von der Mosel nur durch eine Straße getrennt. Programm: alle notwendigen Einrichtungen für die Produktion, Lagerung und Auslieferung von Wein, außerdem Verwaltung und ein eigener Bereich für die Degustation.

Lösung: eine relativ flache, in den Hang geschobene Kiste und ein quer zum Hang verlaufender Verwaltungstrakt mit Restaurationsbereich, schließlich ein vorgeschobener, weithin sichtbarer „Betonpilz", verglast geplant, aber noch offen, als sommerlicher Probierpavillon und Werbezeichen (Buchstaben im Hang, als zweite Werbemaßnahme, wurden nicht genehmigt).

Der schmale Fußweg zum Restaurationsbereich führt links an der Anlage, direkt an Weingärten vorbei. Zufahrten für Autos sind rechts. Wobei die Traubenanlieferung so gelegt ist, dass sie den Erfordernissen hochwertiger Weinproduktion entspricht. Man fährt hinauf und hinter den Bau am Hang, sodass die Trauben nur hinunter gekippt werden müssen, die natürliche Schwerkraft also das künstliche (und für den Wein schädliche) Pumpen ersetzt. Die Produktionsstätte selbst: eine High-Tech-Installation, an deren Umsetzung die Bauherren unmittelbar beteiligt waren (daraus resultieren auch manche formale Brüche, etwa die Wahl der Fliesen).

A sloping site amid the vineyards, only a road separating it from the Moselle. The brief: all the facilities required for production, storage and delivery of wine and, additionally, administration and an area especially for wine tasting.

The solution: a relatively flat box slid into the slope and an administration wing at right angles to the slope with restaurant area and, finally, a clearly visible "concrete mushroom" (intended to be glazed but still open) as a summer wine tasting pavilion and trade mark (letters in the slope planned as additional advertising were not permitted).

The narrow footpath to the restaurant area leads on the left of the complex directly past the vineyards. Vehicular access is on the right. The delivery of the grapes is organised to meet the requirements for the production of high quality wine. The truck drives up the slope behind the building so that the grapes only have to be tipped downwards using the natural force of gravity rather than artificial pumps which are harmful to the wine. The production area itself is a high tech installation, the clients were directly involved in its design (which resulted in several formal lapses such as the choice of tiles).

Vor dem Restaurationsbereich: eine Wasserfläche, die optisch in die Wasserfläche der Mosel übergeht, und über die man hinüber zum „Betonpilz" sieht. Besichtigungstouren durch den Keller können hier enden: denn es gibt eine Treppe hinunter in die Weinkellerei. Drinnen im Degustationsraum: Holzlamellen, bewachsen mit Innenraum-Kletterpflanzen, und ein langer Tresen, auf dem die Flaschen wie Exponate stehen.

Ein Kurzzeitbau: Er wurde im Mai begonnen und Ende September fing die Weinproduktion an. Dazwischen, im August: das Kuriosum der Luxemburger Bauferien, die das Bauen eigentlich verbieten (man muss in dieser Zeit auf Innenarbeiten ausweichen). Also: wenig Zeit, strenge ökonomische Vorgaben – und trotzdem Architektur.

In front of the restaurant area is a pool that links visually to the river and across which one has a view of the "concrete mushroom". Tours through the cellar can end here as there is a staircase at this point leading down into the wine cellars. Inside the tasting room: wooden louvers covered with indoor creepers and a long counter on which bottles stand like exhibits.

A brief construction period: the start was in May, wine production began in September interrupted in August by the curious building-trade holidays in Luxembourg which, in fact, prohibit construction (in this period one has to turn to interior fitting out). This meant little time, strict economic constraints – yet nevertheless architecture.

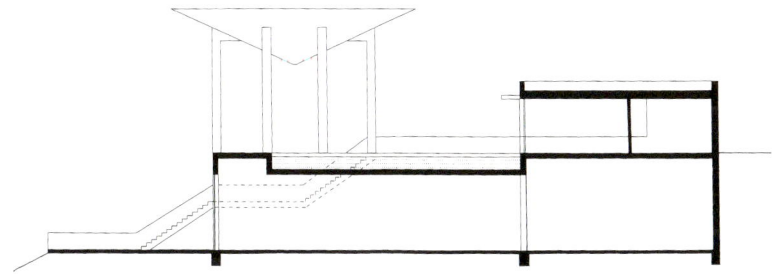

Bauherr | client **Cep d'dor**
Projektleiter | project manager **Axel Christmann**
Grundstücksgröße | size of site **2.634 m²**
Nutzfläche | net floor area **1.437 m²**
Planungsbeginn | start of planning **1/1995**
Baubeginn | start of construction **4/1995**
Fertigstellung | completion **8/1995**

PERFEKTASTRASSE

STEINERGASSE

TELEFONWEG

Bauherr | client
Gesiba Gemeinnützige Siedlungs- u. Bau-AG
Projektleiter | project manager **Sabine Ehrich**
Anzahl der Wohneinheiten | number of dwelling units **65**
Grundstücksgröße | size of site **3.861,50 m²**
Wohnnutzfläche | floor area **5.007 m²**
Wettbewerb | competition **6/1996**
Planungsbeginn | start of planning **4/1997**
Baubeginn | start of construction **11/1998**
Fertigstellung | completion **3/2000**

Bauherr | client
STADT WIEN MA 24
Projektleiter | project manager **Manfred Wagner**
Anzahl der Wohneinheiten | number of dwelling units **74**
Grundstücksgröße | size of site **15.110 m²**
Wohnnutzfläche | floor area **6.710 m²**
Wettbewerb | competition **1993**
Planungsbeginn | start of planning **1993**
Baubeginn | start of construction **4/1998**
Fertigstellung | completion **11/1999**

Bauherr | client
Familienhilfe
Projektleiter | project manager **Peter Frank**
Anzahl der Wohneinheiten | number of dwelling units
22 Reihenhäuser | terrace houses
Grundstücksgröße | size of site **6.760 m²**
Wohnnutzfläche | floor area **1.780 m²**
Wettbewerb | competition **12/1994**
Planungsbeginn | start of planning **12/1994**
Baubeginn | start of construction **1/1999**
Fertigstellung | completion **1/2001**

WOHNBAU IN DER PERFEKTASTRASSE, WIEN-LIESING
HOUSING DEVELOPMENT ON PERFEKTASTRASSE, VIENNA-LIESING

Vorgegebener Städtebau an den Outskirts of Vienna. Eine Mischung aus Turmhäusern und Wohnzeilen, die auf das Umfeld reagieren; das Umfeld: kleine Einfamilienhäuser und Gärten. Daher eine Baukörper-Staffelung bei den Zeilen von zwei auf vier Geschosse, bei den Türmen von vier auf acht Geschosse. Die Dichte steigert sich also mit der Entfernung vom bestehenden Siedlungsgebiet. Außerdem bemerkenswert: die Durchwegung des Areals mit Längs- und Querverbindungen, die Hofsituationen.

H & V haben ein Turmhaus und eine Zeile entworfen. Erste Maßnahme des Entwurfs: ein eingeschossiges Sekundärgebäude parallel zur Straße, sodass die Mietergärten zumindest optisch etwas abgerückt, gewissermaßen privatisiert sind. Zweite Maßnahme: eine räumliche Kerbe zwischen dem hohen und dem niedrigen Gebäudeteil, ein kleiner, interner Hof, über den man hinausschwenkt auf die anderen Wege. Und der, wenn auch nicht „offiziell", nicht der Norm entsprechend, für zusätzlichen Lichteinfall sorgt. Eine sinnvolle Notmaßnahme, Reaktion auf die Gebäudetiefen – immerhin 17 Meter bei der Zeile, sogar 30 auf 25 Meter beim Turmhaus, das dadurch außerdem ein wenig freigespielt ist. Es gibt also keine Wohnung, die nicht zweiseitig belichtet wäre.

Im Turm: durchgehend gleiche Fensterelemente, egal ob Wohnzimmer, Küche oder Bad. Das führt im Bad zu einer eher ungewöhnlichen Lösung. Hier nimmt das Fensterelement die gesamte Breite des Raumes ein, von hier hat man sogar einen Blick über die Stadt. Im übrigen sind im Turm, ausgenommen an den Ecken, die kleineren Wohnungen.

Signifikant an den Zeilen: ein Tragsystem, aber unterschiedliche Wohnungslösungen. Der Scheibenabstand von 7,50 Metern teilt auch die Garage gleich richtig ein, dazwischen jeweils drei Stellplätze. Darüber, im gleichen Raster, je zwei Maisonetten mit der halben Breite, Wohnraum nach Süden, vorgelagert eine zweigeschossige Veranda; lichte Höhe im Wohnraum – durch das Versetzen der Geschossdecke – 3,15 Meter. Darüber Wohnungen über zwei Maisonettefeldern, ein loftartiger Grundriss, durch einen 50 cm abgesenkten Laubengang und über einen kalten Windfang erschlossen.

Ein eigenes Kapitel: die Farbgebung, die Materialisierung. Schwarze Betonfertigteile, rot gestrichener Putz, Streckmetall. Letzteres auch als „Verpackung" des Sekundärbauwerks und der Dachaufbauten, auch als Schattenspender über den Dachterrassen.

Und noch eine Besonderheit: die „grüne" Freiraumgestaltung, mit Bäumen und rankenden Pflanzen und mit einem Biotop, wo man notfalls sogar schwimmen kann.

The brief: the creation of an urban development on the outskirts of Vienna. A mix of tower blocks and long rows that reacts to the surroundings made up of small, single-family houses with gardens. This environment explains why the height of the rows changes from two to four storeys and that of the towers from four to eight. The density increases with the distance from the established developed area. Additionally worth mentioning is the network of pedestrian connections on both long and cross axes, and the courtyard situation.

H & V designed one tower block and one row building. The primary measure in this design was a single-storey secondary building parallel to the street which ensures that, at least visually, the tenants' gardens are set back somewhat, in a sense given privacy. The second measure is a spatial incision between the lower and higher parts of the building, a small internal courtyard via which one moves out onto the other routes and which is a source of additional light (although not officially, as it does not satisfy the norm). A sensible emergency measure that reacts to the depths of the buildings – 17 metres in the case of the rows and 30 to 35 metres in the case of the tower – which is to some degree liberated as a result. There is no apartment without light from two sides.

In the tower the same window elements are employed in the living room, bathroom and kitchen. In the bathroom this leads to an unusual solution: the window element takes up the entire width of the space, one even has a view over the city. Generally speaking, apart from at the corners, the apartments in the tower are smaller.

A significant feature of the row building is the use of a uniform structural system with different apartment types. The distance between the load-bearing slabs of 7.50 metres establishes a suitable layout in the garage, allowing three parking spaces. Above, using the same grid, are two maisonettes each half this width. The living room is south-facing with a two-storey veranda at the front. The room height in the living space is 3.15 metres, thanks to the staggering of the floor slabs. Above are apartments extending across two maisonette bays with a loft-type floor plan. They are reached from an access deck lying 50 cm lower and through an unheated draught lobby.

The colouring and the materials are a chapter of their own: black pre-cast concrete elements, red painted render, expanded metal. The latter is also used to "wrap" the secondary building and the roof-top elements and also provides shade on the roof terraces.

A further special feature is the "green" design of the open space with trees and climbing plants and a biotope in which one could even swim.

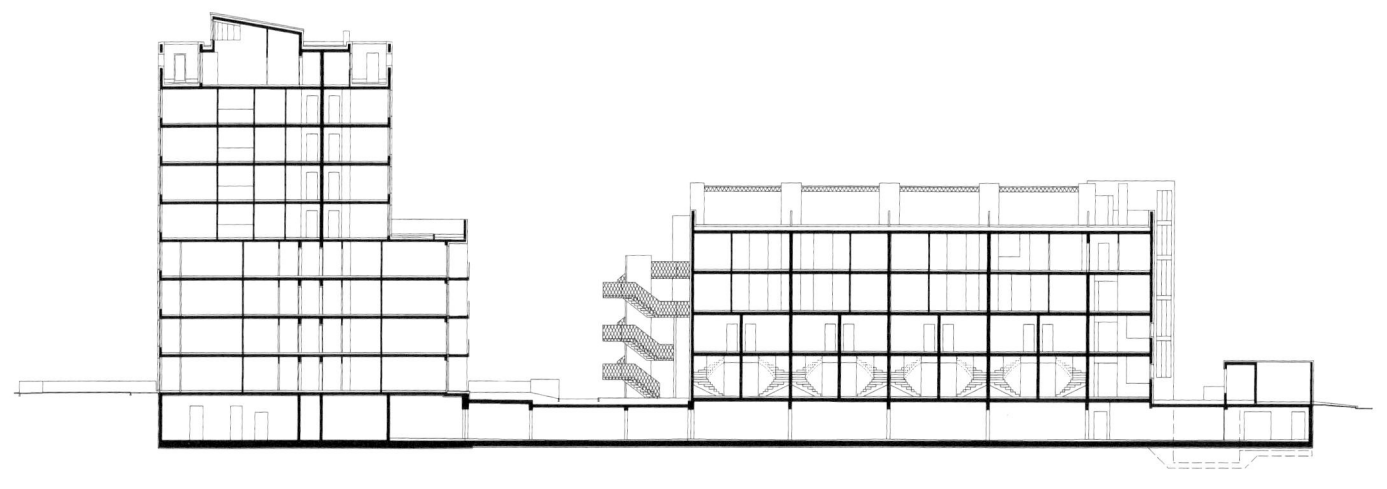

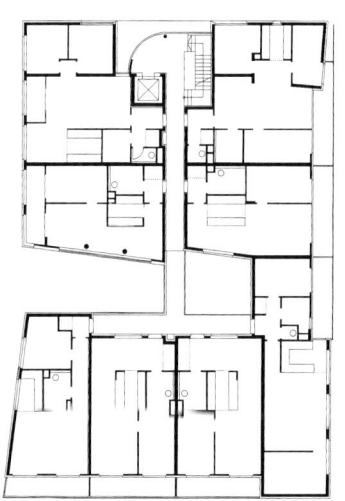

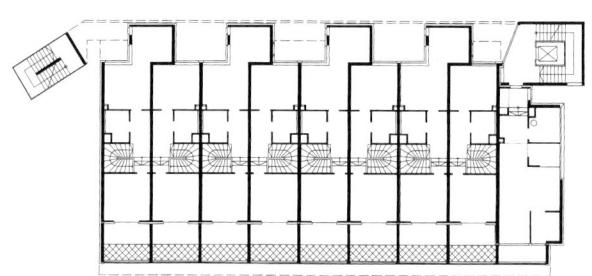

Schnitt
section

Regelgeschoss
standard floor

Erdgeschoss
ground floor

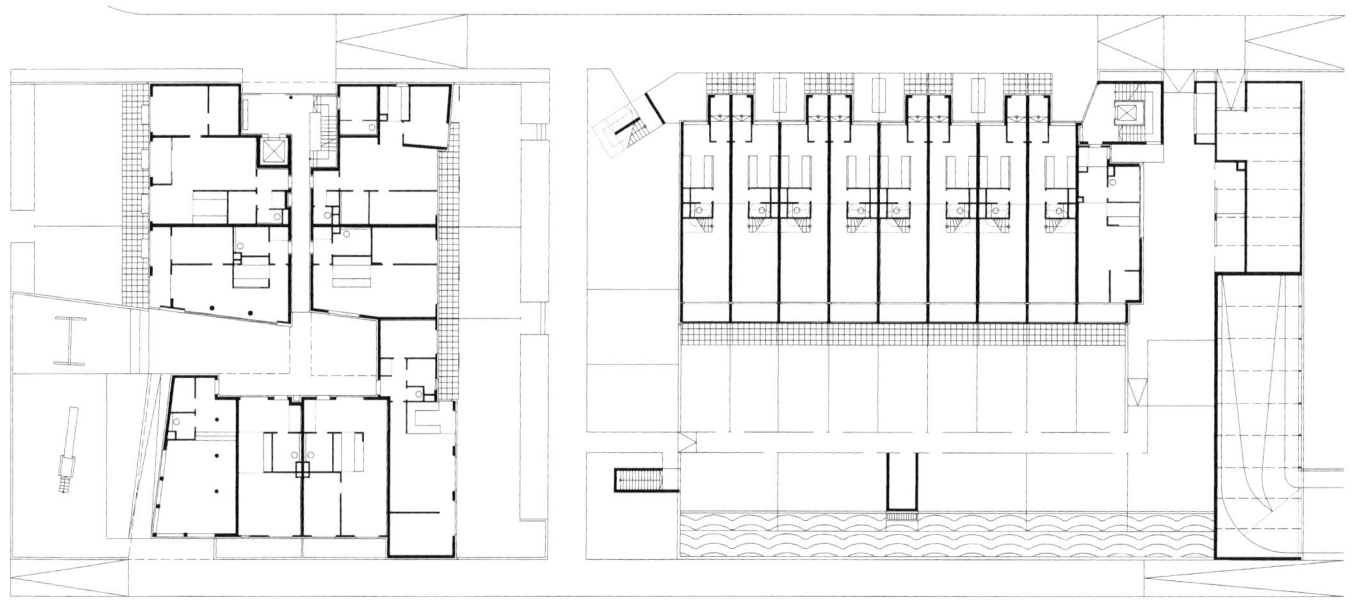

WOHNBAU IN DER STEINERGASSE, WIEN-LIESING
HOUSING DEVELOPMENT ON STEINERGASSE, VIENNA-LIESING

Wieder: sozialer Wohnbau an der Peripherie, vorgegebener Städtebau. H & V haben einen der Kopfbauten entworfen.

Maisonetten im Kopftrakt, dahinter zwei Vierspänner-Typen, angedockt mit laubengangartigen Aufschließungsbereichen. Relativ schmal, also gut belichtet, Loggien und Gärten jeweils zugeordnet. Wohnbau auf dem besseren heutigen Wiener Durchschnittslevel, in der internen Hausorganisation, auch in der Grundrissorganisation durchaus überzeugend gelöst. Dabei sehr kostengünstiger Wohnbau.

Eine weiße Putzfassade, 5,80 Meter Abstand zwischen den tragenden Scheiben. Kein Raster, der für die Tiefgarage Sinn macht, aber die kam auch erst später dazu. Im Übrigen: ein Konfliktpotential, das von der Stadt Wien kraft ihrer Autorität abgewürgt wurde – die angebotenen Leichtbauwände, entweder mit Eternit verkleidet oder auch mit Blechpaneelen, die eine wesentlich interessantere Optik für diesen Wohnbau gebracht hätten. Realisiert wurden Vollwärmeschutz-Fassaden. Eine konventionelle Lösung.

Trotzdem: eine durchgehende Loggienzone, Wohnen und Schlafen entkoppelt, und die Loggia so, dass man in der Wohnung zirkulieren kann. Effekt durch die Maisonette-Lösung an den Ecken: mehrgeschossige Lufträume im internen Erschließungsbereich, stimmungsvoll verkleidet mit Profilit. Letzte Erinnerung an die Industriebauten, die es hier einmal gab.

Once again: social housing on the periphery in an existing urban situation. H & V planned one of the front buildings.

Maisonettes in the front block, behind it two elements (four apartments per floor) attached by means of gallery-like circulation areas. Relatively shallow, therefore well-lit. Loggias or gardens are allotted to the units. Housing of the better modern Viennese standard. The internal organisation of the building and the floor plans are convincing. A highly economical housing project.

A white rendered façade, 5.80 metres between the load-bearing panels but this grid does not derive its logic from the requirements of the underground garage which, in any case, came later. Interesting: a potential source of conflict, eliminated by the Vienna Council in a demonstration of its authority: lightweight walls, clad either with fibre cement or sheet metal panels. Visually they would have been considerably more interesting. Instead a conventional solution – fully thermally insulated rendered façades – was used.

Despite this loss there remains: a continuous loggia zone, separation of living and sleeping, the loggia placed in such a way that one can move freely around the apartment. The maisonette type creates multi-storey circulation spaces at the corners, atmospherically clad with industrial glazing, a lasting memory of the industrial buildings that once stood here.

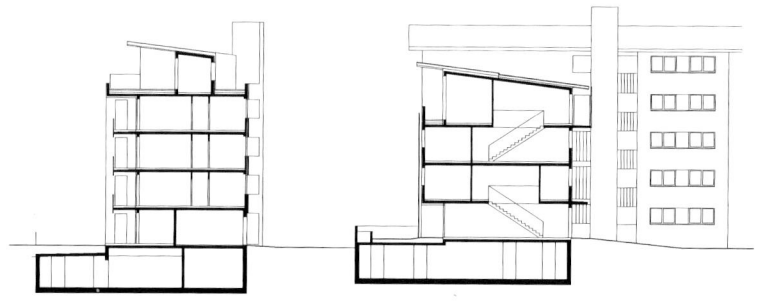

Schnitt
section

Regelgeschoss
standard floor

Erdgeschoss
ground floor

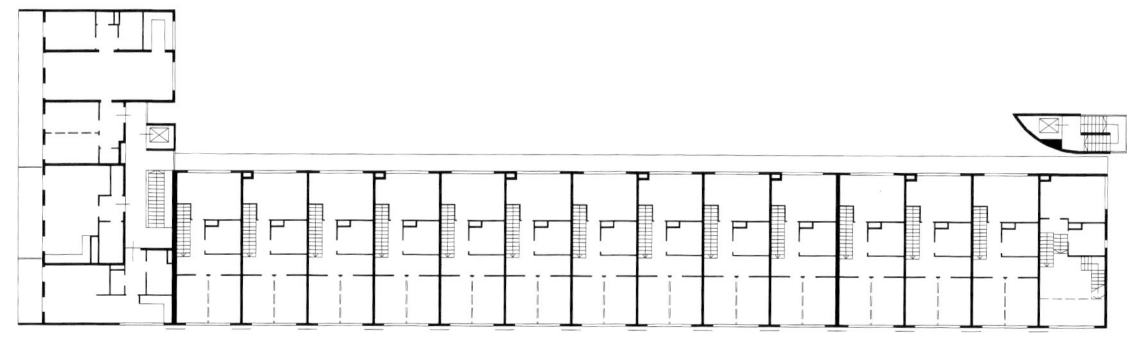

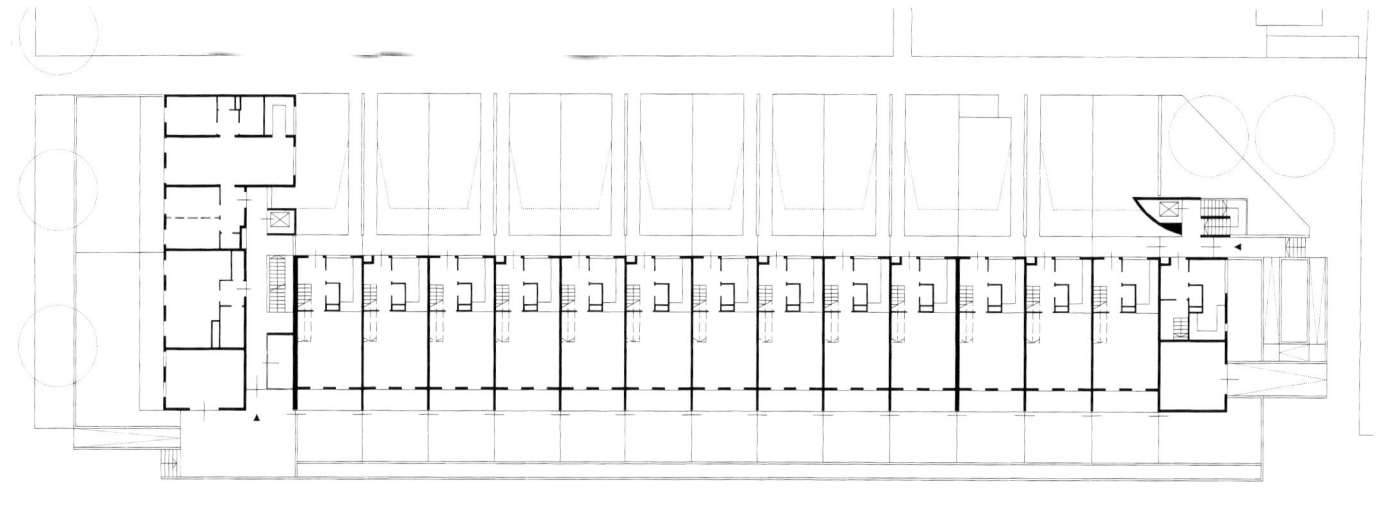

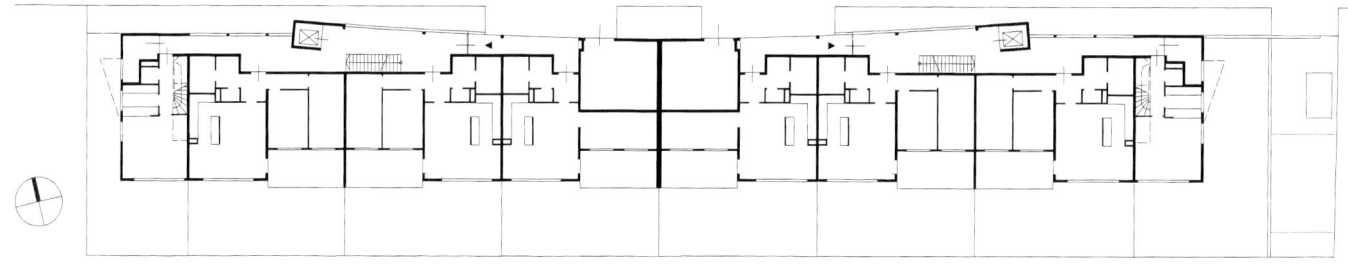

REIHENHÄUSER AM TELEFONWEG, WIEN-DONAUSTADT
TERRACE HOUSES ON TELEFONWEG, VIENNA-DONAUSTADT

Ein 300 Meter langes, sehr schmales Grundstück am Rand von Wien, umgeben von Kleingartenhäusern. Etwa in der Mitte trifft ein zweiter Weg auf den Telefonweg. An dieser Kreuzung steht das eingeschossige, leicht abgesenkte Gemeinschaftshaus, vorgelagert ein Platz, die Reihenhauszeilen (jeweils elf Häuser) ein wenig auseinandergedrückt.

Erste Besonderheit: die Garagenlösung, der auch städtebaulicher Stellenwert zukommt, ein mehrfach nutzbarer, überdeckter Zusatzraum. Zweite Besonderheit: die große Pergola, eine vorgelagerte grüne Schicht an der Ostseite der Häuser, sinnvoller Ersatz für den verordneten vier-Meter-Vorgartenbereich. Wohnraum mit Garten an der Westseite, nur in den beiden Doppelhäusern am Beginn der Anlage auch eine Südterrasse. Die verminderte „Intimität" der Situation hier aber abgefangen durch zusätzliche Dachterrassen.

Ungewöhnlich raffiniert: die innenräumliche Lösung der kleinen Häuser (eigentlich Drei-Zimmer-Wohnungen, Durchschnittsgröße 80 Quadratmeter). Ein wenig hochgehoben der Eingangsbereich, Küche und Essplatz drei Stufen abgesenkt und durch eine Brüstung getrennt die Wohnebene mit direktem Ausgang zum kleinen Gärtchen (kaum mehr als Wohnzimmergröße). Eingeschoben ein Galeriegeschoss, vielfältig interpretierbar – als ein großes Zimmer oder zwei kleine, als Zimmer mit Bad, als offene Galerie, als Arbeitsbereich.

Hier auch die Möglichkeit weiterzubauen, im sechs Meter hohen Luftraum über dem Wohnbereich eine Decke einzuziehen und so ein weiteres Zimmer zu gewinnen. Dann beträgt die lichte Raumhöhe unten 3,05 Meter, darüber 2,55 Meter. Nicht als Wohnraum deklariert, aber isoliert und tatsächlich als solcher nutzbar: das Dachgeschoss (Platz etwa für ein Schlafzimmer mit Bad).

An extremely narrow site on the periphery of Vienna, 300 metres long and surrounded by allotment garden houses. Approximately at the centre a second path meets Telefonweg. At this crossing stands a single-storey, slightly lowered community centre in front of which there is an open space and the rows of terrace houses, each consisting of eleven buildings, are moved apart somewhat from each other.

The first special feature: the handling of the garages which acquires an urban value: a covered space usable in a number of ways. The second feature: the large pergola forming a green layer placed in front of the east side of the houses that offers a sensible alternative to the proscribed, four metre deep front gardens. The living room with garden is on the west side, only in the two double houses at the start of the complex is there also a south-facing terrace. The reduction in the intimacy of the situation here is compensated by additional roof terraces.

Unusually intelligent: the internal planning of the small houses (which are, in fact, three room apartments, average size 80 square metres). The entrance area, kitchen and dining area is slightly elevated, the living area with direct access to the small garden (hardly bigger than the living room) lies three steps lower and is separated by a parapet wall. An inserted gallery level offers a variety of possibilities. It can be used as a single large room or two smaller spaces, as a room with bathroom or a work area.

Here too there is a possibility of extending by inserting a floor slab in the six metre high void to gain additional space. The room height on the upper level would then be 2.55 metres and below 3.05 metres. The attic storey, although not defined as a living space, is thermally insulated and could therefore be used as such (space for a bedroom with bathroom).

Sehr schlicht die Materialisierung: weiße Putzfassaden hinter der Pergola, Lärchenholz an der Westseite, Richtung Garten; eine Art Rahmenkonstruktion schafft hier einen schmalen (1,5 Meter) überdeckten Bereich mit einer Nische für Gartenmöbel oder den Rasenmäher; und sie fungiert als Scheuklappe gegenüber den unmittelbaren Nachbarn. An den schmalen räumlichen Schnittstellen durch die Zeilen: melonengelbe Farbakzente, also auch dort, bei den Zwischenräumen, keine Hinterhofatmosphäre. Gelb außerdem bei den um 90 Grad gedrehten, nach Süden orientierten Doppelhäusern am Beginn der Anlage.

Die Reihenhäuser am Telefonweg sind im Verhältnis zu vergleichbaren Wiener Wohnanlagen ein Vorzeigeprojekt: Hier wurde trotz der rigorosen Förderungsbestimmungen ein maximales Raumangebot zur Verfügung gestellt. Zu äußerst günstigen Preisen. Den Schlüssel zur überdurchschnittlichen Qualität im Wohnbau liefern also nicht Vorschriften oder Normen, den liefert die architektonische Intelligenz.

The materials are extremely simple: white render façades behind the pergola, larch on the west side facing onto the garden. Here a kind of frame construction creates a narrow (1.5 square metre) covered area with a niche for storing garden furniture or the lawn mower and also functions as a screen to the next door neighbours. Along the narrow interface through the rows there are melon yellow colour accents which prevent these intermediate spaces from exuding a backyard atmosphere. Yellow is used also for the south-facing double houses at the start of the complex that are swivelled through 90 degrees.

In comparison to other similar developments in Vienna the terrace houses on Telefonweg represent a model project. Despite the rigorous conditions that apply to the granting of housing subsidies a maximum amount of space is offered here at extremely reasonable price. Proof that the key to above average quality in housing is not supplied by regulations or standards but by architectural intelligence.

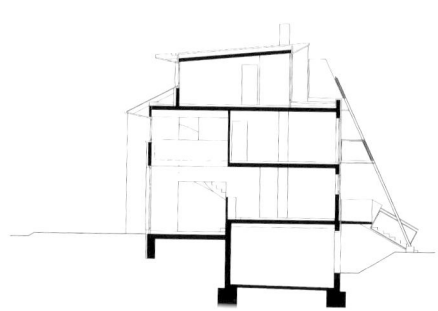

Schnitt
section

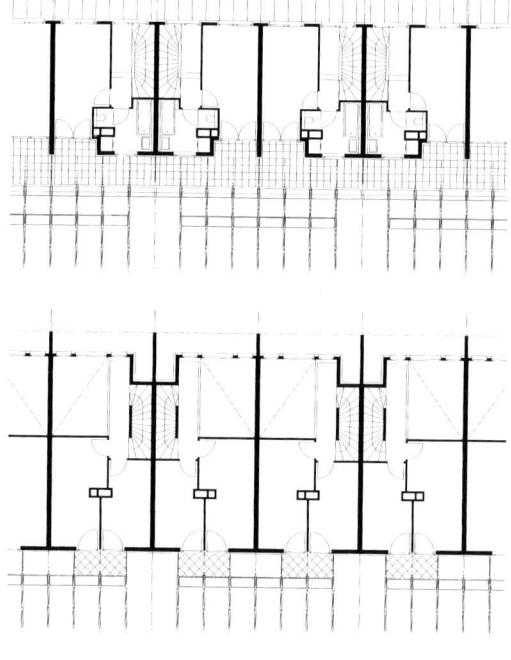

Dachgeschoss
attic storey

Regelgeschoss
standard floor

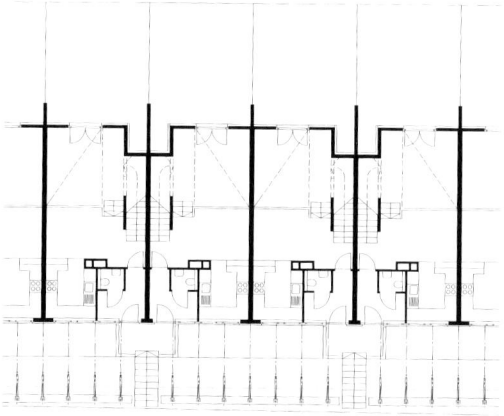

Erdgeschoss
ground floor

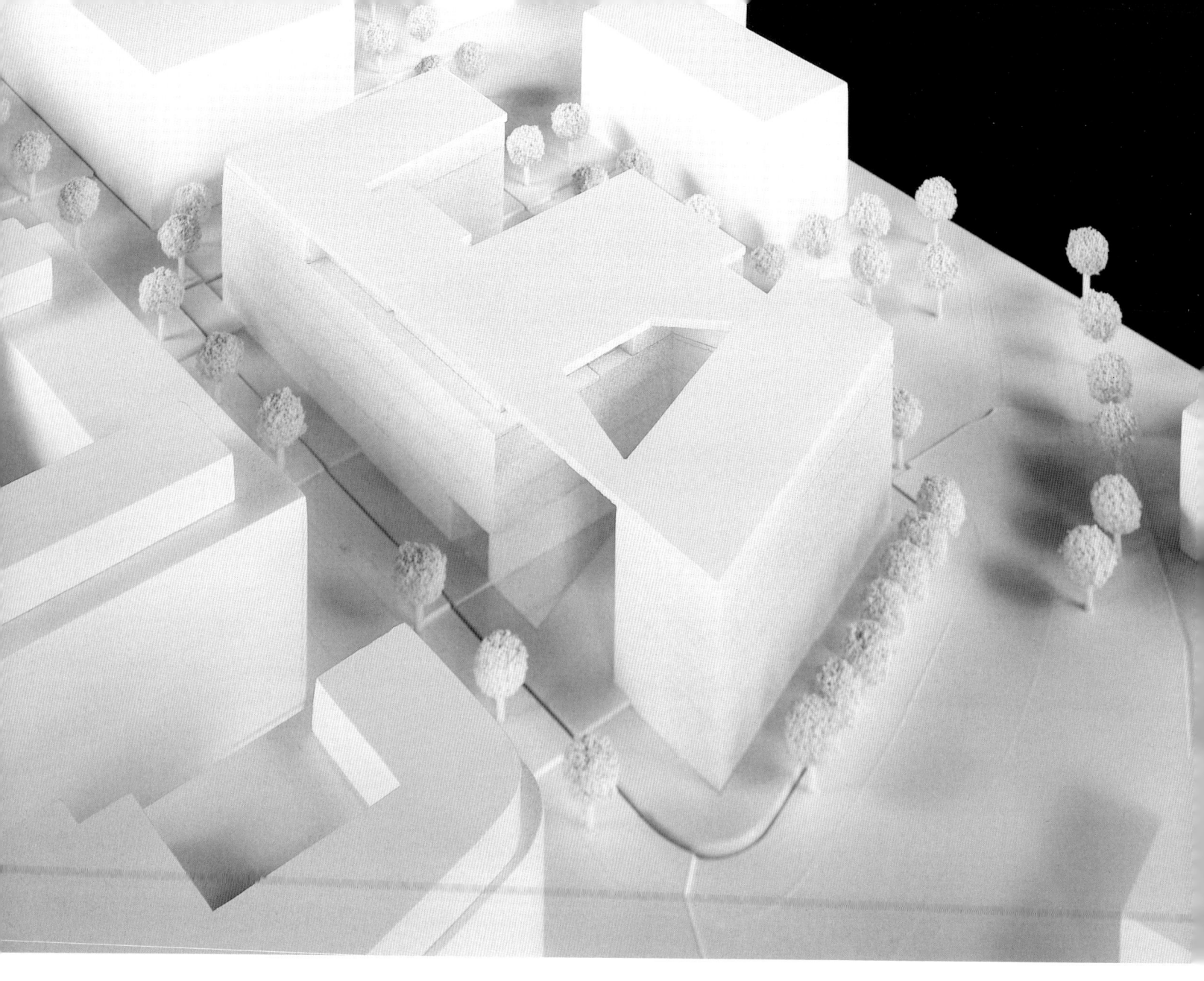

BANKGEBÄUDE AUF DEM KIRCHBERG, LUXEMBURG-STADT
BANK BUILDING ON THE KIRCHBERG, LUXEMBOURG-CITY

Eine Bank, aber zwei unterschiedliche Konzernbereiche auf einem Eckgrundstück im Blockraster des Kirchberges. Kein einfaches Grundstück, in einem Areal, das in Zukunft verdichtet wird. Autoren des Masterplans für diese städtische Entwicklung: H & V.

Verlangt: maximale Flächennutzung bei guter Belichtung der Räume, zusätzlich Freibereiche. Daher die fast mäanderförmige Gebäudekonfiguration, die Verschränkung zweier Bauten, die jeweils über Eck der Baulinie der Nachbargebäude folgen. Naheliegend: der Zugang von Norden – auch die Abfahrt in die Tiefgarage liegt hier –, wo sich aus dem Bebauungsprinzip ein tiefer Einschnitt ins Grundstück ergibt, der die Formulierung einer (überdeckten) Vorplatzsituation ermöglicht. Zwar spezifisch gestaltet durch ein Wasserbecken, aber doch unscharf, fließend im Übergang von öffentlichem und halböffentlichem Bereich. Imposant: die zwischengeschaltete Eingangshalle, fünfgeschossig verglast, die beiden Gebäuden gemeinsam ist und über eingehängte Galerien auch einen Teil der jeweiligen internen Erschließung sichtbar macht. Wichtig: die visuelle Durchlässigkeit dieser Halle, bis an die Südseite und zu einem schön bepflanzten Grünbereich.

Beide Gebäude enthalten vor allem Büros und natürlich auch Besprechungsräume. Hier geht es nicht um alltäglichen Schalterverkehr, sondern um „Private Banking", um Investment. Daher die Kundenparkplätze im ersten Untergeschoss mit direktem Zugang zu den Tresorräumen und jeweils zum obersten Geschoss, das speziell für Kundenberatung ausgelegt ist.

Ein erdgeschossiger Mehrzwecksaal ist zum Grünraum im Süden orientiert. Alle Büros sind durchwegs natürlich belichtet. Das Fassadenmuster aus Beton und geschosshohen, versetzten Fenstern morst unmissverständliche (heutigen Marketing-Strategien von Banken entsprechende) Signale ins urbane Umfeld: Offenheit und Transparenz gepaart mit Standfestigkeit und Sicherheit. Wahrnehmbar für jeden, der vorbei kommt: für den Fußgänger aus seiner verlangsamten Perspektive, für den Autofahrer aus der beschleunigten.

One bank but two different departments on a corner site in the block grid on the Kirchberg. Not an easy site in an area where the density is to be increased. The authors of the master plan for the urban development are H & V.

Requirements: maximum use of the site area, well-lit spaces and, additionally, open areas. The result: an almost meandering building configuration, two interlocking buildings each of which follows the line of the neighbouring buildings around a corner. The approach from the north almost suggested itself here – the ramp down to the underground garage is also at this point – where the development principle produces a deeper incision into the site that allows the formulation of a (covered) forecourt situation. Although the use of a pool gives it a specific design character it remains blurred, a flowing transition between public and semi-public areas. The five-storey glazed entrance shared by both buildings is most imposing. By means of inserted gallery levels it makes part of the internal circulation of both buildings visible. The visual transparency of this hall is important, the view extends through to the south side and to a lovely verdant planted area.

Both buildings contain primarily offices and, naturally, also meeting rooms. What is conducted here is not everyday bank business over a counter but "private banking" relating to investments, which explains the customers' parking places on the first basement level which have direct access to safe rooms and also to the upper floor which is specially laid out for customer services.

A multi-purpose room at ground-floor level faces towards the green space in the south. All the offices have natural light. The façade pattern of concrete and full-height, staggered windows transmits unmistakable messages to its urban surroundings (in accordance with current bank marketing strategy): openness and transparency paired with solidity and security understandable to every passer-by, both to the pedestrian from his slower perspective and to the motorist speeding past.

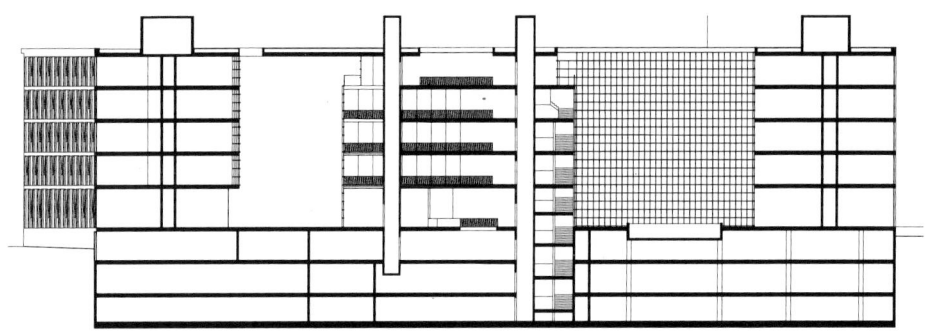

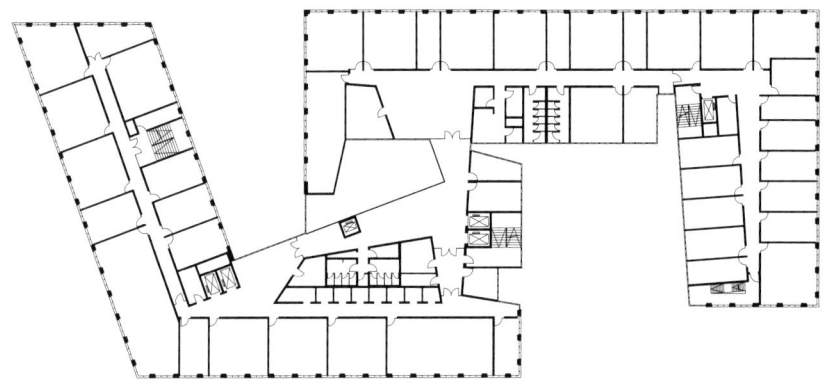

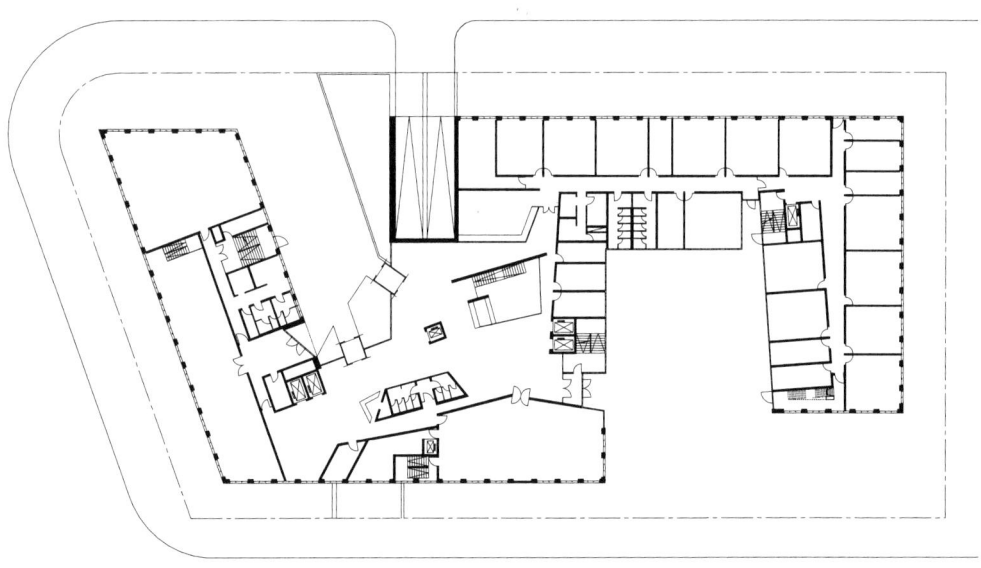

Schnitt
section

Regelgeschoss
standard floor

Erdgeschoss
ground floor

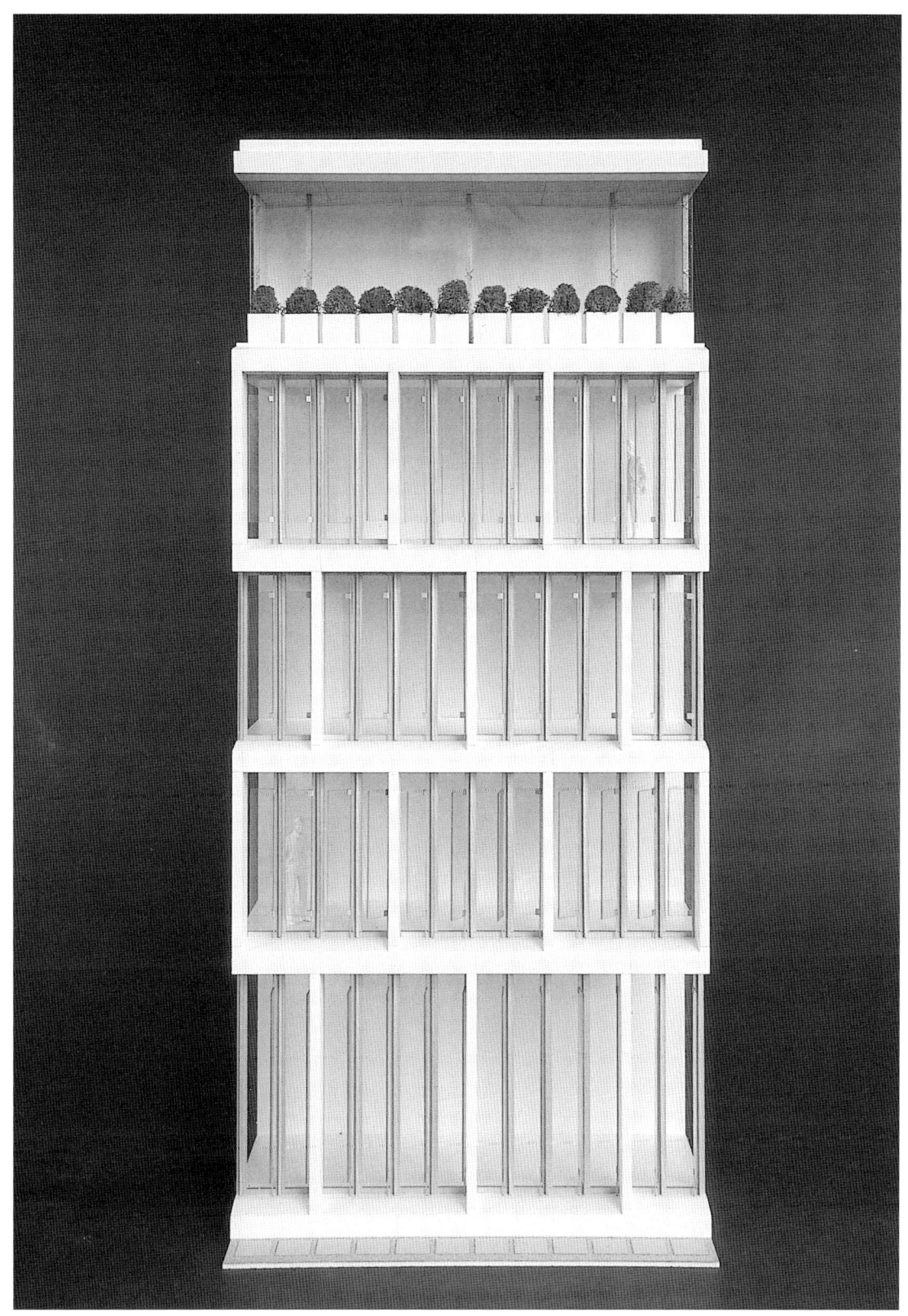

EINFAMILIENHAUS IN KLOSTERNEUBURG, NIEDERÖSTERREICH
SINGLE FAMILY HOUSE IN KLOSTERNEUBURG, LOWER AUSTRIA

Drei Themen, ein Haus.
Thema eins: Die besondere Topographie bedingt das besondere Hauskonzept.
Thema zwei: Die Materialisierung ist mit puren Materialien – Beton und Holz – umgesetzt.
Thema drei: Die in Niederösterreich zwingend vorgeschriebene Dachneigung wird zum bizarren 60-Grad-Giebel überhöht.

Der Baukörper steht oben auf einem steil abfallenden Hang. Man geht von der Straße nahezu ebenerdig ins Wohngeschoss im ersten Stock hinein und von dort hinunter ins Schlafgeschoss und hinauf auf eine Galerie (Arbeitsbereich für die Bauherren, Gästezimmer). Im Zentrum der architektonischen Inszenierung: der wundervolle Fernblick, aber auch das üppige Grün der unmittelbaren Umgebung. Ungewöhnlich spannend: der Umgang mit dem Material. Eine 20 Zentimeter dicke Betonplatte, die sich wie eine schützende Hand über die Andeutung eines Holzhäuschens stülpt. Gegen die Massivität des Betons wirkt der hölzerne Teil mit seiner Auflösung als Schiffsdeck hinter Lamellen fast wie ein Gerippe, wie eine Lattung, der nur noch die Haut fehlt.

Die Realisierung des rigorosen Materialkonzepts – für die Gebäudehaut Beton, Holz und Glas, drinnen etwa Eternit für das Bad – war durch die schwierige Erreichbarkeit der Baustelle – ein LKW kommt kaum hin, ein Kran war nicht aufzustellen – relativ aufwendig. Trotzdem ist die Betonschale in Halbfertigteilen ausgeführt, die mittels Autokran aufgelegt und dann ausgegossen wurden. Mit ihrer Licht-Schatten-Zeichnung für das Haus atmosphärisch unbedingt ein Gewinn: die „zweite" Schicht an der einen Längsseite, das vorgeschaltete hölzerne Deck mit der Lattenhaut.

Three themes, one house.
First theme: the special topography determines the special concept of the house.
Second theme: the house is given material form using pure materials – concrete and wood.
The pitched roof required by the building regulations in Lower Austria is exaggerated in the form of a bizarre 60 degree gable.

The building stands near the top of a steep slope. From the road one enters, almost at ground level, the living area which is on the first floor and from there can proceed down to the sleeping area and onto a gallery (guest rooms and a work area for the clients). At the centre of this architectural drama is the marvellous view into the distance and the luxurious vegetation of the immediate surroundings. The handling of materials is unusually exciting – a concrete slab 20 centimetres thick is placed like a protective hand over something suggestive of a little wooden house. In contrast to the massiveness of the concrete the wooden part, which is reduced at one place to a ship deck behind louvres, seems almost like a skeleton or ribbing, lacking only its skin.

The application of the rigorous material concept – for the skin of the building concrete, wood and glass, inside fibre cement for the bathroom – was relatively expensive due to the difficulty of access to the site which can hardly be reached by truck and where a normal crane could not be erected. Nevertheless the concrete shell is made of semi-prefabricated parts which were placed in position with a two-engine crane and then filled with concrete. The effect of light and shadow it creates undoubtedly benefits the atmosphere of the house. The "second" layer on one of the long sides is the wooden deck with its skin of battens.

Bauherr | client **Susanne Hoffmann / Bernhard Soyka**
Projektleiter | project manager **Marijana Popovic**
Grundstücksgröße | size of site **650 m²**
Nutzfläche | net floor area **224 m²**
Planungsbeginn | start of planning **2/1995**
Baubeginn | start of construction **9/1995**
Fertigstellung | completion **1/1997**

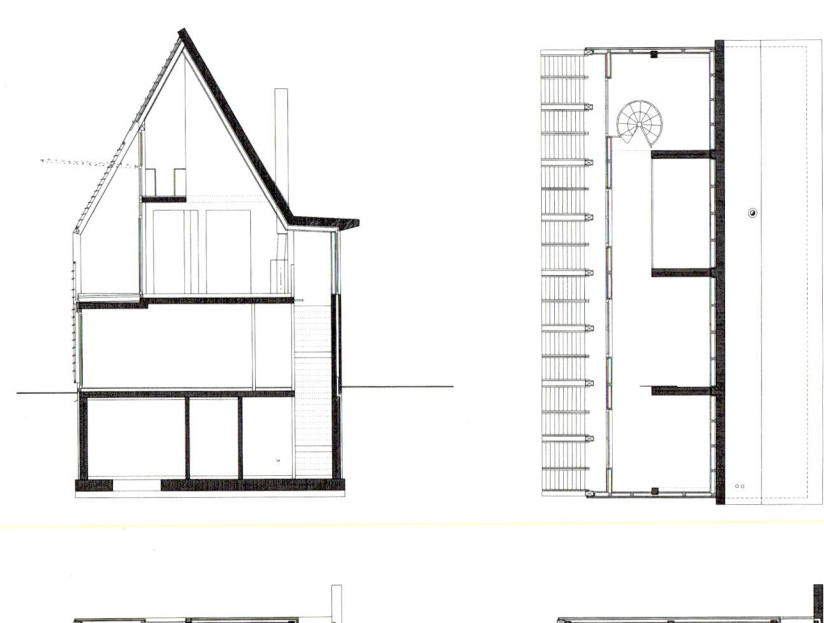

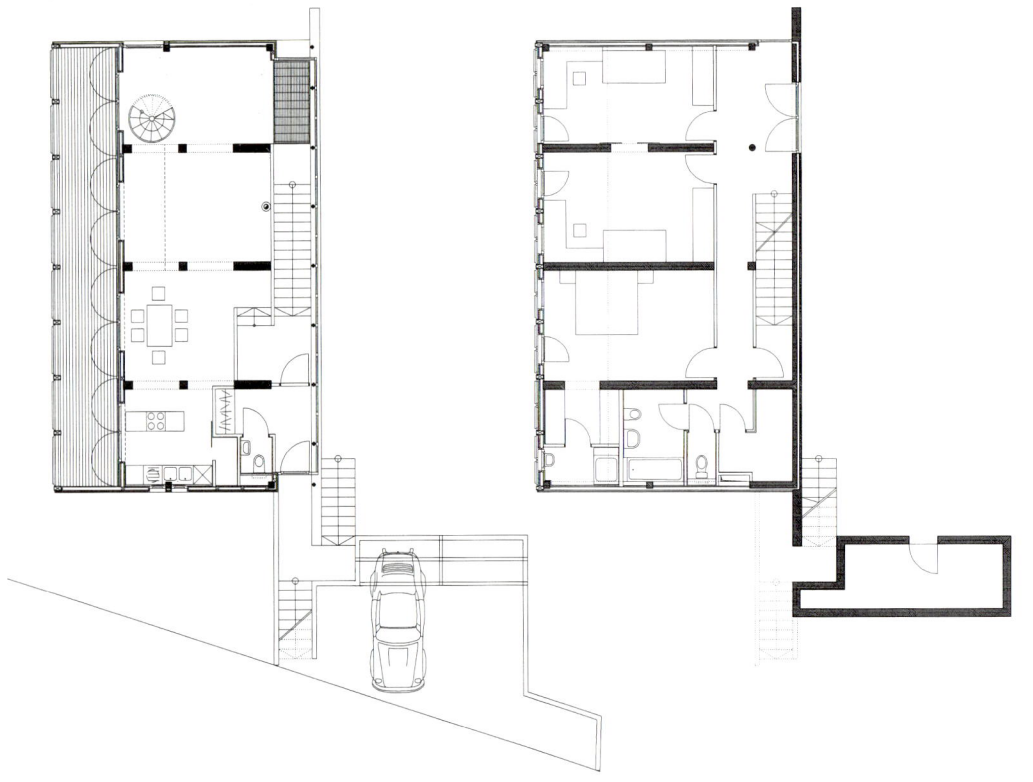

Schnitt
section

Dachgeschoss
attic storey

1. Obergeschoss
1st floor

Erdgeschoss
ground floor

EINFAMILIENHAUS IN WIEN
SINGLE FAMILY HOUSE IN VIENNA

Ein kleines Grundstück, ein großes Haus. Das Umfeld: eine gehobene Wohngegend von Wien, Einfamilienhäuser und Gärten. Hanglage. Das Haus ist von der Straße abgerückt, um einen grünen Vorbereich zu schaffen. Im Übrigen wurde etwa die Hälfte des 600 Quadratmeter großen Grundstückes verbaut.

Das Haus selbst ist entweder als Schachtel lesbar, aus der etwas herausgeschnitten wurde, oder auch als die Verschachtelung von zwei separaten Baukörpern. Neben und unter den größeren dieser beiden Körper ist eine Art Lade eingeschoben, der Versorgungstrakt mit Küche, Kinderzimmer, Gästezimmer und -bad.

Die Garage, natürlich vorne an der Straße, ist ins Gelände eingebettet. Von dort geht es direkt hinauf ins Haus – oder: hinein in das ungewöhnlich attraktive Kellergeschoss. Ein geschwungener Gang – melonengelb gestrichen und raffiniert künstlich belichtet – erschließt die zumindest teilweise auch natürlich belichteten Hobbyräume der Bauherren: das Billardzimmer mit kleiner Bar für den Hausherrn in den Farben tomatenrot und dunkelblau, einen Gymnastikraum für die Hausfrau in pfefferminzgrün und blau.

A small site with a large house. The surrounding area is one of Vienna's better residential districts, mostly single-family houses and gardens. The house is moved back from the road in order to create a green area at the front. About half of the 600 square metre site was built on.

This house can be read either as a box from which a part has been cut out or as two separate interlocking elements. Beside and underneath the larger of these two elements a kind of drawer has been inserted which forms, in a sense, a service wing with kitchen, children's room, guest room and bathroom.

The garage is, naturally, at the front beside the road. From there one can go directly up to the house or inside into an unusually attractive basement. A curved corridor painted melon yellow and artificially lit in a particularly subtle way leads to the clients' hobby rooms which are, at least in part, naturally lit: the billiards room with a small bar for the master of the house which is tomato red and dark blue and an exercise room for his wife in peppermint-green and blue.

Atmosphärisch großzügig: Wohnraum und Essplatz mit ihrer teilweisen Zweigeschossigkeit. Sie sind in der zweiten Ebene räumlich mit dem Schlafzimmer verschmolzen; es ist nur durch eine Glaswand abgetrennt. Sinn dieser ungewöhnlichen Maßnahme: der Blick ins Atrium an der Rückseite des Hauses, einem intimen Außenraum mit Wasserfläche.

Eingehängt ins Obergeschoss: eine Galerie mit Bibliothek; außerdem Ankleide, Bad, ein bescheidener Arbeitsbereich. Und schließlich ganz oben, auf dem Dach: ein kleiner Aufbau, von den Bauherren liebevoll „Gloriette" genannt, ein 14 Meter langes Schwimmbecken, eine strenge, fast japanisch anmutende Dachgartengestaltung.

Ein räumlich luxuriöses Haus. Auch ausgesprochen edel materialisiert: schwarzer Schiefer in den Bädern; helles Ahorn beim teilweise von H & V entworfenen Mobiliar; ein rigoroses Farbkonzept; und außen, an der Fassadenhaut, die Glätte eines zwischen mattem Glattputz und roter Verglasung changierenden Kleides.

The atmosphere is generous. The living room and dining area are in part two storeys high. On the second level they mesh spatially with the bedroom that is separated only by a glass wall. The reason for this unusual measure is the view into an atrium at the rear of the house: an intimate external space with an area of water.

A gallery with library is hung within the upper level: in addition, there is a dressing room, a bathroom, a modest work area, and finally, at the very top, on the roof a small crowning element affectionately dubbed the "Gloriette" by the owners, a swimming pool 14 metres long and a severe, almost Japanese, roof garden.

In spatial terms a luxurious house, the materials are particularly fine: black slate in the bathrooms, light maple wood for the furnishings, some of them designed by H & V. A rigorous colour scheme and, externally, on the façade skin the smoothness of a cladding that changes between matt render and red glazing.

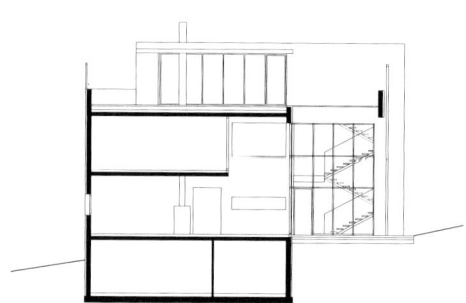

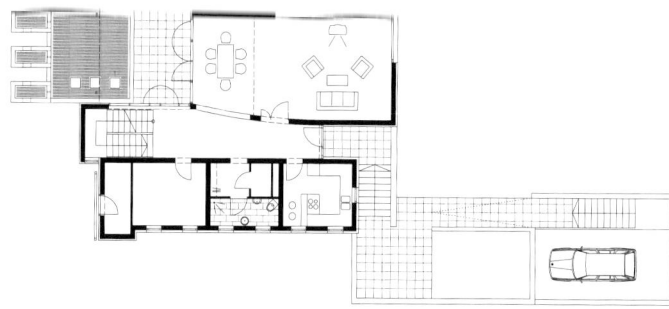

Bauherr wird nicht bekanntgegeben | client not stated
Projektleiter | project manager **Manfred Wagner**
Grundstücksgröße | size of site **590 m²**
Nutzfläche | net floor area **305 m²**
Planungsbeginn | start of planning **7/1997**
Baubeginn | start of construction **8/1998**
Fertigstellung | completion **12/2000**

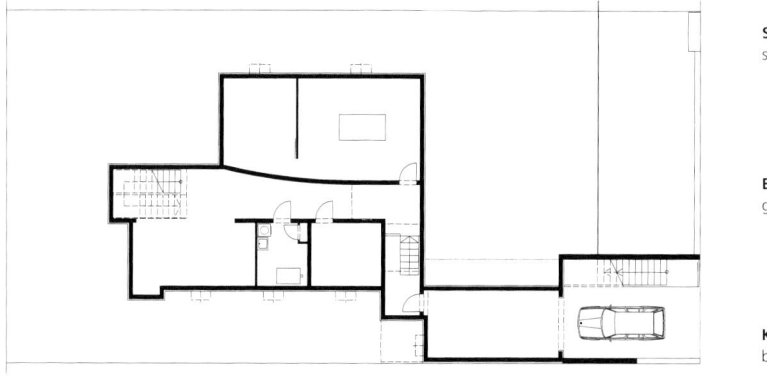

Schnitt
section

Erdgeschoss
ground floor

Kellergeschoss
basement

UMBAU EINES EINFAMILIENHAUSES IN GROSSAU, NIEDERÖSTERREICH

REDESIGN OF A SINGLE FAMILY HOUSE IN GROSSAU, LOWER AUSTRIA

Metamorphose eines Hauses aus den sechziger Jahren. Standort: auf einem Hang, der den Blick über die Ortschaft und hinüber in die unverbaute Landschaft frei gibt. Die ursprüngliche Dachform: unsäglich, zwei gegeneinander verschnittene Pultdächer. Durch den Umbau eines davon – das hangseitige – abgetragen und ersetzt durch eine überdachte Terrasse mit phänomenaler Weitsicht. Trickreich die Materialisierung: ein haushohes Stahlgerüst als zweite Schicht, das den fragwürdigen Zubau eines Wintergartens (aus neuerer Zeit) in den Hintergrund drängt, ihn relativiert. Seitlich eine Verletzung am Haus, melonengelb gestrichen: ein vergittertes Wohnzimmer im Freien für die Katzen der Hausherrin. Weitere architektonische Eingriffe – unter anderem ein über den Hang vorkragendes Schwimmbecken – sind noch nicht realisiert.

Metamorphosis of a house dating from the sixties. Located on a slope with a view across the town and of the open countryside beyond. The original roof was unspeakably awful: two intersecting mono-pitch roofs. In the course of the redesign the roof on the slope side was demolished and replaced by a covered terrace with a phenomenal view. The use of materials reveals a number of tricks: a steel frame the entire height of the house forms a second layer that pushes the questionable (more recent) addition of a winter garden into the background. At the side an "injury" to the house is painted melon yellow: a caged open-air living room for the client's cats. Further architectural interventions – including a swimming pool projecting above the slope – have not been realised yet.

Bauherr | client **Monika Maderbacher/Horst Foidl**
Projektleiter | project manager **Claude Giger**
Grundstücksgröße | size of site **650 m²**
Planungsbeginn | start of planning **1997**
Baubeginn | start of construction **1997**

GASOMETER IN WIEN-SIMMERING
GASOMETER IN VIENNA-SIMMERING

Eines der problematischsten Bauvorhaben in Wien: eine Gratwanderung im Unschärfebereich zwischen Denkmalschutz, Umnutzung und zeitgenössischer architektonischer Intervention.

Die vier gewaltigen Gasometerhüllen – zylindrisches Sichtziegelmauerwerk auf einem Sockel, jeweils gedeckt mit einer flachen Kuppel – umschließen die wahrscheinlich eindrucksvollsten (kalten) Innenräume, die es in Wien in historischen Gebäuden noch gibt. Sie sind so groß, dass in jedem solchen Innenraum das Wiener Riesenrad Platz finden würde. Und sie stehen in einer peripheren Gegend der Stadt, wo sich Wohnen und Gewerbe schon sehr verschränken. Gesucht wurde nach einer neuen Nutzungsmöglichkeit für diese Industriebauten. Und entschieden wurde zugunsten von Wohnbauten, die in der – nunmehr durchlöcherten – historischen Hülle realisiert werden.

H & V formulieren dagegen eine krasse, unmissverständliche Aussage, die im extremen Widerspruch zur realisierten Lösung steht. Das Büro packt genau das, was im Gasometer-Innenraum Platz finden sollte, in der historischen Hülle, in einen eigenen Baukörper hinein, der als überdeutliches Architektur-Statement hinter die vier Zylinder gestellt ist. Ein Protest-Projekt: 300 Meter lang und 27 Geschosse hoch. Also eine Größenordnung, an der Schmerzgrenze der Verkraftbarkeit.

Der offensichtliche Gewinn: Die infrastrukturellen Maßnahmen, die jetzt zur Aufwertung des bisher unentwickelten, aber durch einen eigenen, neu geschaffenen U-Bahn-Anschluss interessanter gewordenen Gebietes unter eingeschränkten Bedingungen in die Umgebung gestellt werden, die hätten in den Gasometern selbst Platz gefunden. Damit wäre das eigentliche Spektakel dieser Denkmäler, das eindrucksvolle Raumvolumen, weitgehend erhalten geblieben.

One of the most problematic building projects in Vienna that represents a tightrope walk in an imprecisely defined area lying somewhere between conservation, new uses for old buildings and contemporary architectural intervention.

The four mighty gasometers: cylinders made of fair-faced brick, each roofed by a shallow dome. These shells encase what are probably the most impressive (unheated) interiors still existing in any historical building in Vienna. They are so large that the giant Ferris wheel in the Prater could fit inside any one of them and are located in an area on the periphery of the city where housing and industrial premises stand cheek by jowl. The objective was to find a new use for these buildings; the final decision was made in favour of housing which is presently being constructed in the historical shells now perforated by a number of openings.

H & V formulate a blunt statement impossible to misunderstand that is the extreme opposite of the solution actually built. This architectural practice packs precisely what was meant to be accommodated in the interior of the gasometer, i.e. in the historic shell, in an independent element, a mighty slab that forms a kind of background architecture but is above all an emphatically clear architectural statement placed behind the four cylinders, This project is a protest made with an unsurpassable clarity. It is 300 metres long and 27 storeys high and thus of a size which unmistakably steers towards the limits of what is acceptable.

The clear advantage: the infrastructural measures, undertaken (under restricted circumstances) in the area in order to enhance a district previously underdeveloped but now more interesting due to its own newly built Underground railway connection, could have been placed in the gasometers themselves. The truly spectacular aspect of these monuments, the impressive spatial volumes, would have been for the most part preserved.

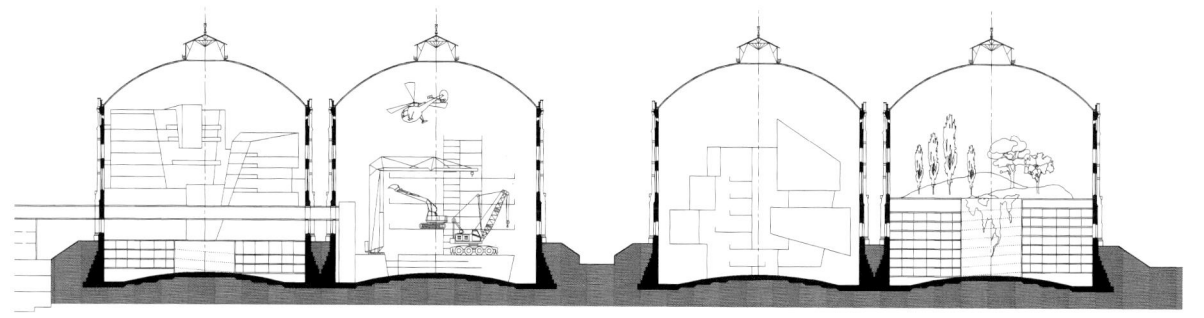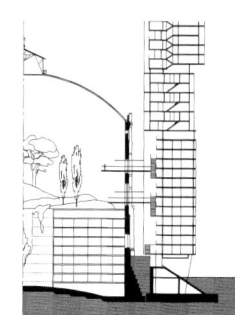

Die Wohnscheibe selbst – ein Entwurf in Schichten. Aufgeständert, drei Typologien übereinander. Die unterste im Dialog mit dem Backstein-Mauerwerk der Gasometer, darüber Maisonetten, schon teilweise durchgesteckt, und wieder darüber – mit 18 Metern – ein ganz tiefer Split-Level-Typ. Erschließungsgänge nur in jedem zweiten Geschoss; hier gibt es auch die besondere Attraktion der Draufsicht auf die Gasometerkuppeln.

Das Projekt hätte übrigens ein spannendes, ausgesprochen innovatives Potential enthalten. Die Möglichkeit nämlich, unterschiedliche Architekten mit den einzelnen typologischen Schichten zu beauftragen – also eine handschriftlich individuelle horizontale Schichtung statt der üblichen vertikalen Addition. Allein das wäre einen Versuch wert gewesen.

The housing block itself: a design made up of layers carried on struts, three typologies one above the other. The lowest enters into a dialogue with the brick masonry of the gasometers, above are maisonettes, some extending the full depth of the building, and above again – 18 metres high – an extremely deep split-level type. Access decks only on every second floor, here too a special attraction is offered: a view from above of the gasometer roofs.

This project would have harboured an exciting, extremely innovative potential i.e. the possibility of commissioning different architects for the different typological layers resulting in horizontal layering carrying individual signatures rather than the standard vertical stacking of floors. This alone would have justified making the attempt.

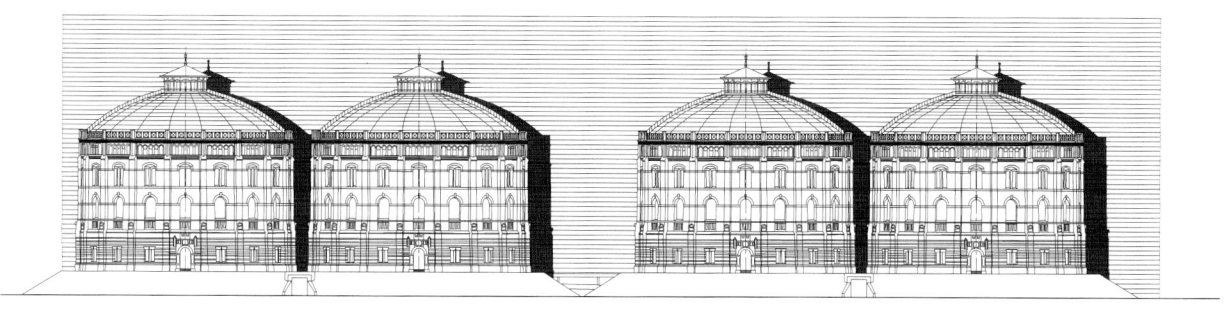

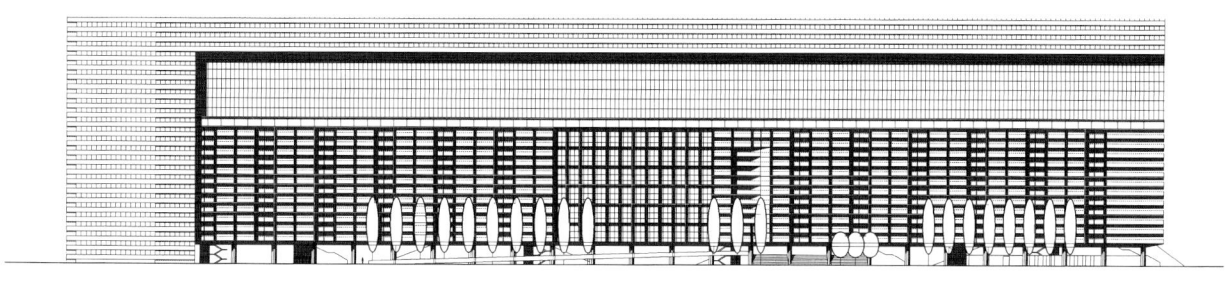

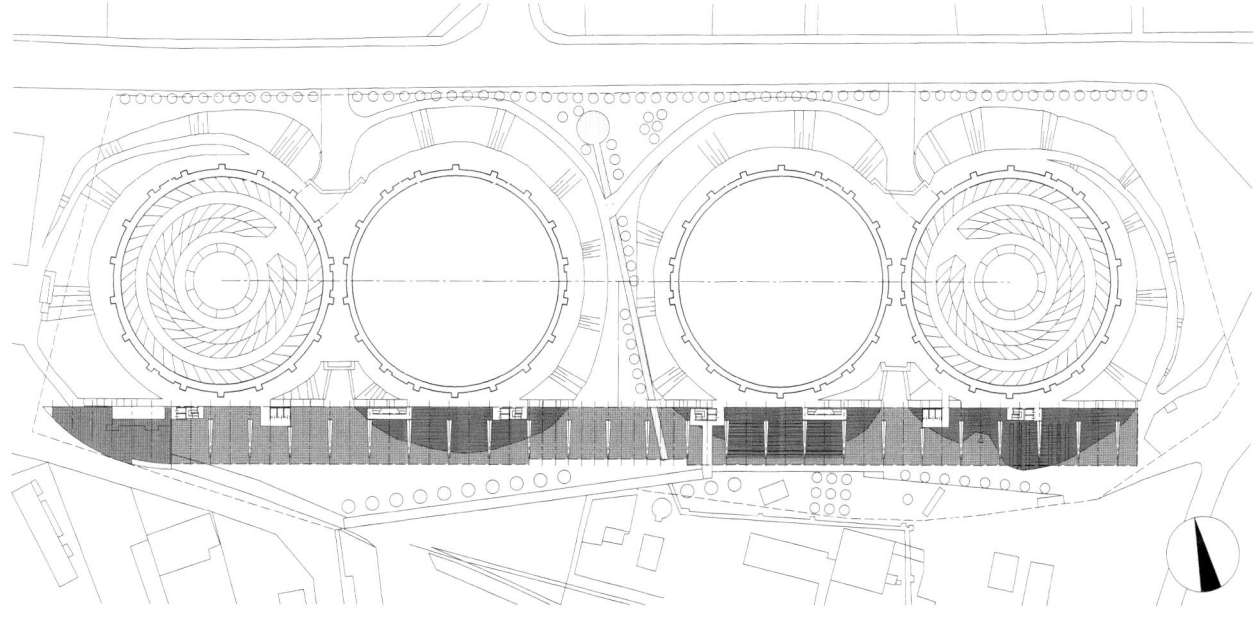

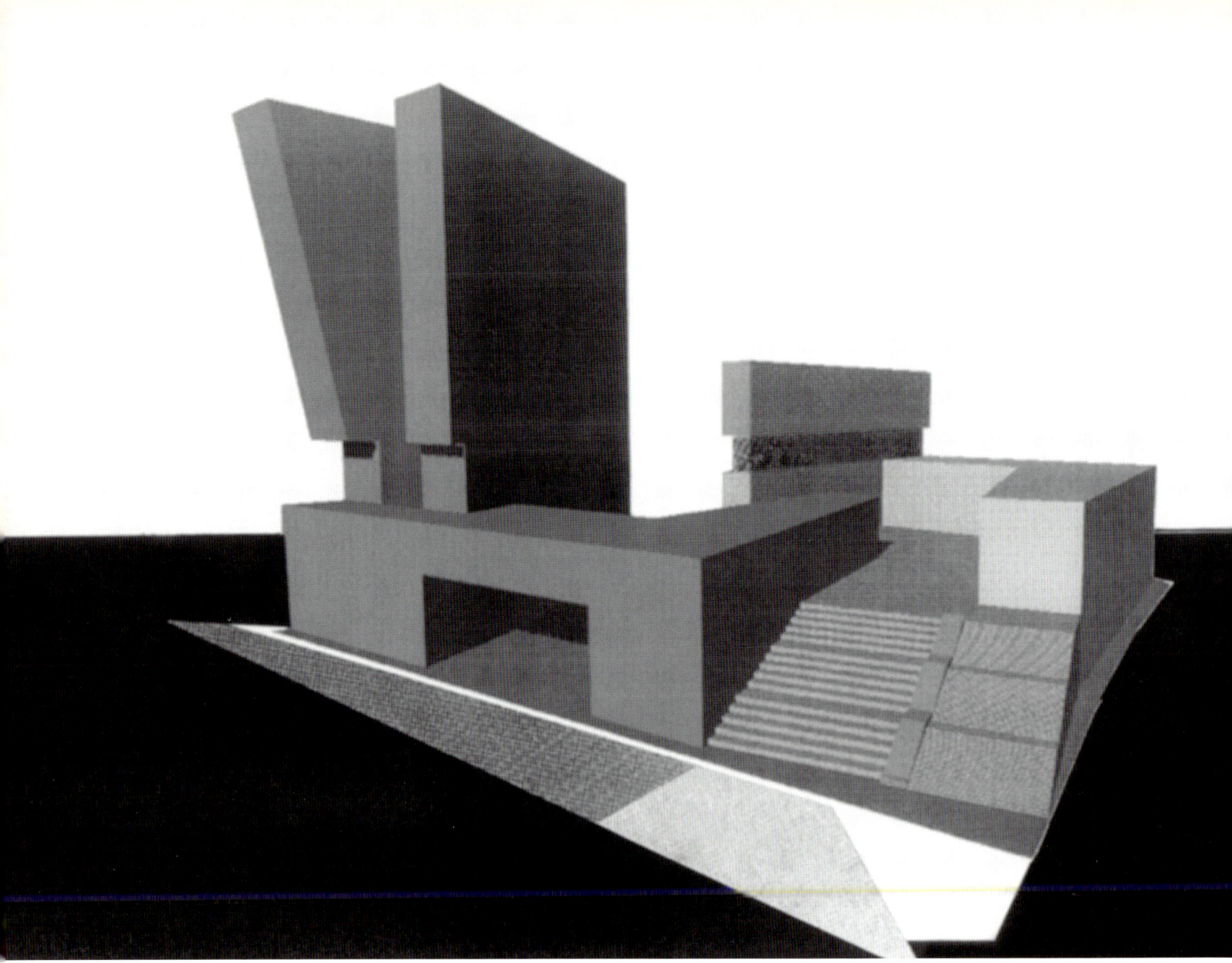

BÜRO-, GESCHÄFTS- UND GEWERBEBAUTEN
MODECENTERSTRASSE, WIEN-SIMMERING
OFFICE, RETAIL AND COMMERCIAL BUILDINGS,
MODECENTERSTRASSE, VIENNA-SIMMERING

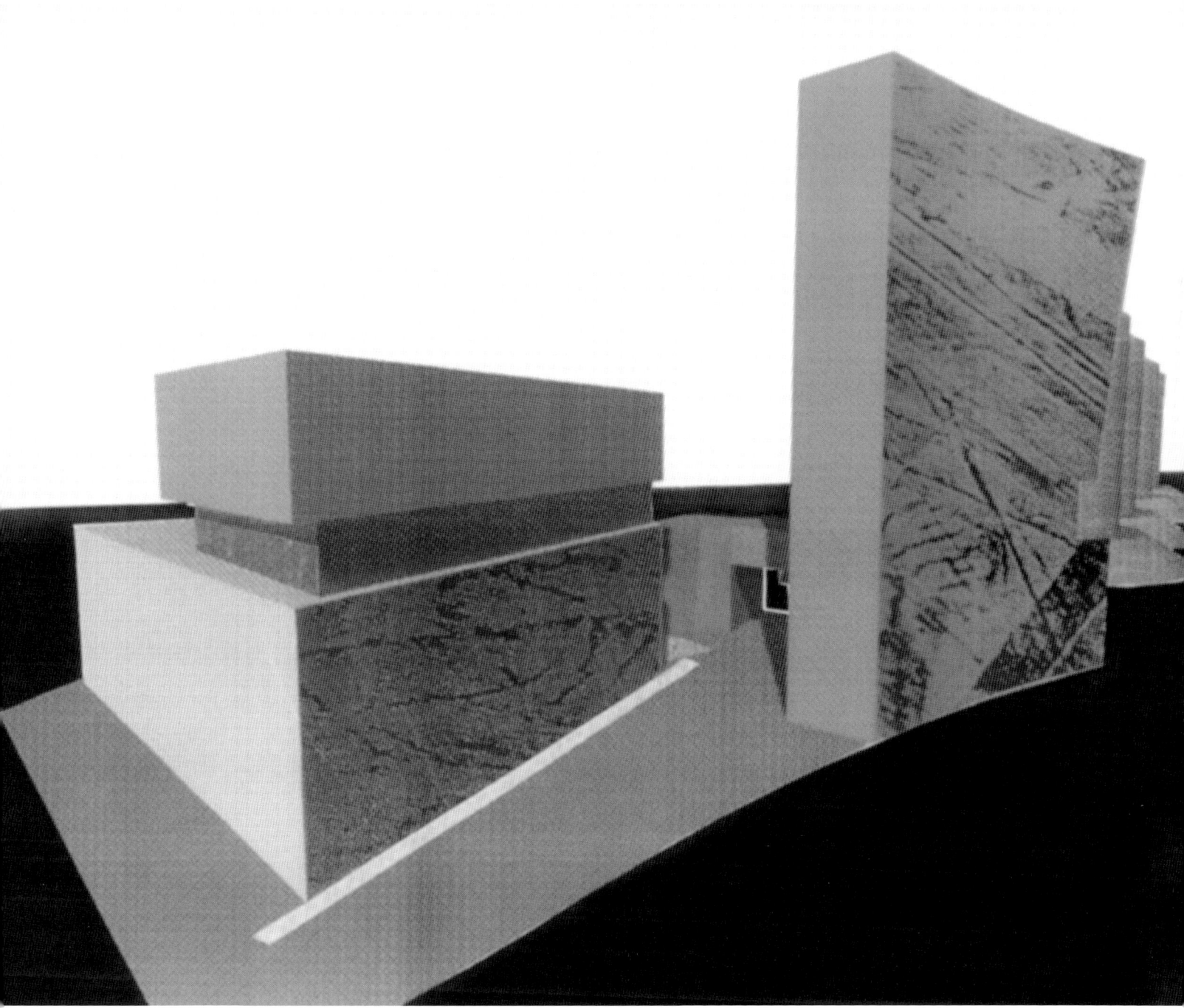

Eine Initiative der Stadt Wien, die im Zusammenhang mit dem Gasometer-Projekt gesehen werden muss. Die Wohnungen in den vier Gasometern sind durch die U-Bahn gut ans (ferne) Stadtzentrum angebunden, es fehlt ihnen jedoch ein entsprechend städtisches Umfeld im Nahbereich. Entlang der Modecenterstraße sind in jüngster Zeit einige Bürobauten entstanden, zwischen den Gasometern und diesen Bürobauten gibt es hingegen, von einem neuen Kinocenter abgesehen, ein weitgehend leerstehendes Areal, das sich auf drei verschiedene Eigentümer aufteilt. Aufgabe war es, ein Gesamtkonzept für diese Fläche zu entwickeln.

Städtebaulich nimmt der Vorschlag von H & V vor allem zweierlei auf: die gewaltige Flucht der vier Gasometer, die im Bebauungsvorschlag gewissermaßen weitergeführt und zu einem Ende gebracht wird; und den Bezug zur U-Bahn-Station als Drehscheibe für die Verbindung zur Stadt.

Der ursprünglich geforderte Nutzungsmix wurde im Verlauf der Planung zugunsten reiner Büro- und Gewerbeflächen aufgegeben, nur entlang der mäandrierenden Passage, die das Areal durchzieht, sind auch Geschäfte vorgesehen. Themen, die bei den Gasometern eine Rolle spielen, kehren im Bebauungsvorschlag von H & V wieder, der Unterschied liegt in der Interpretation. So stehen die vier Gasometer auf einem Sockel – er taucht auch an der Modecenterstraße wieder auf, aber genutzt als Gewerbefläche. Der Vorteil: für die Gebäude auf diesem Sockel entstehen weite Blickachsen, städtebauliche Verbindungen sind also wahrnehmbar. Auch mit der Höhenentwicklung der Gebäudekonfiguration reagieren H & V auf die Nähe der Gasometer: Ein Bauteil, wie ein Fingerzeig Richtung Himmel, ragt sogar 80 Meter auf, also über die Traufe der historischen Nachbarn.

Architektonische Feinarbeit: Die höhenmäßig sehr differenzierten Baukörper nehmen den leichten Schwung der Grundstücksgrenze auf, sie geben eine Richtung an; eine große Freitreppe führt hinauf in diese Arbeitslandschaft; Bürohöfe stellen attraktive Freibereiche zur Verfügung; aber niemand, der hier arbeitet, sieht nur in einen Hof oder hinüber zu seinem Visavis. Das wäre heute, sagt Hubert Hermann, unzumutbar.

An initiative of the City of Vienna that should be viewed in conjunction with the gasometer projects. The apartments in the four gasometers are well connected to the (distant) city centre by the Underground, but lack appropriate urban surroundings in their immediate vicinity. In recent times several office buildings have been erected along Modecenterstrasse, but between these buildings and the gasometers, apart from a new cinema centre, there is a largely empty area made up of sites belonging to three different owners. The task was to develop an overall concept for this area.

In urban planning terms H & V's suggestion makes two primary responses: firstly to the powerful line of the four gasometers which is, in a sense continued and terminated and secondly to the Underground station as the turntable for the connection to the city.

In the course of planning the originally required mix of uses was abandoned in favour of office and commercial space and it is only along the meandering passageway extending through the site that shops are also envisaged. Themes which play a role in the gasometers reoccur in H&V's development proposal, the difference lying in the way they are interpreted. For example the four gasometers stand on a base, an element which crops up again along Modecenterstrasse, but in this case used as commercial space. The advantage is that the buildings on this plinth have axial views into the distance making the urban connection visually perceptible. The heights of the configuration of buildings in H & V's design also react to the proximity of the gasometers. An element pointing like a finger towards the heavens extends 80 metres upwards, that is above the eaves height of its historic neighbours.

Precision architectural work: the buildings, which differ considerably in height, take up the gentle curve of the site boundary and indicate a direction. A large external set of steps leads up to this landscape of workplaces. Office courtyards offer attractive outdoor spaces, but no-one working here has a view into a courtyard or across to his neighbour opposite only. Nowadays, says Hubert Hermann, that would be unacceptable.

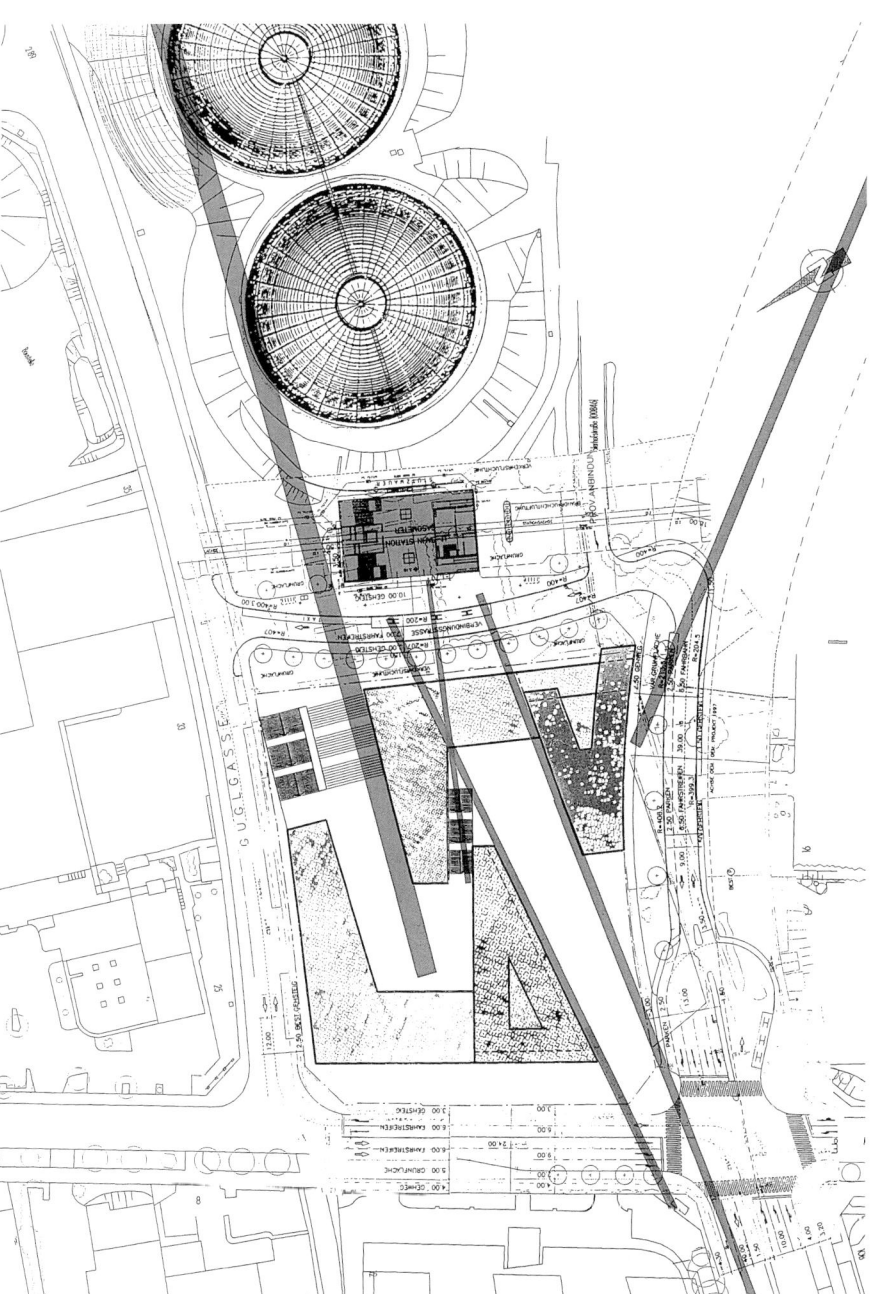

Studie Sichtbezüge
study of the visual relationships

Erdgeschoss
ground floor

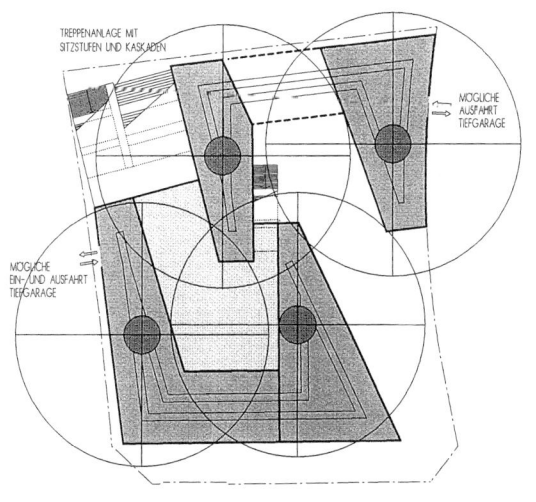

GEMEINDEZENTRUM IN BECH-KLEINMACHER, LUXEMBURG
TOWN COUNCIL BUILDING IN BECH-KLEINMACHER, LUXEMBOURG

Eine dörfliche Struktur, in die sich das Gemeindehaus maßstäblich einfügt. Ein altes Pfarrhaus – aus Stein gebaut und verputzt –, umgenutzt und um einen Zubau erweitert. Das unmittelbare Umfeld, einschließlich Platzraumgestaltung und der vorhandenen, gestalterisch modifizierten Aufbahrungshalle, neu und einheitlich interpretiert. Und – gerade was das Umfeld betrifft – auch sehr stimmungsvoll: mit einer Wasserfläche an der (straßenabgewandten) Breitseite des Zubaus und der gezielt eingesetzten Begrünung.

Besonderheit des Gemeindehaus-Zubaus: Er ist schwarz und roh und schimmert (Basaltbeton). Ein wirkungsvoll inszenierter Kontrast zur bloß instand gesetzten weißen Putzfassade des ehemaligen Pfarrhauses. Beibehalten der Eingang in den Altbau, die Erschließung im Inneren allerdings geklärt und in aller Bescheidenheit neu inszeniert; im Neubau weitergeführt die Sockelzone des Bestands, die nun aber durchgehend in schwarzem Basaltbeton ausgeführt ist. Signifikant die Schalungstechnik: im Sockel schmal und reliefartig strukturiert, darüber so, dass horizontale Betonbänder – im Nachhinein teilweise abgeschlagen oder „aufgeraut", damit der Basaltanteil Wirkung entfaltet – die Fassade des Zubaus gliedern. Auffällig auch der skulpturale Zuschnitt des Betonbaus. Alle Öffnungen symmetrisch beziehungsweise axial gesetzt; durch den Einsatz von Holz an der Fassade speziell hervorgehoben – also auch von außen lesbar – der große Ratssaal.

Der Ratssaal: ein zeitgenössisches Beispiel manieristischer Verunsicherung. Die leintuchartig eingehängte Decke, „durchhängend" wie ein Sonnensegel, lässt die Wände optisch kippen. So, als wäre die „Geduld des Raumes" angesichts der Alltäglichkeit der Gemeinderatsdebatten, die hier stattfinden, überstrapaziert.

This building housing the local town council is inserted with a respect for the existing scale into the village structure. An old presbytery originally built of stone and then rendered was adapted and extended. The immediate surroundings, including the open spaces and the existing funeral chapel (modified in design terms) were reinterpreted and given coherence. Particularly as regards the surroundings this is a highly atmospheric place with an area of water on the broad side of the extension, facing away from the street, and a careful use of planting.

The special quality of the extension to the council building derives from the fact that it is black, bare and shimmers (basalt concrete), making an effectively staged contrast to the white render façade of the former presbytery which was merely renovated. The entrance in the old building was preserved but the internal circulation clarified. The plinth zone of the existing building is repeated in the new structure albeit in black basalt concrete. The formwork used is important. In the base it left a narrow, relief-like pattern, above this are horizontal concrete bands (chiselled or "roughened" allowing the basalt aggregate to achieve a particular effect) that articulate the façade of the extension. Its sculptural form is striking, all openings are placed symmetrically or axially. The large council chamber is emphasised by the use of wood on the façade that makes it legible externally.

The council chamber reveals a contemporary unsettling mannerist quality. The suspended ceiling is a cloth that "sags" like an awning making the walls tilt visually. It is as if the "patience of the space" had been exhausted by the monotony of the council debates that take place here.

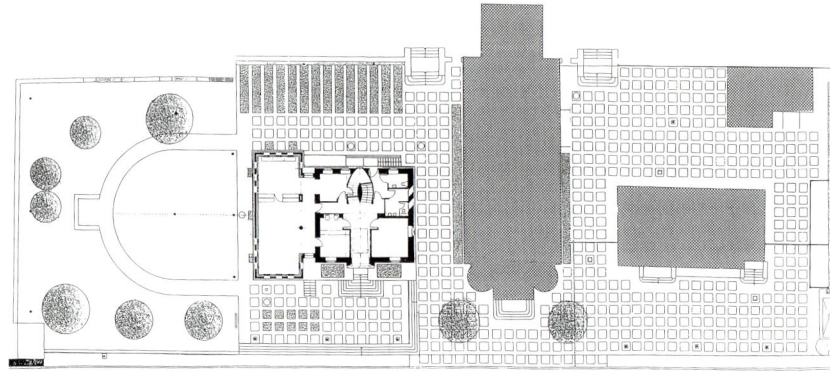

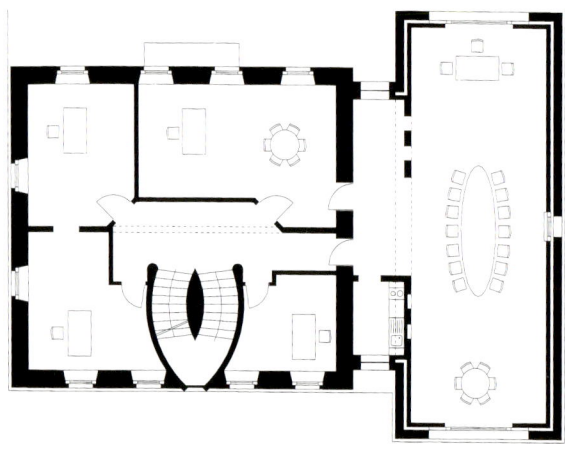

1. Obergeschoss
1st floor

Bauherr | client **Gemeinde Wellenstein**
Projektleiter | project manager **Sergio Soto, Axel Christmann**
Grundstücksgröße | size of site **1.775 m²**
Bruttofläche | total floor area **535 m²**
Planungsbeginn | start of planning **7/1993**
Baubeginn | start of construction **9/1994**
Fertigstellung | completion **11/1995**

UMBAU UND AUFSTOCKUNG
GEMEINDEHAUS IN DALHEIM, LUXEMBURG
REDESIGN AND ADDITION OF A STOREY
TO THE COUNCIL BUILDING IN DALHEIM, LUXEMBOURG

Erweiterung eines bestehenden Gebäudes aus den sechziger Jahren. Programm: ein neuer Sitzungssaal, zusätzliche Büros, ein Aufzug und eine Fluchttreppe.

Das Gemeindehaus, im Zentrum eines geschichtsträchtigen Ortes (römisches Amphitheater), liegt neben einem Kulturzentrum und an einem kurz vor dem Umbau neu gestalteten Platz. Der Eingang ist seitlich, weil dort früher eine Straße vorbeiging. Heute fungiert dagegen eine Schmalseite des Hauses als „Schauseite" Richtung Straße. Daher auch die Notwendigkeit einer kräftigen architektonischen Geste: eine schwarze Betonscheibe in Bretterschalung, dahinter die Fluchttreppe, davor ein Wasserbecken.

Wichtigste Maßnahme im Zug der Aufstockung: ein großes, flaches Holzdach, das vor bis zur Straßenkante und hinüber zum Kulturzentrum reicht. Es wird von ungewöhnlich schlanken, vier Geschosse hohen Betonstützen (Zentrifugalbeton) getragen. Unter der neuen Holzkassettendecke der Sitzungssaal, rundum verglast, mit zwei zusätzlichen Lichtkaminen im Dach, durch die Streiflicht einfällt. Farbakzente drinnen: melonengelb für das Treppenhaus und die Lichtkamine, pfefferminzgrün für den Lift und tomatenrot für die Holzkassetten, die Leimbinder und die Fenster; ebenfalls rot – der neue Anstrich an der sonst unrenovierten Fassade.

Extension to an existing building dating from the sixties. The brief: a new meeting room, additional offices, a lift and an escape staircase.

The council building lies at the core of a historical town (Roman amphitheatre), beside a cultural centre and on a new square redesigned shortly before this project. The entrance is at the side as a street once ran along there. Today, on the other hand, it is a narrow side of the building that forms the "principal façade" towards the street. Hence the necessity for a powerful architectural gesture: a black concrete slab cast in timber boarding formwork, behind it the escape staircase and in front a pool of water.

The most significant measure made in the course of the addition of a storey is a large flat wooden roof extending to the edge of the street and across to the cultural centre. It is carried by unusually slender, four-storey high concrete columns (centrifugal concrete). Beneath this new coffered wooden ceiling is the meeting room, glazed on all sides, with two additional chimney-like roof lights through which light slopes into the space. The colour scheme in the interior: melon yellow for the staircase and the roof lights, peppermint green for the lift, and tomato red for the wooden coffering, the laminated timber beams and the window frames. The new coat of paint on the otherwise unrenovated façade is also red.

Die geforderten zusätzlichen Büros wurden im Bestand des alten Sitzungssaales eingerichtet.

Vorteil der Dachlösung: Es war vorgefertigt und in knapp zwei Wochen montiert. Danach blieb die Baustelle „trocken" – ein Glücksfall im regenreichen Luxemburg. Außerdem: Das Dach überdeckt die neu angelegte Treppe zwischen Kulturzentrum und Rathaus. Ein vielfach nutzbarer Freibereich, der auch bei Regen seine Dienste tut. Erwähnenswert als kleines (mehr spielerisches) Aperçu: Es gibt oben, im neuen Geschoss, einen Punkt, an dem alle drei markanten Farben sehr effektvoll zusammentreffen; wenn man genau schaut, sieht man es sogar von der Straße.

The requisite additional offices were placed in the former meeting room.

The advantages of this roof were that it could be prefabricated and erected in barely two weeks. After that the site remained dry, most fortunate in rainy Luxembourg. The roof also covers the new staircase between the cultural centre and the town hall. An outdoor space which can be used in a variety of ways, even when it is raining. A small playful aperçu is worth mentioning: at the top, on the new floor, there is a point where all three striking colours meet in a most effective manner. If you look very carefully you can even see this point from the street.

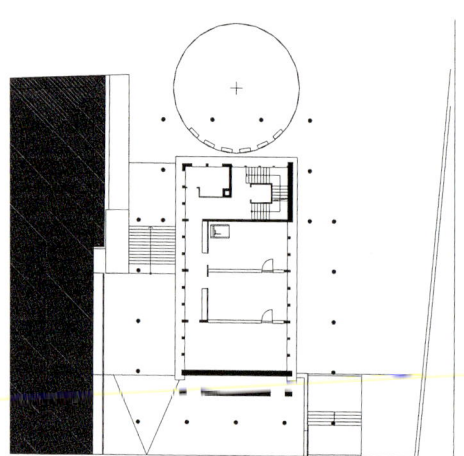

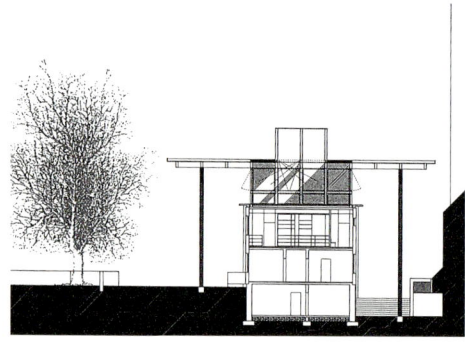

Schnitt
section

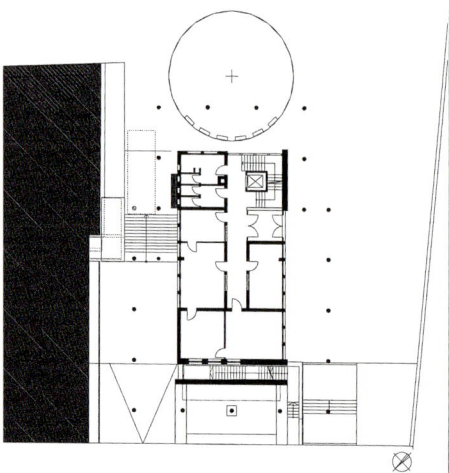

1. Obergeschoss
1st floor

Erdgeschoss
ground floor

Bauherr | client **Gemeinde Dalheim**
Projektleiter | project manager **Werner Feltes**
Bruttofläche | total floor area **167 m²**
Planungsbeginn | start of planning **7/1998**
Baubeginn | start of construction **9/1999**
Fertigstellung | completion **5/2000**

MUSEUMSUM- UND ZUBAU IN LUXEMBURG-STADT
REORGANISATION OF AND EXTENSION TO A MUSEUM IN LUXEMBOURG-CITY

Das Museum liegt am alten Fischmarkt, im ältesten Teil der Stadt. Es enthält kunstgeschichtliche Sammlungen, aber auch archäologische und naturhistorische Fundstücke. Die historische Bausubstanz – alte Wohnbauten, wie sie auch noch im unmittelbaren Umfeld stehen – wurde Anfang des 20. Jahrhunderts umgebaut, durch einen Zubau ergänzt und als Museum umgenutzt. Denkmalgeschützt: die authentischen Gebäudeteile, vor allem die Außenwände. Ein in Stein gehauenes Gewölbe unter dem U-förmigen Vorplatz war ebenfalls zu erhalten.

Wichtigste Maßnahmen des Projekts: Entkernung in der durch den Umbau bereits verfälschten Substanz, neue Geschossebenen für die verschiedenen Sammlungsteile; und statt des massiven Zubaus vom Anfang des Jahrhunderts ein gläserner Baukörper. Der Eingang: mittig im Glasteil.

Der viergeschossige Glaskörper ist nach Süden orientiert. Daher: eingelegte Lamellen als Sonnenschutz und zusätzlich über dem – ebenfalls gläsernen – Dach eine feine Struktur, die Sonnenkollektoren hätte tragen können. Das Modul dieser Dachstruktur kehrt in der Vorplatzgestaltung wieder, hier in Granit und Glas interpretiert. Von oben, vom Platz aus belichtet und einsehbar: das historische Gewölbe und ein neuer Vortragssaal.

Hauptfunktionen des Glaskörpers: Eingang, Kassa, ein Kaffeehaus, das auch extern nutzbar ist, Verteiler; man kommt von hier, ohne das eigentliche Museum zu betreten, auch in den Vortragssaal. Besonders wichtig: Die einzelnen Ausstellungsgalerien wachsen in den Glaskörper hinein, man sieht von außen, was drinnen Sache ist.

The museum lies on the old fishmarket in the oldest part of the city. It houses art collections along with archaeological and natural history finds. The historic building substance – old dwelling houses like the buildings surrounding the museum – was altered at the beginning of the last century, extended and used as a museum. The authentic parts of the building, above all the external walls, are under a preservation order. A stone vault beneath the U-shaped courtyard had also to be preserved.

The most important aspects of the project: the removal of the substance falsified in the course of the earlier conversion, new floor levels for the various parts of the collection and, in place of the massive extension dating from the start of the previous century, a glass element. The entrance is at the centre of this glass part.

The four-storey glass building faces south which explains the louvers that provide shade and, in addition, above the roof – also of glass – a delicate structure that could have carried solar collectors. The module of this rooftop structure reoccurs in the design of the forecourt where it is interpreted using granite and glass. The historical vault and a new lecture hall are top-lit from the square, where one can see into them.

The main functions of the glass element: entrance, cash desk, a coffee shop – also open to people not visiting the museum – a distributor from where, without going into the museum proper, one can also enter the lecture hall. Particularly important: the individual exhibition galleries grow into the glass element. From outside one sees what is contained inside.

1. Obergeschoss
1st floor

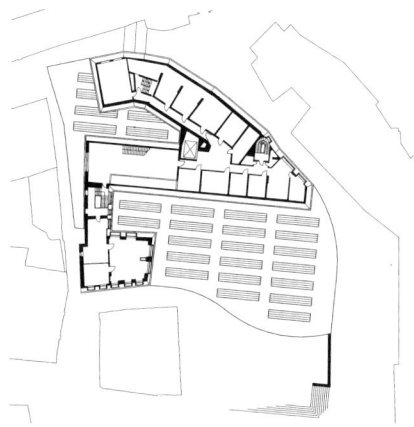

4. Obergeschoss
4th floor

GESCHÄFT IN WIEN-INNENSTADT
SHOP IN VIENNA'S INNER CITY

Ein Eckgeschäft in der attraktiven Wiener Wollzeile, das Fachgeschäft Thun für Porzellan und Glas. Altbestand, räumlich verschachtelt. Der Hauptverkaufsraum im Erdgeschossbereich mit Schaufenstern zur Straße, etwas tiefer gelegen ein schmaler, langer Raum, noch weiter unten ein fast tresorartiger Ausstellungsraum, wo auch das wertvollste Porzellan ausgestellt ist, ganz unten schließlich der Basar.

Wichtigste Maßnahme: die Klärung der verschachtelten Innenräume, sodass der Kunde schon im Hauptverkaufsraum erkennt, dass und wie es weitergeht. Es musste also die Treppe freigespielt werden und es ging darum, die spezifische Qualität der unterschiedlichen Räume herauszuarbeiten.

Die Problematik in einem Porzellangeschäft: eine Vielzahl kleinteiliger Einzelwaren, üblicherweise in Regalsystemen präsentiert, die von den unterschiedlichen Herstellern zur Verfügung gestellt werden. Dagegen im Laden von H & V: eine sehr reduzierte Auswahl an Hintergrundmaterialien, vor und auf denen die unvermeidliche Warenfülle so inszeniert wird, dass der Eindruck der Überfülltheit vermieden ist.

Durchgängiges Thema im Geschäft: rund 300 Hintergrundwände für das Regalsystem aus gewachsenem, aber rohem Stahl, gestampfte, nur acht Zentimeter starke, mit Hirschhaar bewehrte Lehmplatten; ein sehr flexibles Belichtungssystem, das magnetisch angeklippt werden kann, wo man es braucht; und eine ganz einfach lesbare Wegführung auf dem Boden, ein hölzerner Teppich, der im Stoßbereich Richtung Wände in Flusskiesel eingebettet ist.

Ein elegantes Innenstadtgeschäft. Offenheit, Großzügigkeit im Hauptverkaufsraum zu ebener Erde, spielerische, kaum bewusst wahrnehmbare Eingriffe in den Räumen darunter. Etwa die Verspiegelung der vorhandenen Wandnischen im schmalen, tiefen Ausstellungsraum weiter unten; oder die Irritation am Ende dieser Sackgassen-Situation, wo man auf Anhieb nicht genau weiß, ob es nicht doch noch weiter geht. Schließlich der Tresorraum mit seinen schlichten Glaseinbauten – die Griffe nur aufgeklebtes Leder, der Verschlussmechanismus ganz zart. Und die Ausleuchtung gezielt in Szene gesetzt. Ein Minimalprogramm mit maximaler Wirkung.

A corner building on the attractive Wollzeile in Vienna houses Thun, a specialist china and glass retailers. The existing shop was a spatial muddle. The main sales area at ground-floor level has windows onto the street, somewhat lower there is a long, narrow room and lower still a display space almost like a safe where the most valuable china is displayed and finally, at the lowest level, the "bazaar".

The most important measure was to clarify the layout of the interior so that the customer, on entering the main sales space, realises that the shop extends further and in which direction he/she should go. The staircase had to be liberated and the specific qualities of the individual spaces underlined.

The problem in a china shop is the large number of rather small individual goods usually presented on shelving systems supplied by the different manufacturers. The design by H & V is a complete contrast: a much reduced selection of background materials in front of and upon which the inevitably rich variety of goods is presented in such a way that an impression of overcrowding is avoided.

A reoccurring theme in the shop: about 300 background walls for a shelving system made of waxed but otherwise untreated steel, compounded loam slabs only eight centimetres thick reinforced with deer hair, an extremely flexible lighting system which can be attached magnetically wherever required and a simple, legible indication of the route along the floor: a wooden "carpet" which, near the walls, is lined by beds of pebbles.

An elegant inner city shop: an open and generous quality in the main sales area at ground-floor level, playful, almost imperceptible, interventions in the spaces below. An example is the mirroring of the existing wall niches in the deep, narrow display space further below, or the irritant at the dead-end where one is not sure whether the space might extend further. Finally, the safe room with its simple glass cabinets, the leather handles simply glued on, the locking mechanism extremely delicate. The lighting is most carefully employed. A minimal programme used to maximum effect.

Bauherr | client **Mag. Thun**
Projektleiter | project manager **Bébé Branss**
Nutzfläche | floor area **600 m²**
Planungsbeginn | start of planning **4/1995**
Baubeginn | start of construction **2/1996**
Fertigstellung | completion **3/1996**

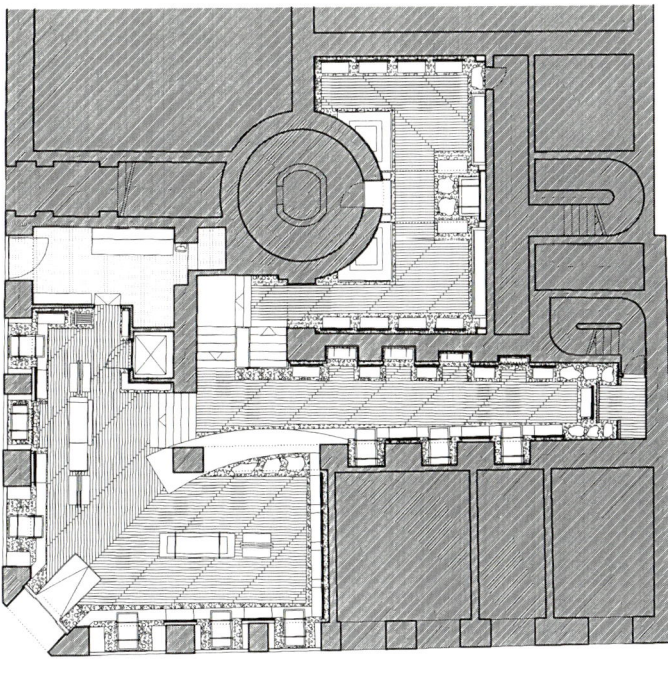

Erdgeschoss
ground floor

GALERIE RACKEY IN BAD HONNEF, DEUTSCHLAND
GALLERY RACKEY IN BAD HONNEF, GERMANY

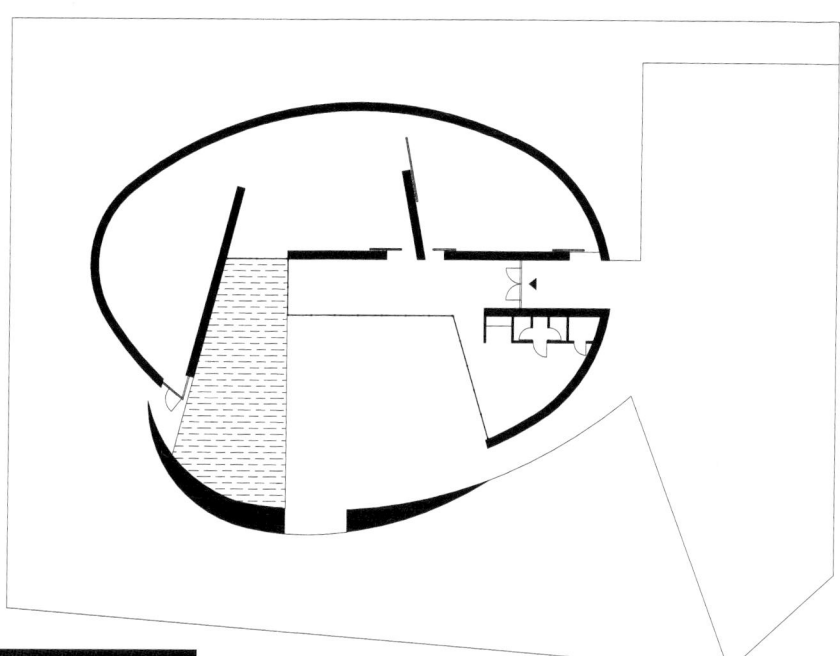

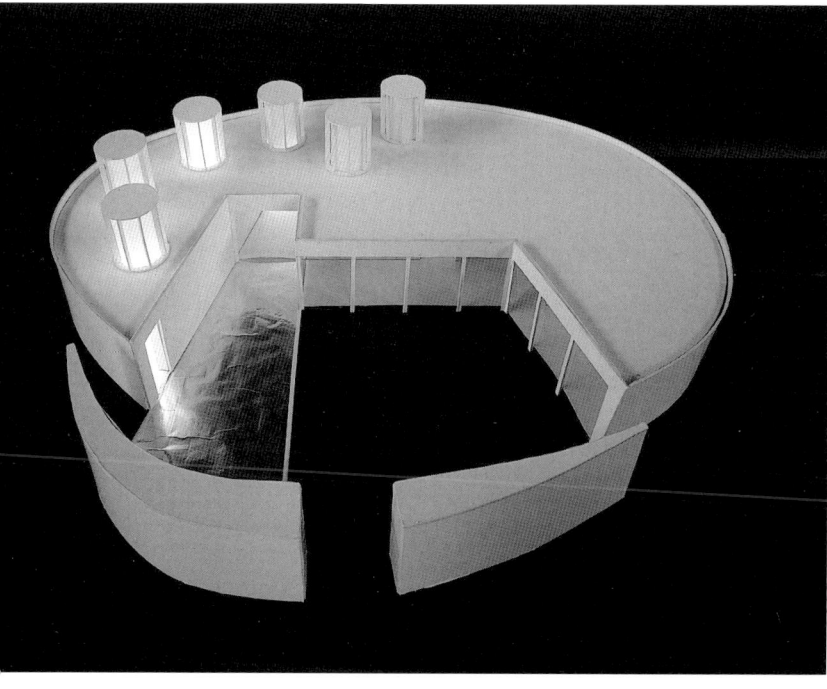

Lage: ein Industriegebiet zwischen Bonn und Köln, eine stark befahrene Straße. Aufgabe: ein Ausstellungsraum für einen Kunsthändler (im Unterschied zu einem Galeristen), der hier seine „Ware" inszenieren möchte.

Das Gebäude: ein Oval. Zur Straße hin geschlossen, ausgeführt in Sichtbeton mit Bretterschalung. An der straßenabgewandten Seite: ein Schnitt durch die Gebäudekonfiguration. Der Schnitt – eine sichelförmige Wand – vom Gebäude abgerückt aufgestellt. Dadurch zwischen Hauptraum und Sichelwand: ein Hof, ein Garten. Hierher auch die Vollverglasung der Galerie-Rückfassade.

Der Hauptraum gegliedert durch eine trennende Wand, die aber nicht ganz an die Fassade vorstößt. Belichtet auch von oben: durch – voraussichtlich – sechs höchst markante Lichtkamine im Dach. Die Sichelwand als schließende Definition des Terrains.

Eine gebaute Skulptur. Ein roher Raum – Bodenbelag womöglich nur Asphalt? –, ein raues Outfit. Keine Details, nur Fläche und Raum. Genau das Richtige für Kunst. Die braucht kein zusätzliches Design, die braucht Neutralität, einen Raum, in dem sie sich in all ihrer Individualität, vor allem aber auch im richtigen Licht entfalten kann. Insofern – ein idealer Ort.

Location: an industrial area between Bonn and Cologne, a very busy road. Commission: an exhibition space for an art dealer (as opposed to gallery owner) who wanted to display his "wares" here.

The building is an oval, closed on the street side, made of exposed concrete that shows the pattern of the shuttering boards. On the side away from the street a cut is made through the configuration of the building. The cut piece line is a sickle-shaped wall erected at a distance from the building itself producing a courtyard or garden between the main space and the wall. The rear façade of the gallery is entirely glazed.

The main space is articulated by a partition wall that does not extend quite as far as the façade. It also receives light from above through – presumably – six extremely striking protruding roof lights. The sickle wall provides a terminating definition of the site.

A built sculpture. A raw space. The flooring possibly just asphalt? A rough outfit: no details, just surface and space, exactly right for art which does not need additional design but rather neutrality, a space in which it can develop its individuality, most importantly in the right light. Consequently – an ideal place.

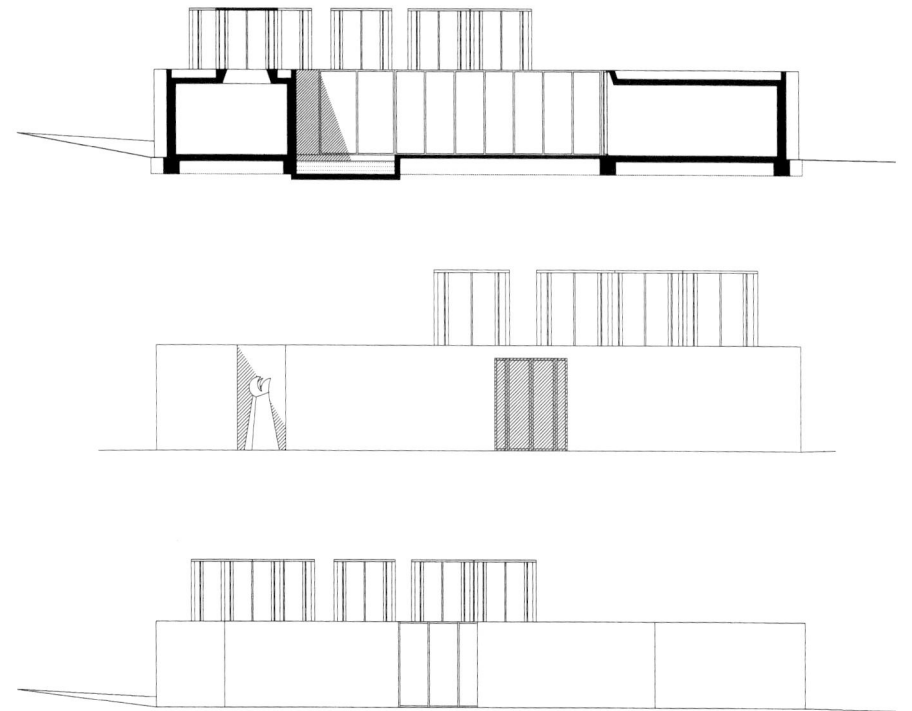

Schnitt
section

Ansicht
view

GALERIE CLAIREFONTAINE UND WOHNUNG IN LUXEMBURG-STADT
GALLERY CLAIREFONTAINE AND APARTMENT IN LUXEMBOURG-CITY

Ein sieben Meter schmales Haus im geschützten Altstadtbereich mit drei Ebenen für eine Fotogalerie und darüber die Wohnung der Galeristin. Denkmalgeschützt: die Außenhaut des Gebäudes. Drinnen war nicht viel zu erhalten. Daher: Entkernung und eine neue Betonstruktur mit neuer Treppe, die einläufig von unten nach oben führt und in der Galerie und der Wohnung übereinander geschoben ist.

Die Galerie: Archiv und Arbeitsraum im Keller, der nur drei Meter breite Eingangsbereich und ein zweigeschossiger Ausstellungsraum zu ebener Erde, darüber eine weitere Ausstellungsebene. Die Wohnung zweieinhalbgeschossig: Wohnraum und offene Küche unten, darüber Schlafzimmer, Bad und Ankleide und ganz oben, im Dachgeschoss – nur durch eine Sambatreppe erschlossen – das Zimmer der Tochter. Im hinteren Teil eine eingeschnittene Terrasse, mit Glasbausteinen ausgelegt, sodass in den Galerieraum darunter Licht fällt.

Wichtigster Eingriff an der Fassade: der Eingang der Galerie und der separate Zugang zur Wohnung. Beide aus Glas, ersterer fast wie ein Bilderrahmen, der die Blicke ins Innere der Galerie zieht, letzterer mit Holzlamellen überzogen. In die Galerie geht es durch einen schmalen, schlauchartigen Korridor. Rechter Hand schalungsrauer Beton, links eine Rigipswand als Hängefläche. In der leicht gewölbten Decke ist die Beleuchtung raffiniert verborgen. So lenkt in dieser beengten Eingangs- und Durchgangssituation nichts von den Exponaten ab.

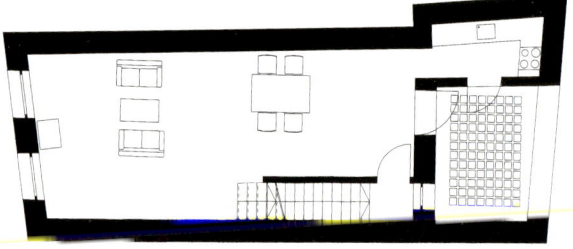

Der zweigeschossige Ausstellungsraum dahinter: durch die Glasbausteine auf der Terrasse auch natürlich belichtet und mit einer matt gestrichenen, tomatenroten Wand. Zweifel der Galeristin an dieser Lösung wurden glücklicherweise ausgeräumt. Besonders für schwarzweiß-Fotografien stellt sie einen überaus effektvollen Hintergrund dar. Und inzwischen ist sie wohl – neben dem Schriftzug „Clairefontaine" an der Fassade – auch zum Signet dieses Kunstraumes geworden.

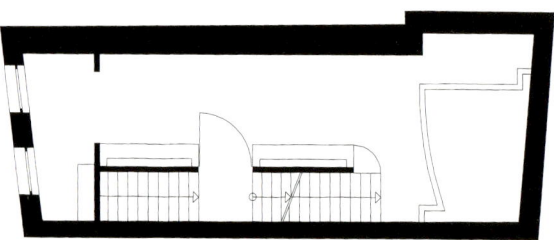

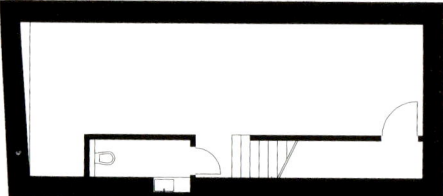

2. Obergeschoss
2nd floor

1. Obergeschoss
1st floor

Untergeschoss
basement

Bauherr | client **Marita Ruiter**
Projektleiter | project manager **Axel Christmann, Thomas Letz**
Grundstücksfläche | site area **77,25 m²**
Bruttofläche | total floor area **345 m²**
Planungsbeginn | start of planning **2/1995**
Baubeginn | start of construction **11/1995**
Fertigstellung | completion **10/1996**

A house, only seven metres wide, in the preserved old city with three levels accommodates a photography gallery and, above it, the apartment of the gallery owner. The external skin of the building is under a preservation order. Internally not much needed to be preserved hence it was stripped out and a concrete structure, with a new staircase leading in a single line from below to above, added. In the gallery and apartment the flights are above each other.

The gallery: archive and work space are at basement level, the entrance area, only three meters wide, and a two-storey exhibition space are at ground-floor level, above this is a further exhibition level. The apartment is two-and-a-half storey high: living room and open-plan kitchen below, bedroom, bathroom and dressing room above. At the very top, in the attic which is reached only by a split staircase, is the daughter's room. At the rear is an incised terrace paved with glass blocks allowing light to enter the gallery below.

The most important intervention in the façade: the gallery entrance and separate access to the apartment. Both are of glass: the former is almost like a picture frame directing the view into the interior of the gallery, the latter is clad with wooden louvers. Access to the gallery is along a narrow, tube-like corridor. On the left bare concrete, on the right a plasterboard wall providing hanging space. The lighting is cleverly concealed in the gently vaulted ceiling. In this tight entrance and passageway nothing distracts from the exhibits.

The double-height exhibition space behind: naturally lit from the glass blocks on the terrace and with a matt painted, tomato-red wall. The gallery owner's doubts about this solution could fortunately be dispelled. It forms a most effective background, particularly for black and white photographs. And in the meantime it has become, alongside the sign "Clairefontaine" on the façade, a symbol of this gallery.

KINDERTAGESSTÄTTE IN BETTEMBURG, LUXEMBURG
CHILDREN'S DAY CARE CENTRE IN BETTEMBOURG, LUXEMBOURG

Ein Schlüsselprojekt in Bezug auf die Einsicht von H & V, dass der architektonische Ausdruck eines Gebäudes nicht zwangsläufig aus seinem Inhalt abgeleitet werden muss. Daher: ein Kindergarten, dem man den Kindergarten nicht ansieht. Kein niedliches, sondern ein „erwachsenes" Gebäude, so, als wäre es für eine allerhöchste Instanz bestimmt, voller raffinierter Raumverschränkungen, dabei ungemein präzise komponiert.

Lage: Versteckt hinter einem gründerzeitlichen Gemeindehaus, im Zentrum des Ortes. Ein mit 2000 Quadratmetern sparsam bemessenes Grundstück, das aber einen wunderbar nutzbaren Freibereich für die Kinder einschließt. Letzterer architektonisch „gefasst" – durch eine Pergola und begrünte Mauern zu den Nachbarn –, also definiert gegenüber seinem heterogenen, auch maßstäblich divergenten Umfeld.

Der Baukörper: eine schwungvolle Bewegung hinter dem Gemeindehaus. Besonders artikuliert: Vorplatz, Gebäudeeingang, Haupterschließung. Letztere aus dem Gebäude herausgeschält in Form eines Liftturms, der mit blauen Glasbausteinen ummantelt und durch Brücken an die Geschossebenen angekoppelt ist. Auch die Treppe ist speziell formuliert, als ausladende Freitreppe vor dem Haus. Über allem das Vordach, ein acht Meter ausladender Baldachin.

A key project in terms of H & V's view that the architectural expression of a building must not inevitably be derived from its content. Hence a kindergarten which one does not recognise as such. Not a sweet little building but a grown-up one as if intended for an ultimate authority, filled with sophisticated interlocking spaces yet incredibly precisely composed.

Location: hidden behind a 19th century town council building at the centre of the town. A tight site, only 2000 square metres, that yet includes a wonderfully usable outdoor space for the children. This space is architecturally "contained" by a pergola and walls with planting that face the neighbours. It forms a contrast to its heterogeneous surroundings that are divergent in terms of scale.

The building: a lively movement made behind the town council building. Forecourt, building entrance and main circulation are particularly emphasised. The latter is extracted from the building and takes the form of a lift tower clad with blue glass blocks that is linked to the building by bridges at the floor levels. The staircase too is specially formulated: a projecting external stairs in front of the building. A roof canopy – a baldachin projecting eight metres –, extends above the ensemble.

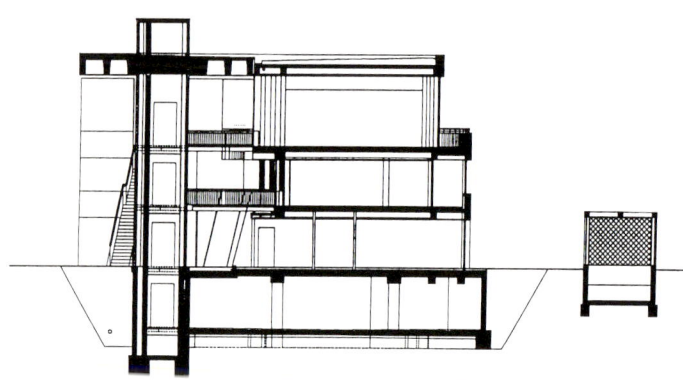

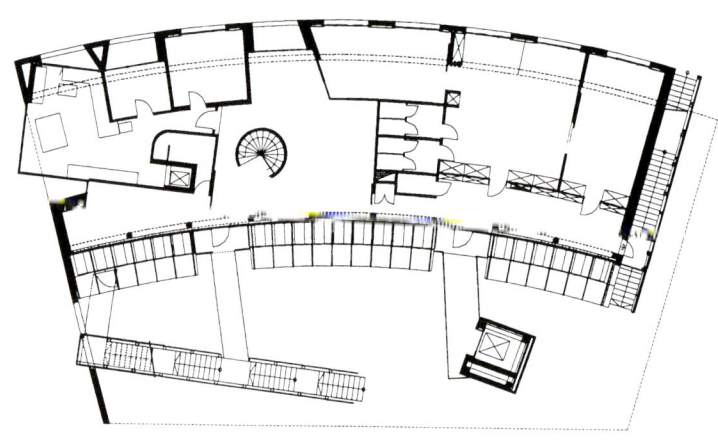

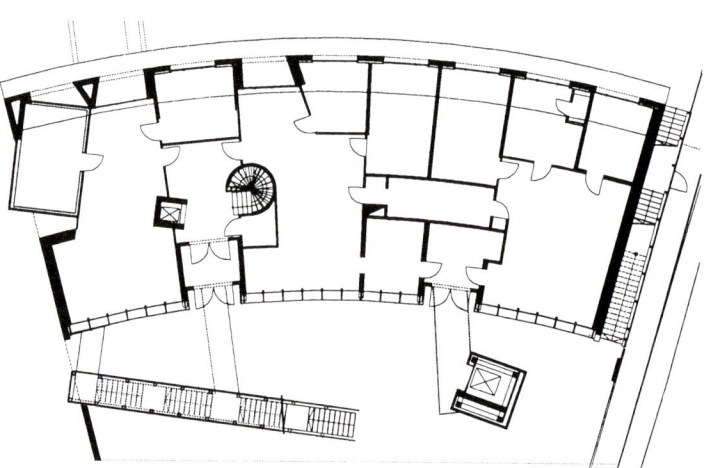

Schnitt
section

1. Obergeschoss
1st floor

Erdgeschoss
ground floor

Holz: Es liegt auf dem Vorplatz, der auch als geschützter Spielplatz für die Kinder dient, es ist das Material der Vordach-Untersicht. Es kontrastiert zum scheinbar „harten" Streckmetall, das die Freitreppe semitransparent abschirmt (übrigens auch den Raum unter dieser Treppe, der als „Parkgarage" der Kleinen dient, für ihre Dreiräder und Roller); und es bildet den Rahmen für die großflächigen Verglasungen an der Gebäudevorderseite. Beton: in markant gestreifter Bretterschalung ausgeführt, dominiert er die drei anderen Gebäudefassaden. Blauer Glasbaustein: draußen, am Liftturm, ein erstes Signal; drinnen wiederkehrendes, raumdefinierendes Element,

Wood: covers the forecourt, which doubles as a protected play area for the children, and is used for the soffit of the projecting roof. It contrasts with the apparently hard expanded metal that provides a semi-transparent screen to the external staircase (and also to the space beneath this stairs, a kind of "garage" for the kids, their tricycles and roller-boards) and forms the frame for the large areas of glazing at the front of the building. Concrete: striking, poured in stripes using boarded shuttering, it dominates the three other façades of the building. Blue glass block: externally, at the lift tower, it provides a first signal then reoccurs inside as a spatially defining

Mantel der internen Erschließung (des kurzen Weges für das Personal), auch festliches Spektakel im großen (extern nutzbaren) Saal auf der Ebene des zweiten Obergeschosses. Ungewöhnlich reizvoll gelöst: die künstliche Belichtung, die aus Ausstanzungen in den eingehängten Decken strahlt.

Ein Haus für Kinder, architektonisch ernst gemeint. Nichts, das mit scheinbar kindlichen Gefühlswelten spekuliert. Eine räumliche Komposition, besonders, kompliziert, komplex. Insofern ein Erlebnis: für Klein und Groß.

element lining the internal circulation (the short route for the staff) also provides a festive spectacle in the large hall (that is also available for non-school related activities) on the second floor. The artificial lighting is solved in an unusually delightful manner: in a sense it radiates from areas stamped out of the suspended ceilings.

A building for children that is intended as serious architecture. Not a single element speculates with an imagined world of children's emotions. A spatial composition that is special, complex and complicated providing as a result an experience for both young and old.

Bauherr | client **Administration communale de Bettembourg**
Projektleiter | project manager **Thomas Letz, Werner Feltes**
Grundstücksfläche | site area **2.015 m²**
Bruttofläche | total floor area **2.145 m²**
Planungsbeginn | start of planning **7/1994**
Baubeginn | start of construction **3/1995**
Fertigstellung | completion **3/1999**

KAUFHAUS IN WIEN-FAVORITEN
DEPARTMENT STORE IN VIENNA-FAVORITEN

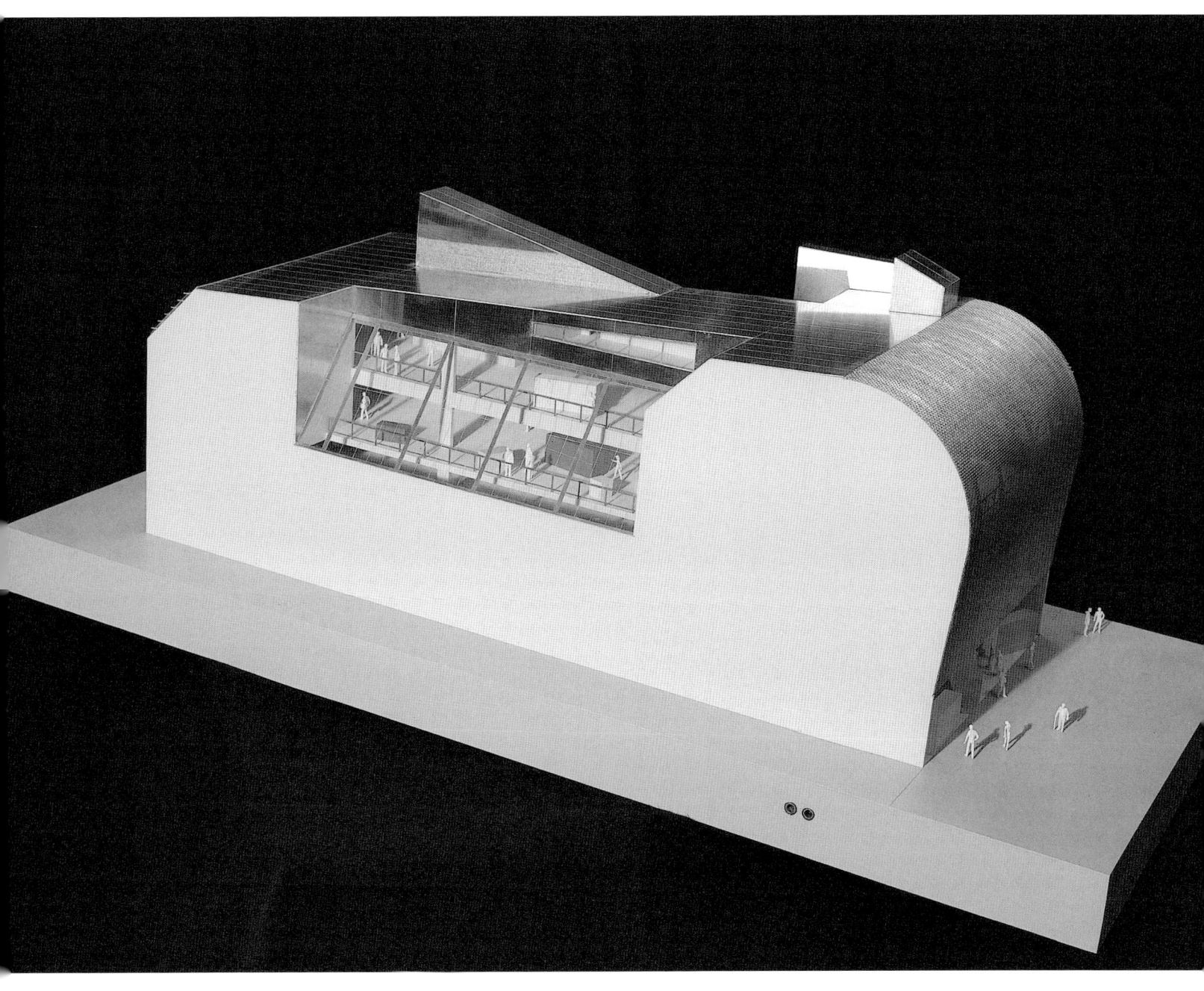

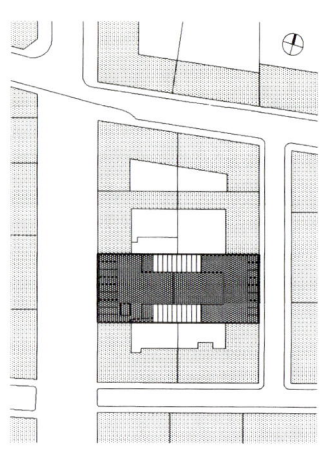
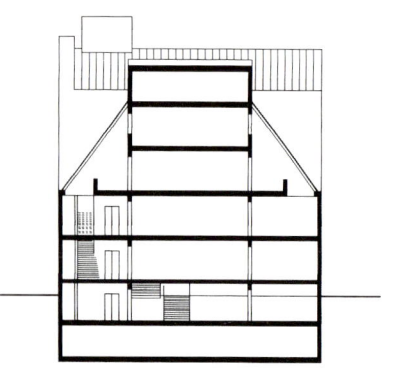
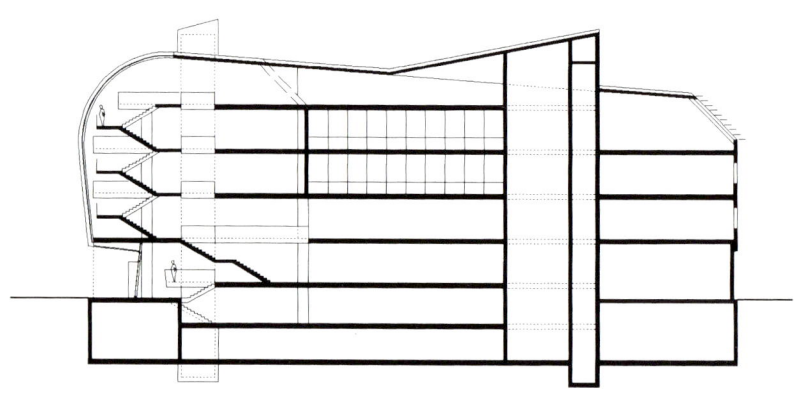
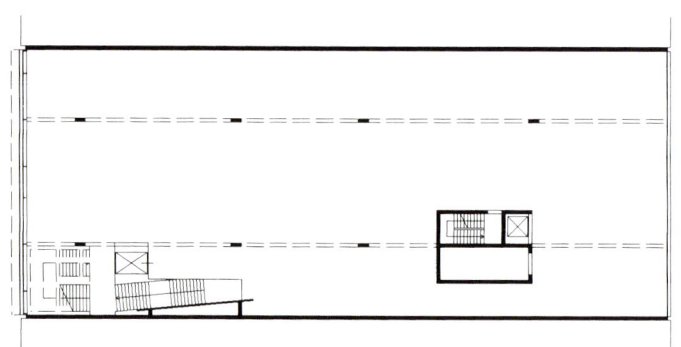
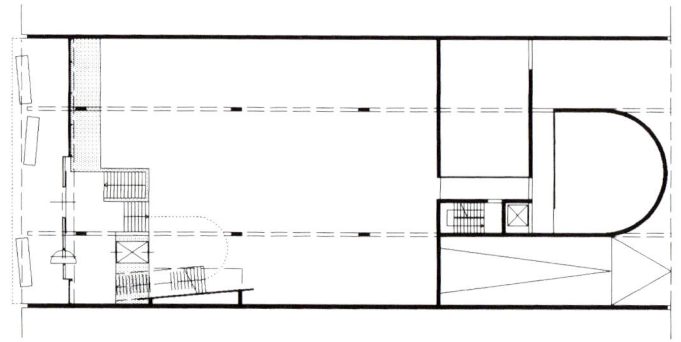

Lageplan
site plan

Schnitte
sections

1. Obergeschoss
1st floor

Erdgeschoss
ground floor

Eine 15 Meter tiefe Gebäudestruktur. Und eine Baulücke mitten im Bestand einer Fußgängerzone Wiens, die der Erneuerung bedarf. Aufgabe: ein kleines Kaufhaus.

Kurios ist die vorgeschriebene Arkadierung an der Fußgängerzone, die keine Fortsetzung findet. H & V nutzen sie zur Formulierung eines gedeckten Vorbereiches, zu dem die Erdgeschosszone und der Blick hinunter, in einen halbgeschossig versetzten Verkaufsraum im Souterrain, offen sind. Ausschlaggebendes Thema drinnen: die Verlegung der Erschließung an die Fassade und damit die sichtbare Inszenierung der Kundenbewegungen. Wichtig für die Außenansicht: eine vorgelagerte, bauchig ausgeformte Membran – Streckmetall? Lochblech? Metallgeflecht? –, die für Blicke durchlässig, aber doch als Werbeträger geeignet ist. Ein zweifellos interessanter Kick für die – aus budgetären Gründen – voraussichtlich eher simple Verglasung der Warmhaut des Hauses.

Innenraumkonzept: ein attraktiver Raum in der Tiefe des Gebäudes, durch verglaste „Verletzungen" auch natürlich belichtet; und eingehängte Galerien, die trotz der Kompaktheit der Lösung Lufträume erlauben. Unter dem Haus sind die Garagen, Lagerräume und die Anlieferung, auf dem Dach die Haustechnik, Nebenräume (zum Beispiel für Werkstätten und dergleichen), ein Restaurant.

Der vielversprechende Versuch, mit architektonischen Mitteln das Konzept für ein – an sich „regelwidriges", herkömmlichen Erfahrungen widersprechendes – Kleinkaufhaus zu entwickeln, das trotz allem das räumliche Potenzial hat, zu funktionieren.

A building pattern 15 metres deep, a vacant site in need of renewal, centrally situated in an existing pedestrian zone in Vienna. The commission: a small department store.

The proscribed arcade along the pedestrian zone, which is not continued, is most strange. H & V exploited this requirement of the planning authorities to formulate a covered front area onto which the ground-floor and the view downwards into the sales area located half a storey lower, are open. The dominant theme in the interior is the way that the circulation is moved to the façade placing the movement of the customers on stage, so to speak. In the external elevation a curved external membrane is dominant – expanded metal, perforated metal sheeting, mesh? It allows a view through, but can also carry advertising. Without doubt it lends an interesting "kick" to the (for budgetary reasons) probably rather simple glazing that forms the warm skin of the building.

Interior concept: an attractive space in the depth of the building, also naturally lit by means of glazed "injuries", with inserted galleries which, despite the compactness of the solution, allow the creation of voids. The garages are underneath the building, along with store rooms and delivery area. The services and ancillary spaces (e.g. workshops etc.) and a restaurant are at roof level.

This promising attempt at using architectural means to develop a small department store that is itself "irregular" and at variance with all established experience has, nevertheless, the spatial potential to function.

UM- UND ZUBAU EINES GYMNASIUMS IN DIEKIRCH, LUXEMBURG
REDESIGN OF AND EXTENSION TO A SECONDARY SCHOOL IN DIEKIRCH, LUXEMBOURG

Die Schule ist auf zwei Gebäude aufgesplittet, die fast einen Kilometer auseinander liegen. Der eine Teil ist um eine alte Kaserne herum organisiert, zu dem schon in den sechziger Jahren ein Trakt hinzukam; ein weiterer, neuer Trakt ist derzeit im Bau. Zwischen diesen Bauteilen: ein geschlossener Hof, außen verglast, mit einem Baum in der Mitte. Eine geschützte Aula, aber doch ein Kaltraum.

Der zweite Gebäudekomplex stammt aus den siebziger Jahren und ist ganz aus Beton-Sandwich-Elementen errichtet. Hier kam als neuer Bauteil eine große Sporthalle hinzu, außerdem eine Bibliothek, Ateliers und Büros. Der Bestand wurde ganz in Streckmetall eingepackt, die Waschbeton-Oberfläche schimmert also durch. Eine Art „Kreuzgang" schließt die Platzsituation, um die sich die Gebäude gruppieren. An die Sporthalle mit Zuschauertribünen – darunter die Garderoben, darüber Ateliers – ist eine „Bibliothek" angedockt. Eine spezifische Bibliothek: Denn sie besteht aus einem Bus, der hier einfährt und von einer Art Kai oder Laderampe aus mit Büchern aus dem Bücherspeicher bestückt wird. Oben drüber: Büros, denen der Luxus von Balkonen zugeordnet ist, die direkt auf einen dicht bewaldeten Hang schauen.

This school is split up into two buildings almost one kilometre away from each other: one part is organised around an old barracks to which a wing was added in the sixties, a further new wing is at present under construction. Between these two building elements lies an enclosed, externally glazed courtyard with a tree at the centre: both a protected aula and outdoor space.

The second building complex dates from the seventies and is built entirely of concrete sandwich elements. A new sports hall was added along with a library, ateliers and offices. The existing substance was packed in expanded metal through which the exposed aggregate concrete surface shimmers. A "cloister" terminates the square around which the buildings are grouped. A "library" is docked against the sports hall with its spectator stands (the changing rooms lie below and the ateliers above). This is a special type of library as it consists of a bus which drives in here and is loaded from a kind of quay or loading ramp with books out of the book store. Above are offices which enjoy the luxury of balconies and have a direct view of a densely wooded slope.

Ein äußerst großzügiger Schulkomplex. Schlicht in der Materialisierung, dabei unerhört signifikant, auch geradezu respektvoll im Umgang mit dem Siebzigerjahre-Bestand. Die architektonischen Maßnahmen sind sparsam, aber gezielt gesetzt. Dadurch: räumlich ein besonderes, ein bestechendes Angebot, eine überzeugende Lösung.

An extremely generous school complex. The materials chosen are simple, yet the building is extremely significant. A respectful handling of the seventies building. The economical architectural measures are applied in a focussed way. The result is a particularly impressive series of spaces and a convincing solution.

Bauherr | client **Administration des Bâtiments Publics**
Projektleiter | project manager **Thomas Letz, Axel Christmann**
Grundstücksfläche | site area **20.475 m²**
Bruttofläche | total floor area **3.985 m²**
Planungsbeginn | start of planning **3/1996**
Baubeginn | start of construction **10/1997**
Fertigstellung | completion **4/1998**

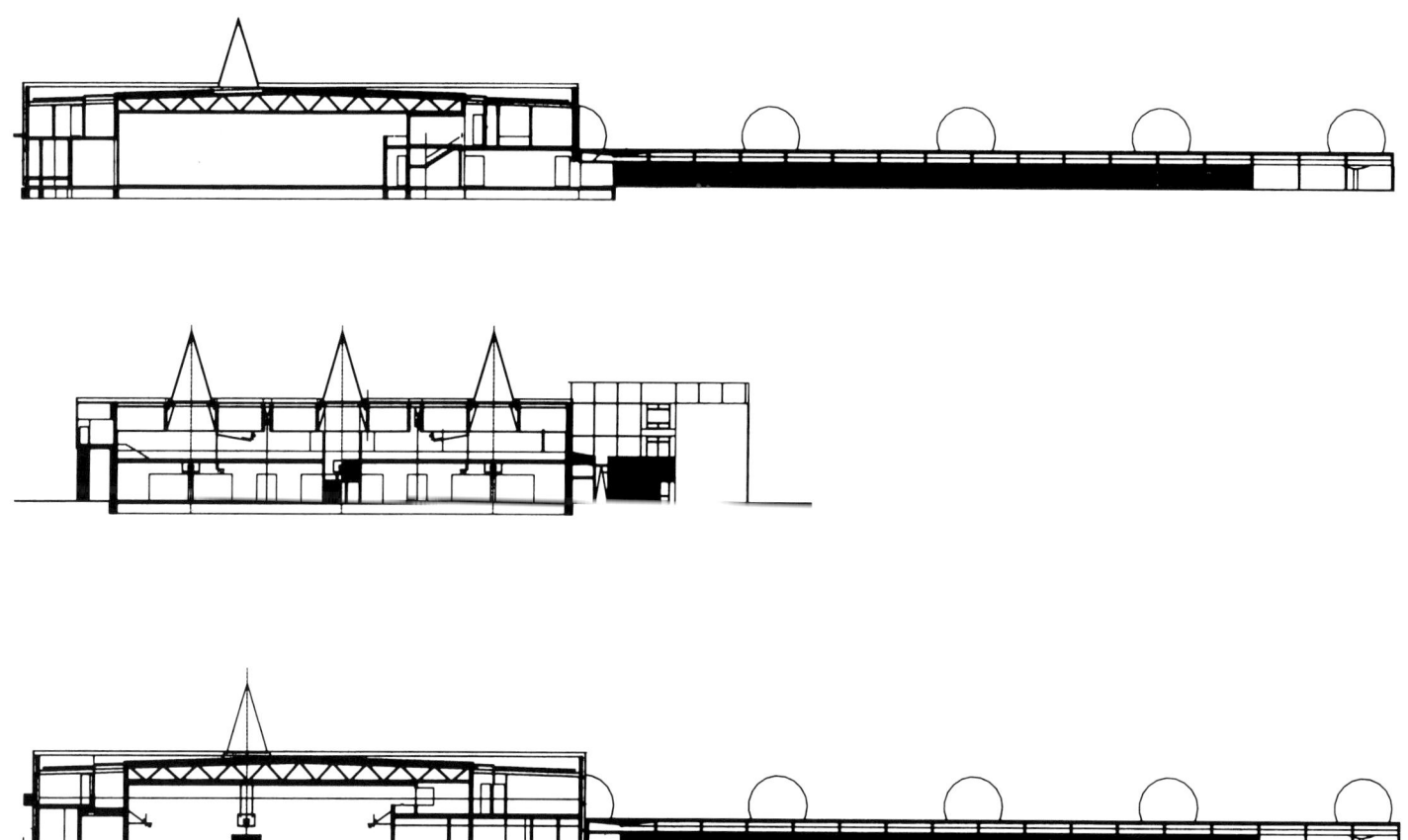

Schnitte
sections

Erdgeschoss
ground floor

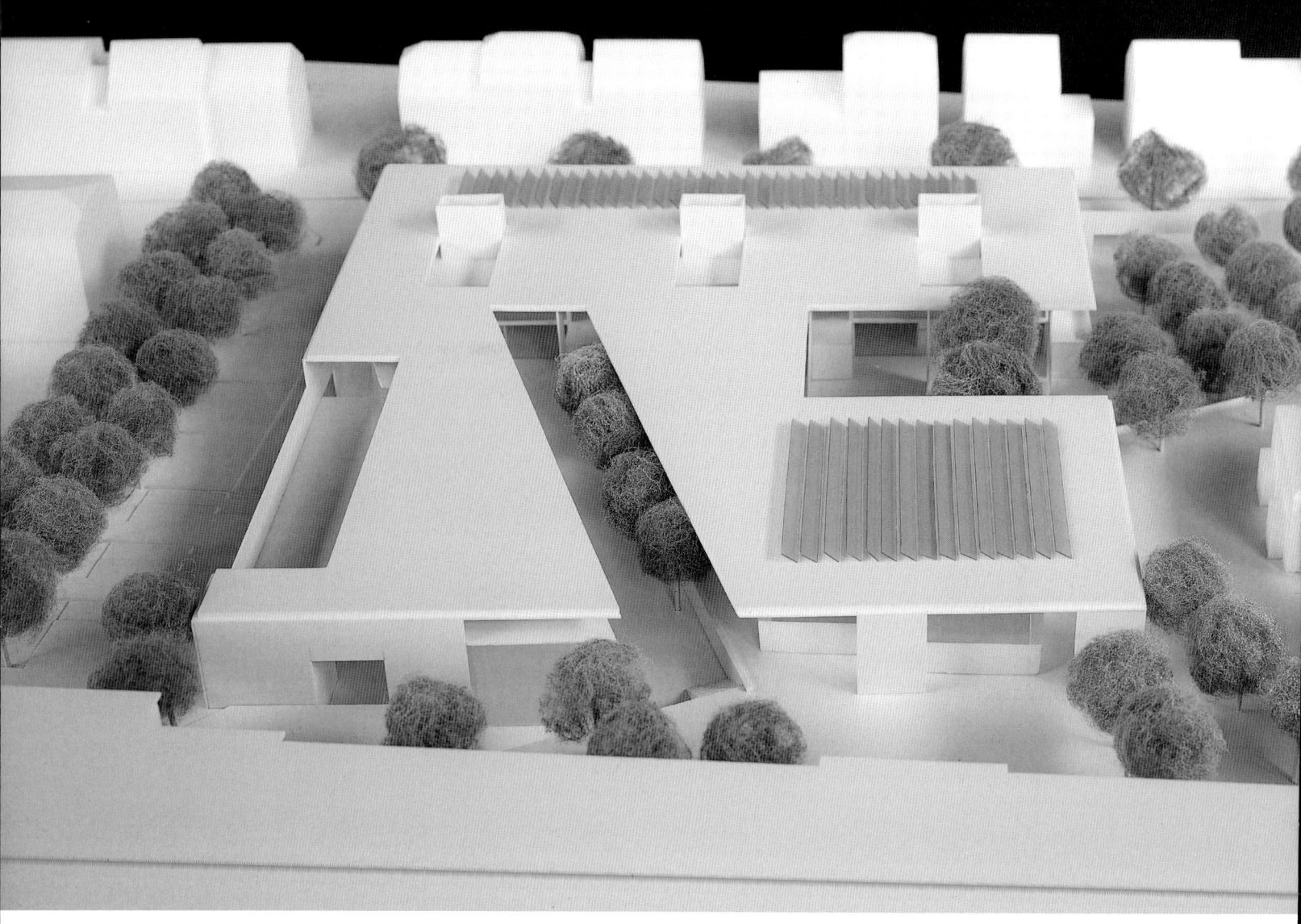

VOLKSSCHULE, VORSCHULE UND KINDERGARTEN IN SCHÜTTRANGE, LUXEMBURG
PRIMARY SCHOOL, PRE-SCHOOL AND NURSERY SCHOOL IN SCHÜTTRANGE, LUXEMBOURG

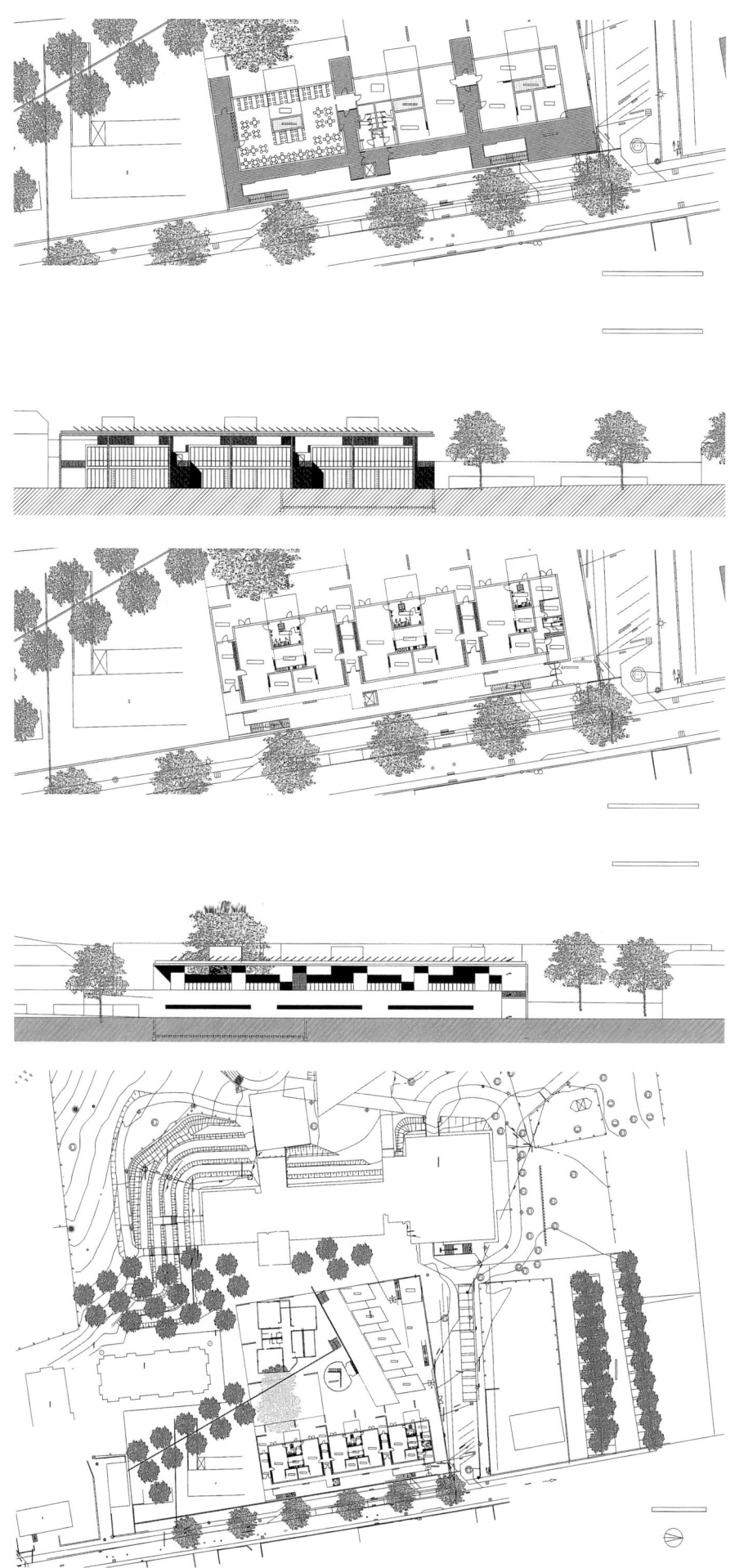

Ein Bau im Dorf – jedenfalls in ländlicher Umgebung. Und ein Projekt, das konzeptuell viel mit einem zweiten, ähnlich gelagerten Bauvorhaben zu tun hat, mit einem Schulkomplex in Remerschen. Beiden gemeinsam: Unter einem schützenden, alles überspannenden Dach versammeln sich die verschiedenen Bauteile – neue ebenso wie vorgefundene.

Im Fall von Schüttrange zählen Container zum Bestand, in denen der Vorschulbereich untergebracht ist (in Remerschen ist es eine Turnhalle, die besteht). Sie werden beibehalten, sie können auch erweitert werden. Drum herum gruppiert die zweigeschossigen Neubauten, durchwegs einhüftig konzipiert, mit einer durchgehenden (kalten) Erschließungshalle. Letztere dient als Aufenthalts-, als Pausenraum, ein gedeckter Bereich, vielfach nutzbar. Ebenso die – hofartigen – Freiräume zwischen den Bauten: wettergeschützte Außenräume, interessant zu jeder Jahreszeit.

Ein besonderes, ein innovatives Konzept: nicht gerade platzsparend in seiner Ausdehnung (eine schlichte Schachtel wäre zweifellos kompakter); dafür ein räumliches Angebot, das seinesgleichen sucht. Und zu einem Preis, der nicht höher liegt als jener für die zitierte Schachtel. Ein Prototyp, der sich bewähren wird.

A building in a village or at least in rural surroundings and a project that in conceptual terms is closely related to a second, similarly located project, a school complex in Remerschen. Both have much in common: the various parts of the building, both new and old, are gathered under a protective roof that extends above all the elements.

In the case of Schüttrange containers form part of the existing building substance. They house the pre-school department (in Remerschen it is a gym, which still exists). They have been preserved, could also be extended, new two-storey buildings are grouped around them, based on a single-sided corridor system with a continuous (unheated) circulation hall. This serves as a space to linger in, is used during school breaks: a covered space with a variety of functions. The same applies to the courtyard-like external spaces between the buildings. These outdoor rooms protected from the weather are interesting at any time of the year.

A particularly innovative concept: its extent means it is not exactly economical in its use of space (a simple box would doubtless have been more compact) but it offers an exceptional variety of spaces and at a price no higher than that of the aforementioned box. A prototype that will prove its worth.

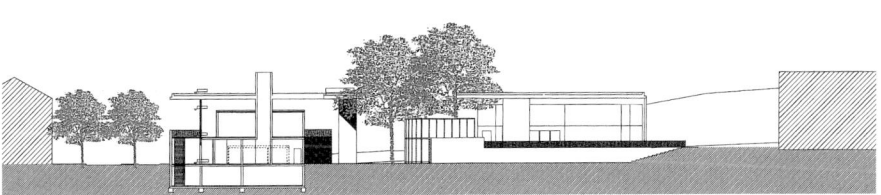

EINFAMILIENHAUS IN SANEM, LUXEMBURG
SINGLE FAMILY HOUSE IN SANEM, LUXEMBOURG

One could say: the first building in a small "series" of concrete houses. A blinkered house that screens out the existing buildings on either side. It stands in a newly-built area (as usual somewhat problematic) full of single-family houses on relatively tight sites. The only positive aspect is the view of a small valley with a field of rape and behind a plateau covered with trees.

The shape of the building possesses its own logic. A "U" enclosed on three sides. A completely glazed front opens to the fine view. Wooden trellises planted with wisteria to the left and right of this side provide additional screening to the terrace in front of the house.

The house is almost a cube: the projecting, very gently inclined tent roof (a requirement of the building regulations) seems in fact flat. The concrete walls surrounding on three sides that reach up to the upper storey have a specific structure as is always the case with H & V. Horizontal beads "deliberately" produced by the boarded form-work were later broken off in part, creating a particularly rough and rocky façade. The area between roof and concrete and also the cut made for the entrance, which is shifted somewhat away from the centre, are "filled up" with wood, in this particular case reddish Okoumé. This layer of wood seems to be pinned under the roof, placed between concrete brackets on either side.

Innenräumlich ein flächiges Sparprogramm, dabei von fulminanter Großzügigkeit. Über dem zweigeschossigen Wohnraum mit vollverglaster Front schwebt die Erschließungsgalerie zu den Schlafräumen und das – abends kristallin leuchtende, weil in Profilit gepackte – Badezimmer. Auch von dort oben also: der Fernsehblick auf die Aussicht. Dabei rohe, raue Industriematerialien. Und minimalisierte, aber effektive Belichtungsausschnitte zu diesen Räumen im Obergeschoss.

Ein „Masterpiece" an räumlicher und budgetärer Ökonomie, wohl kaum zu überbieten in seinem Preis-Leistungs-Verhältnis.

The interior reveals an economical use of floor area yet is impressively generous. The access gallery leading to the bedrooms hovers above the two-storey living room with its fully glazed front as does the bathroom that gleams like a crystal in the evening because it is packed in industrial glass. From the upper level too one sees the broad panorama of the view – like on a TV screen. Bare, basic industrial materials. Minimal but highly effective cut-outs allow light to enter the rooms on the upper floor.

A "masterpiece" of spatial and budgetary economy offering value for money which could hardly be surpassed.

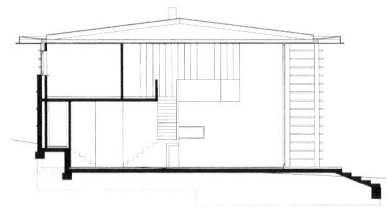

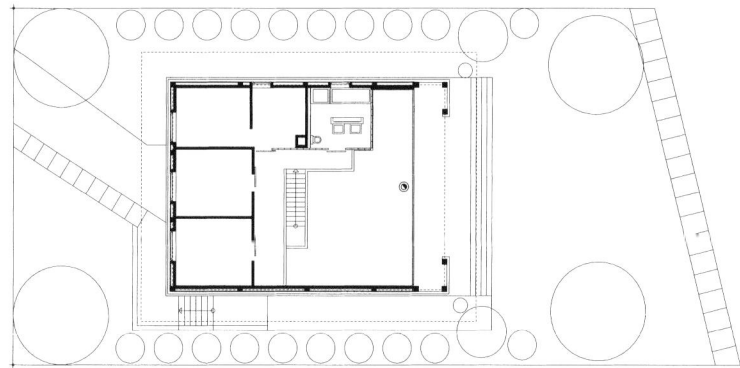

Schnitt
section

Obergeschoss
upper floor

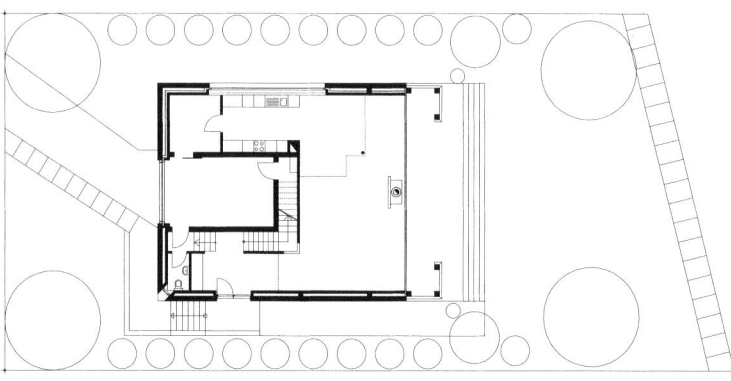

Erdgeschoss
ground floor

Bauherr | client **Nathalie und Alain Ierace**
Projektleiter | project manager **G.G. Kirchner, Mario T. Reinert**
Grundstücksfläche | site area **623 m²**
Bruttofläche | total floor area **230 m²**
Planungsbeginn | start of planning **12/1995**
Baubeginn | start of construction **6/1996**
Fertigstellung | completion **6/1997**

EINFAMILIENHAUS IN REMICH, LUXEMBURG
SINGLE FAMILY HOUSE IN REMICH, LUXEMBOURG

Der zweite Entwurf in der Betonhaus-Serie. Eine Variation. Auch hier das (dicht verbaute) Umfeld problematisch, diesmal außer Einfamilienhäusern zu beiden Seiten sogar ein viergeschossiger Wohnbau vis-à-vis. Der Garten daher voll einsehbar.

Das Grundstück liegt auf einem sanften Hang, in den das L-förmige Haus eingeschoben ist. Man geht, an einem Wasserbecken vorbei, seitlich hinein, der Wohnraum ist teilweise wieder zweigeschossig, anschließend Essplatz, Küche und ein Wirtschaftsraum. Im Obergeschoss die Schlafzimmer und das Bad. Küche, Wohnzimmer, Schlafzimmer sind alle in eine Richtung, nach Osten orientiert: mit Blick auf die Mosel. Besonderheit dieses Haustyps: der kleine, eingeschnittene Hof, der durch einen massiv gebauten Schenkel mit vorgesetzter Garage vor den Blicken der Nachbarn und des Gegenübers geschützt ist. Ein durchgehender Querbalken, der die Oberkante des Hauses definiert, bewirkt die visuelle Integration dieses Hofes ins Haus (und wurde mittlerweile – das war von vornherein eine Option – von den Bauherren verglast, so dass sie nun einen wettergeschützten Freibereich haben).

Die Betonhaut zeigt wieder die Merkmale der H & V-spezifischen Schalung mit den bekannten Wülsten als horizontale Gliederung. Abgesehen von der zweigeschossigen Holz-Glas-Außenfassade des Wohnraums und der Verglasung zum Innenhof sorgen streng symmetrisch gesetzte Öffnungen in der Betonhülle – über dem Eingang in Form eines signifikanten Musters aus ganz kleinen, quadratischen Ausschnitten – für die Belichtung der Räume.

The second design in the concrete house series. A variation: here too the densely built-up surroundings represent a problem. In this case, in addition to single-family homes on either side, there is also a four-storey apartment block opposite which means that the garden can be looked into.

The site lies on a gentle slope into which the L-shaped house is inserted. After passing a pool one enters the building from the side. The living room is again partly two-storey, adjoining it are the dining area, kitchen and a utilities room. The bedrooms and bathroom are on the upper floor. Kitchen, living room and bedroom all look in one direction (eastwards) and enjoy a view of the Moselle. This house type has a particular quality: the small, incised courtyard protected by a solidly built wing of the building with a garage at the front. A continuous cross-beam defining the upper edge of the house effects the visual integration of the courtyard into the house (in the meantime the owners have glazed in this yard – an option considered from the very start – so that they now have an open area protected from the weather).

Here too the concrete skin illustrates the characteristic H & V-shuttering with the familiar beads providing horizontal articulation. In addition to the two-storey wood and glass external façade and the glazing onto the inner courtyard openings placed with strict symmetry in the concrete shell provide daylight for the rooms – above the entrance they take the form of an interesting pattern of extremely small square cut-outs.

Bauherr | client **Fam. Vandenberg**
Projektleiter | project manager **Werner Feltes**
Grundstücksfläche | site area **1.361 m²**
Bruttofläche | total floor area **340 m²**
Planungsbeginn | start of planning **2/1997**
Baubeginn | start of construction **10/1997**
Fertigstellung | completion **12/1998**

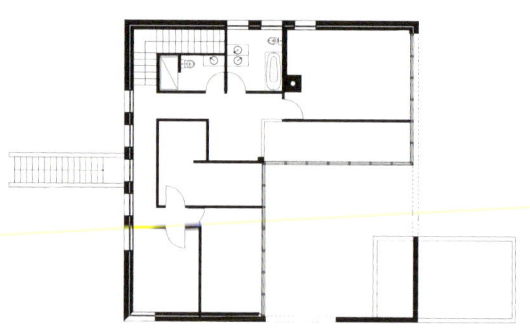

Obergeschoss
upper floor

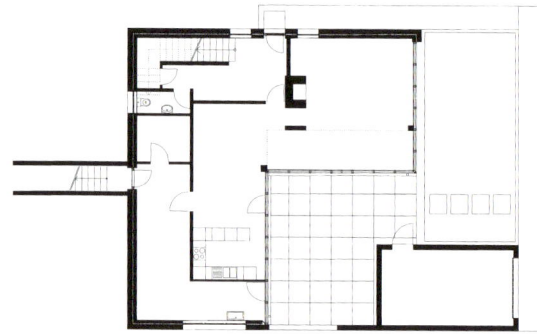

Erdgeschoss
ground floor

EINFAMILIENHAUS IN WELLENSTEIN, LUXEMBURG
SINGLE FAMILY HOUSE IN WELLENSTEIN, LUXEMBOURG

Der dritte Entwurf in der Serie. Gelegen am Ortseingang zu einem kleinen Weinbaudorf, im Umfeld Weinberge und eine große Weinkellerei. Lage des Grundstücks: ein leichter Hang.

Im Sprachgebrauch des Büros: das Sokrates-Haus. Also ein Haustyp, den es so als Typ eigentlich gar nicht gibt. Ein Trichterhaus. Zufahrt im Norden, Öffnung nach Süden. Eine große Öffnung, genau genommen nach Südosten, in Richtung eines ganz sanft ansteigenden Hanges mit Apfelbäumen, dahinter die Weinberge. Die Öffnung des Trichters: großflächig verglast, davor ein Wasserbecken, dahinter der Wohnraum. Im Nordwesten die Zufahrt zur Garage, seitlich links – über eine kleine Treppe – der Hauseingang. Seitlich: die Küche als plastisch vorspringendes Element, das gleichzeitig einen Balkon für die Schlafzimmer im Obergeschoss formuliert.

Sokrates' Sonnenhaus: ein Trichter. Und wieder konzipiert in Basaltbeton, in Bretterschalung. Architektur pur. Roh, rauh. Aber geradezu unheimlich gut bewohnbar.

The third design in this series. It lies at the entrance to a small wine-growing village surrounded by vineyards and a large winery. The site has a slight slope.

Known in the architects' office as the Socrates house, i.e. a house type which, as a type, does not in fact exist. A funnel house: the approach road is on the north side, the building opens towards the south. A large opening, more precisely south-east facing, in the direction of a gently rising slope with apple trees and vineyards behind. The opening of the funnel has a glazed façade: in front of which there is a pool, behind it the living room. In the north-west is the approach to the garage, to the left the entrance to the house via a short flight of steps. The kitchen is a sculptural element that projects at one side and also formulates a balcony for the bedrooms on the upper floor.

Socrates' solar house: a funnel, also made of basalt concrete using board form-work. Pure architecture – raw, rough but unbelievably easy to live in.

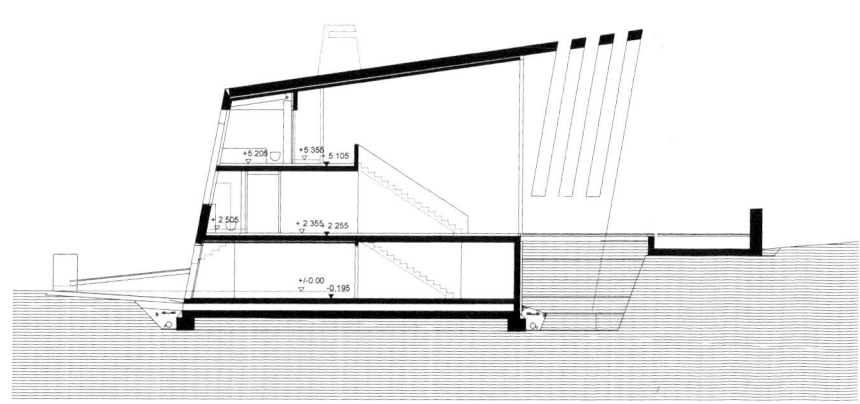

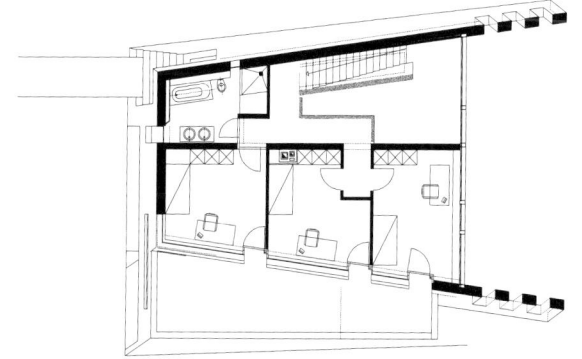

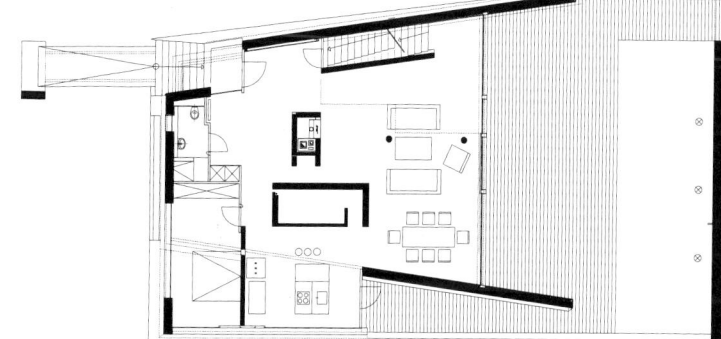

ER (SOKRATES) MEINE AUCH, DIESELBEN HÄUSER SEIEN SCHÖN UND NÜTZLICH, UND ES SCHIEN MIR, ALS WOLLE ER DAMIT LEHREN, WIE MAN SIE BAUEN MÜSSE. ER ÜBERLEGTE ABER FOLGENDERMASSEN: WENN JEMAND EIN HAUS HABEN WILL, WIE ES SEIN MUSS, SOLL ER ES DANN SO EINRICHTEN, DASS DAS LEBEN DARIN ANGENEHM UND NÜTZLICH SEIN WIRD? ALS MAN DIES ZUGAB, FUHR ER FORT: IST ES NUN NICHT ANGENEHM, WENN ES IM SOMMER KÜHL, IM WINTER WARM IST? ALS MAN DIES ZUGESTAND, MEINTE ER WEITER: SCHEINT NICHT IN DEN NACH SÜDEN GELEGENEN HÄUSERN DIE SONNE IM WINTER UNTER DIE VORHALLE, IM SOMMER ABER WANDERT SIE ÜBER UNS UND DIE DÄCHER HINWEG, DASS WIR SCHATTEN HABEN? WENN ES NUN ANGENEHM IST, DASS ES SO GESCHIEHT, MUSS MAN DANN NICHT DIE SÜDLICHEN ZIMMER HÖHER BAUEN, DAMIT DIE WINTERSONNE NICHT ABGESCHLOSSEN WIRD, DIE DER NORDSEITE ABER NIEDRIGER, DAMIT DIE KALTEN WINDE NICHT EINFALLEN KÖNNEN? UM ES KURZ ZU SAGEN: DAS DÜRFTE MIT RECHT DIE SCHÖNSTE UND ANGENEHMSTE BEHAUSUNG SEIN, IN DER MAN SICH IN JEDER JAHRESZEIT WOHL FÜHLT UND SEINEN BESITZ AM SICHERSTEN VERWAHRT.

HE (SOCRATES) ALSO MAINTAINS THAT A HOUSE CAN BE BOTH BEAUTIFUL AND USEFUL AND IT SEEMED TO ME AS IF HE WISHED IN THIS WAY TO GIVE A LESSON IN THE ART OF BUILDING HOUSES AS THEY SHOULD BE. HE REFLECTED AS FOLLOWS: IF SOMEONE WISHES TO HAVE THE RIGHT SORT OF HOUSE OUGHT HE MAKE IT AS PLEASANT TO LIVE IN AND AS USEFUL AS POSSIBLE? WHEN THIS WAS AGREED HE CONTINUED: IS IT NOT PLEASANT WHEN IT IS COOL IN SUMMER AND WARM IN WINTER? AS THIS WAS CONCEDED HE SAID FURTHER: IN SOUTH-FACING HOUSES DOES NOT THE SUN SHINE INTO THE PORCH IN WINTER WHEREAS IN SUMMER IT PASSES OVER OUR HEADS AND ABOVE THE ROOF SO THAT WE ARE IN SHADE? IF THIS IS FELT TO BE THE BEST ARRANGEMENT SHOULD WE NOT BUILD THE SOUTH-FACING ROOMS HIGHER TO CAPTURE THE WINTER SUN AND THE NORTH SIDE LOWER TO KEEP OUT THE COLD WINDS? TO PUT IT CONCISELY: A HOUSE IN WHICH THE OWNER CAN FIND AN AGREEABLE RETREAT AT ALL SEASONS AND CAN STORE HIS BELONGINGS SAFELY IS PRESUMABLY THE LOVELIEST AND MOST PLEASANT.

aus | from Xenophon, *Memorabilia of Socrates*

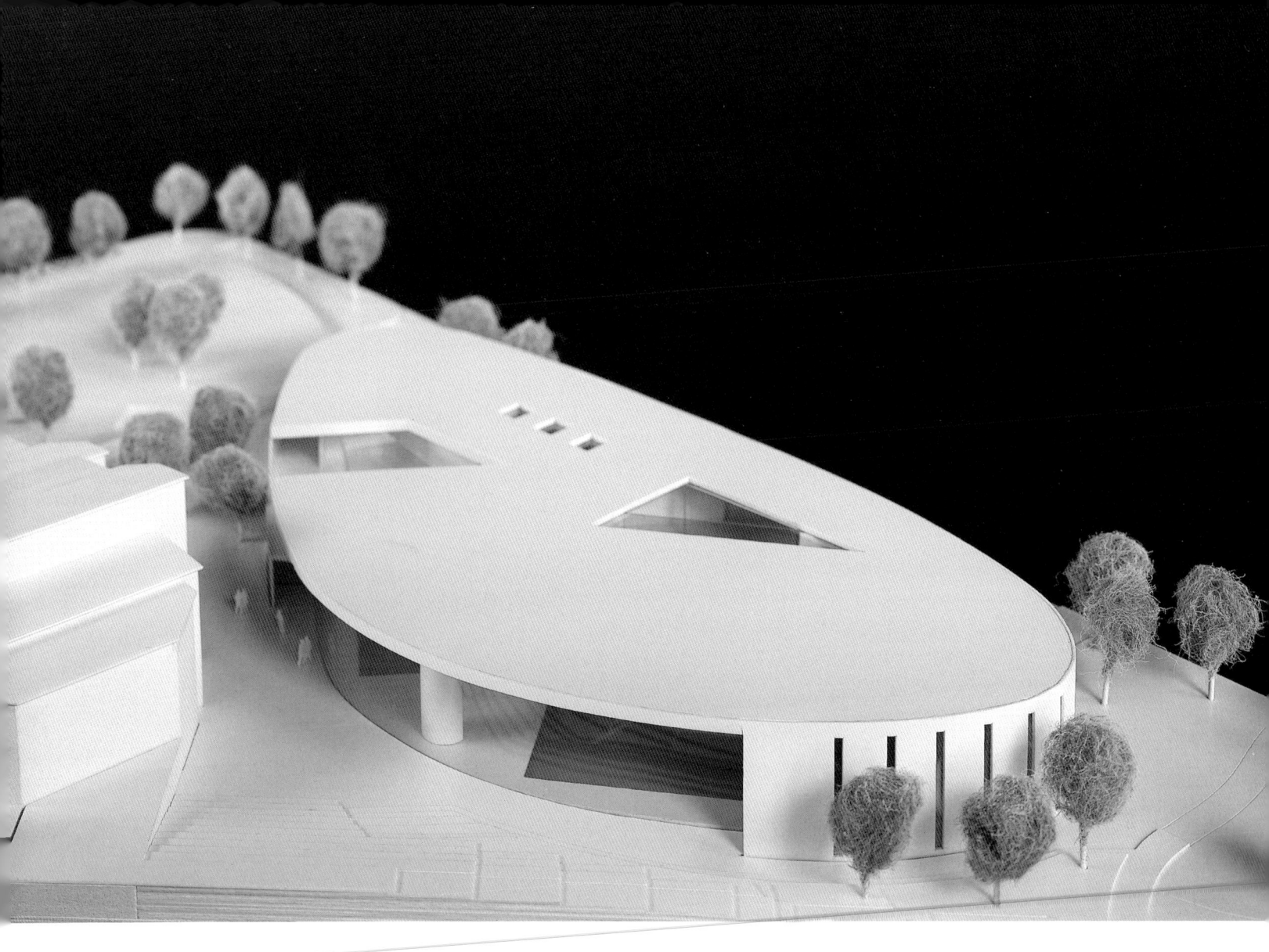

SCHWIMMBAD IN BONNEVOIE, LUXEMBURG-STADT
PUBLIC SWIMMING POOL IN BONNEVOIE, LUXEMBOURG-CITY

Ein neues Hallenbad (statt des unbrauchbar gewordenen alten) inmitten einer grünen Insel im städtischen Verband, also an einem privilegierten Standort: Luftdistanz zum Zentrum – ein Kilometer. Grundgedanke des Entwurfs: ein luft- und grünumspültes Gebäude, räumlich spannend, aber flächenmäßig nicht ungebührlich dominant. Einzig mögliche Realisierungsstrategie: Das neue Hallenbad wird im Grünraum errichtet, das alte danach abgerissen und an seiner Stelle (im Loch) eine Tiefgarage gebaut, die Platte darüber wird anschließend begrünt.

Das Bad: eine große, dreidimensionale Nierentischform. Keine viereckige Schachtel mit linear angeordneten Schwimmbecken, letztere vielmehr platzräumlich situiert, auch mit Blick auf pyramidenförmig eingeschnittene und begrünte Lichthöfe als reizvollen Ausblick für alle Besucher und in jeder Situation (auch beim Schwimmen). Programm: ein großes Becken mit Tribünen, geeignet für sportliche Events; ein Kinderbecken; ein großer Sauna- und Fitness-Bereich; die Umkleiden so organisiert, dass sie auch für den Schulbetrieb geeignet sind.

A new indoor swimming pool to replace an old one no longer usable. Situated at the centre of a green island within the urban area, i.e. in a privileged location only one kilometre from the town centre as the crow flies. The basic idea of the design: a building surrounded by air and greenery, spatially exciting but in terms of the area covered not unsuitably dominant. The only possible strategy: to build the new indoor baths in the green area, demolishing the old one and putting the underground car park in its place (in a hole in the ground). The slab covering it to be subsequently planted.

The baths: like a large, three-dimensional kidney-shaped coffee table and not a rectangular box with the pools arranged in linear fashion. In fact they are positioned to create a space with a view of the incised pyramid-shaped planted courtyards that offer a delightful glimpse of the outdoors to all visitors and in every situation (even while swimming). The brief: a large pool with spectator stands suitable for sporting events, a children's pool, a large sauna and fitness area. The changing rooms are planned so that they can be used by school groups.

Natürlich vorgesehen: eine gastronomische Einrichtung. Sie ist in einem Einschnitt des Gebäudes gelegen – das Potential einer Außenterrasse besteht – und sowohl intern als auch extern zugänglich.

Räumliche Besonderheit: die ins Dach großflächig eingeschnittene, geschützte Terrasse für die Sauna-Benutzer, mitten in der Stadt ein außergewöhnliches Angebot.

A restaurant was naturally included in the planning. It is placed in an incision in the building, has a potential external terrace and is accessible from both inside and outside.

One particular spatial feature: the screened terrace for visitors to the sauna generously cut out of the roof. An unusual facility in the centre of a city.

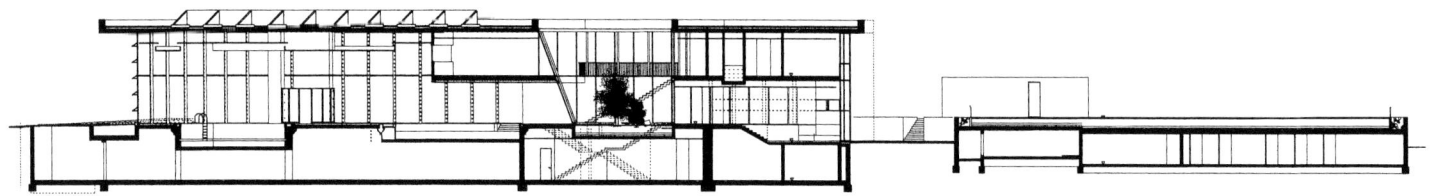

Schnitte
sections

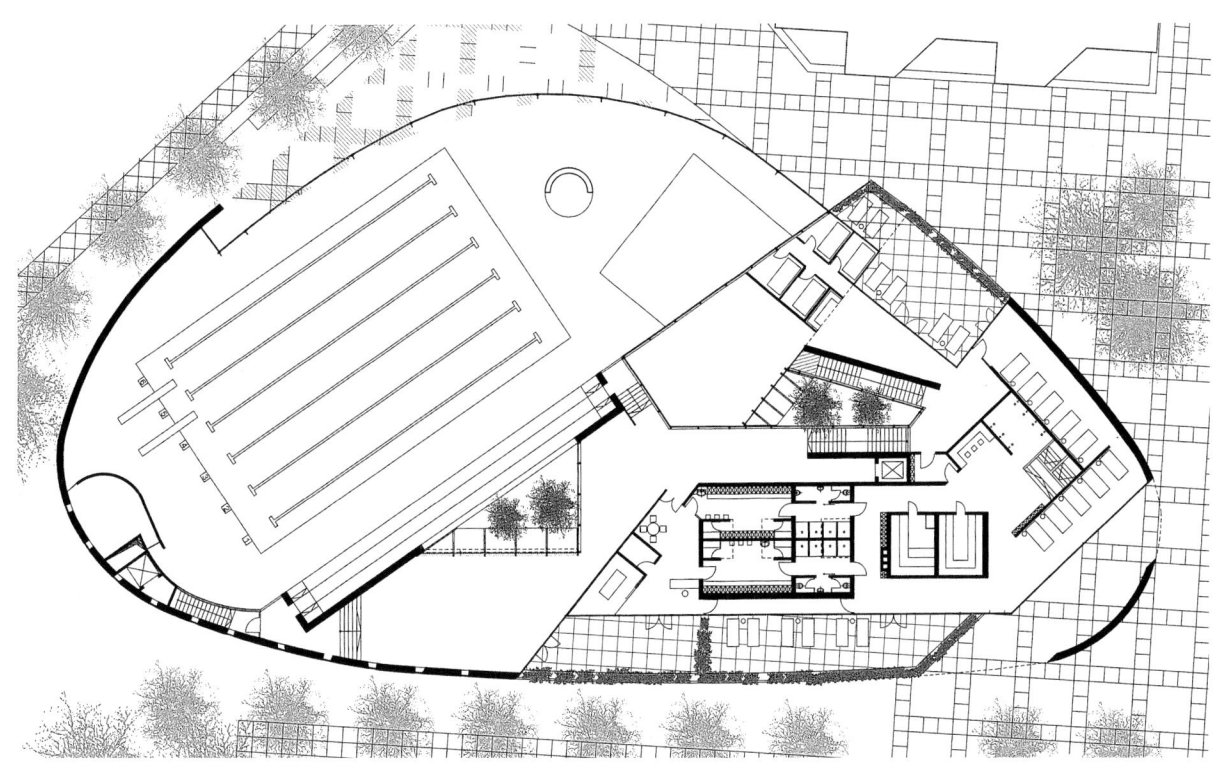

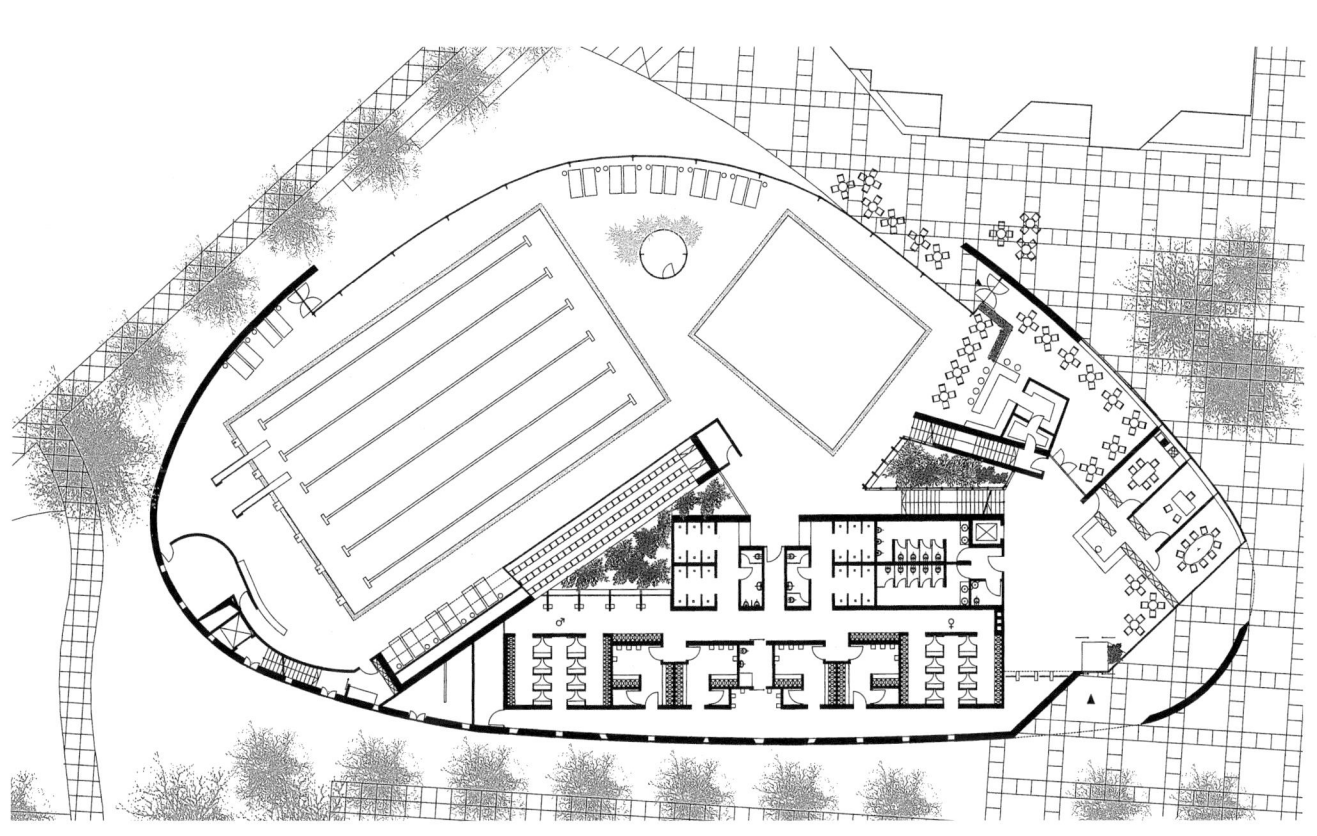

KIRCHBERG

DUDELANGE

DESSAU-ZIEBIGK

Bauherr | client **Reimerwe Giogetti S.a.r.L.**
Projektleiter | project manager **Axel Christmann**
Anzahl der Wohneinheiten | number of dwellings
    34 Haus 3,
    34 Haus 4
Grundstücksfläche | site area
    3.475 m² Haus 3,
    3.475 m² Haus 4
Bruttofläche | total floor area
    3.4266 m² Haus 3,
    3.4266 m² Haus 4
Planungsbeginn | start of planning **2/1994**
Baubeginn | start of construction **5/1996**
Fertigstellung | completion **2/1998**

Bauherr | client **Fonds pour le Logement à Coût Modéré**
Projektleiter | project manager **Axel Christmann, Karin Kist**
Grundstücksfläche | site area **5.557,50 m²**
Bruttofläche | total floor area **4.101 m²**
Planungsbeginn | start of planning **6/1993**
Baubeginn | start of construction **5/1994**
Fertigstellung | completion **9/1996**

Bauherr | client **Aachener & Münchener Lebensversicherung AG / Aachen**
Projektleiter | project manager **Thomas Letz**
Anzahl der Wohneinheiten | number of dwellings
    18 WE Reihenhaus 1
    18 WE Reihenhaus 2
Grundstücksfläche | site area
    2.246 m² Reihenhaus 1 | terrace 1
    2.294 m² Reihenhaus 2 | terrace 2
Bruttofläche | total floor area
    1.104 m² Reihenhaus 1
    1.104 m² Reihenhaus 2
Planungsbeginn | start of planning **2/1995**
Baubeginn | start of construction **5/1996**
Fertigstellung | completion **3/1997**

WOHNBAUTEN AUF DEM KIRCHBERG, LUXEMBURG-STADT
HOUSING DEVELOPMENT ON THE KIRCHBERG, LUXEMBOURG-CITY

Zwei schwarze, langgestreckte Wohnblöcke, die einen Platz flankieren, Zentrum einer wachsenden Wohnanlage. Langzeit-Ergebnis eines Wettbewerbes vom Ende der achtziger Jahre, das bis heute nicht vollständig realisiert ist: ein dritter Wohnblock von H & V steht nach wie vor aus.

Kirchberg: einer der Hügel, über die sich Luxemburg-Stadt in den letzten Jahrzehnten erweitert hat. Ein „internationaler Distrikt" voller Verwaltungsbauten und insofern weitgehend monofunktional. Dagegen Ziel der aktuellen Stadtentwicklung: urbane Durchmischung. Also Kulturbauten wie das Philharmonie-Projekt oder das Pei-Museum, aber auch Wohnungen. In dieser speziellen Situation allerdings kein sozialer Wohnbau, sondern relativ anspruchsvolles Eigentum.

Die Blöcke von H & V: fast siebzig Meter lang und fünf Geschosse hoch. Den Wohnungen ebenerdig zugeordnete Freiflächen liegen an der Rückseite, alle anderen haben vielfach ungewöhnlich große Loggien und Balkone. Besonders zum Platz hin prägt die großflächige Loggienverglasung auch das Fassadenbild: Sie ist als streng axialer Ausschnitt aus der Gebäudehaut formuliert und gibt den beiden Wohnblöcken einen eigenen Ausdruck.

Zwei ausgesprochen städtische, sehr elegante Wohnhäuser. Darin ganz unterschiedliche Wohnungen – von 50 bis 150 Quadratmetern Größe. Aber allen gemeinsam nicht nur der Luxus zugeordneter Freibereiche, sondern auch des inszenierten Außenbezugs, des Ausblicks. Fast „edel" zu nennen: die Materialisierung. Schwarzer Klinker an der Fassade (vorgesehen war ursprünglich schwarzer Beton – siehe Bech-Kleinmacher), Aluminium natur an der Untersicht des vorstehenden Daches, an den Untersichten der Balkone, in den Fensterlaibungen; auch die Sonnenschutz-Lamellen sind aus Aluminium; nur die Fenster selbst wurden in Holz ausgeführt. Alles jedenfalls angelegt auf ein „Alter in Schönheit".

Markantes Zeichen auf dem Platz: Vor der Tiefgaragenabfahrt steht ein Trafohäuschen. H & V nutzten (und entschärften) es als Sockel für eine große Skulptur aus Corten-Stahl. Ein rostiger König Artus, mitten in einer Wohnanlage, die „Avalon" heißt.

Two long, black blocks that flank an open space, the centre of a growing residential complex. The final result of a lengthy competition held in the eighties which to date has not been completely realised: a third housing block by H & V still awaits construction.

Kirchberg: one of the hills around which Luxembourg town has extended in recent years. An "international district" filled with administration buildings and, in this sense, by and large mono-functional. Hence the goal of current urban development is an urban mixture i.e. cultural buildings like the Philharmonie project or the Pei museum but also apartments. In this special situation there is no social housing but relatively high-standard, privately owned dwellings.

The blocks by H & V: almost seventy metres long and five storeys high. The open areas allotted to the ground-floor apartments lie at the rear, all the others have unusually large loggias and balconies. Particularly on the side facing the square the large areas of glazing of the loggias determine the appearance of the façade. They are formulated as a strictly axial cut made in the skin of the building that gives both blocks an individual expression.

Two particularly urban and extremely elegant housing blocks. Inside there are very different apartment types ranging in size from 50 to 100 square metres: all have not only the luxury of their own outdoor spaces but also a staged relationship to the outside and to the view that could almost be described as "noble". The materials: black engineering brick on the façade (black concrete was originally planned, see Bech-Kleinmacher), natural aluminium for the soffit of the projecting roof and of the balconies and in the window reveals. The sun screen louvers are also of aluminium, only the window frames themselves are made of wood. Everything planned to allow "ageing gracefully".

A striking symbol on the open space: in front of the ramp leading down to the underground garage is a small transformer building. H & V used (and defused) it as a base for a large sculpture made of Corten steel. A rusty king Arthur at the centre of a housing development named "Avalon".

3. Obergeschoss
3rd floor

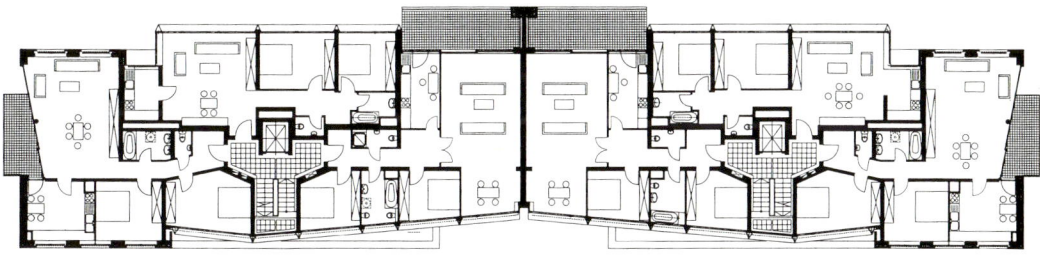

WOHNBAU IN DUDELANGE, LUXEMBURG
HOUSING DEVELOPMENT IN DUDELANGE, LUXEMBOURG

Sozialer Wohnbau auf einem ehemaligen Industriegelände, direkt an der Bahn. Die Gleise führen in südöstlicher Richtung daran vorbei. Der Bebauungsplan sah drei Baublöcke vor, was bedeutet: drei Stiegenhäuser, drei Lifte – also hohe Erschließungskosten. Dagegen der Vorschlag von H & V: ein großes Dach über alle drei Bauteile, Laubengänge und – nur zwei Stiegenhäuser und zwei Lifte.

Es sind viergeschossige Häuser, an den – auch höhenmäßig – modifizierten Ecken mit Maisonette-Typen. Die anderen Wohnungen sind west-ost-orientiert. Ein simpler, aber effektiver Grundrisstyp (mit Variationen): Eingang vom Laubengang im Osten, von der Seite der Bahn, links Küche, rechts Kinderzimmer, dann Bad und Elternschlafzimmer, schließlich der Wohnraum nach Westen samt den zugeordneten Loggien oder Balkonen. Der Laubengang ist um drei Stufen abgesenkt, sodass man in die Wohnungen nicht hineinsieht. Die drei Stufen liegen in einem Einschnitt, der über Eck verglast ist. Konstruktiv eine traditionelle, weil besonders ökonomische Lösung: Scheiben, die jeweils eine Wohneinheit definieren.

Architektonische Besonderheit: eine gewaltige, schräg gestellte, begrünte Pergola, an der die Laubengänge aufgehängt sind. Eine strategische Maßnahme. Einerseits semitransparenter Sichtschutz gegenüber dem Bahngelände. Andererseits: Traggerüst für die Laubengänge. Insofern doppelter Gewinn: die Wandkonstruktion musste die Kräfte der Laubengänge nicht aufnehmen; und die Pergola ist nicht dem Rechenstift zum Opfer gefallen.

A social housing development on a former industrial site, directly beside a railway line. The tracks run past south-eastwards. The development plan envisaged three blocks which meant three staircases and three lifts i.e. high circulation costs. H & V's proposal is a contrast: a large roof above all three building elements, access decks and only two staircases and two lifts.

Four-storey buildings: at the corners, which are also differentiated in terms of height, maisonette-type apartments are located. The other apartments face east/west. A simple but effective floor plan (with variations). Entrance is from the access deck on the railway line side, to the left the kitchen, to the right the children's room followed by the bathroom and parents' room and, finally, the west-facing living room with its own loggia or balcony. The access deck is three steps lower so that people cannot see into the apartments. The three steps lie in an incision with corner glazing. The structural system is a traditional, particularly economical solution: cross walls defining a single dwelling unit.

Architectural speciality: a powerful, sloping pergola covered with creeper. A strategic measure: providing, on the one hand, semi-transparent screening of the railway tracks and, on the other, a supporting structure for the decks. A double advantage: the walls do not have to carry the load of the decks and the pergola was not eliminated on budgetary grounds.

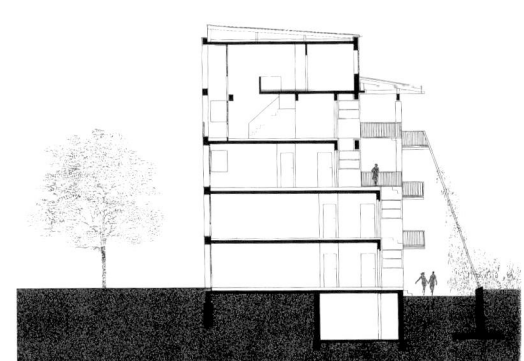
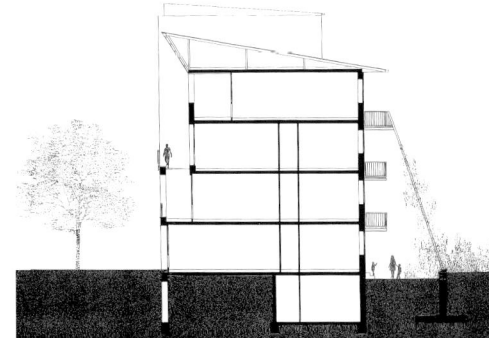

Schnitte
sections

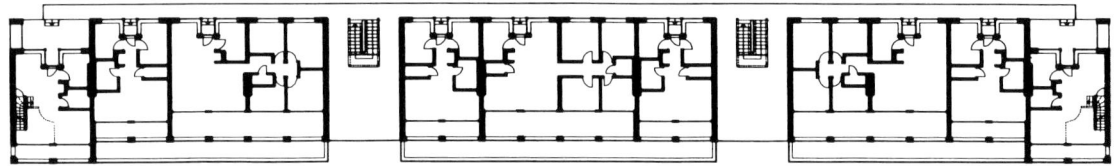

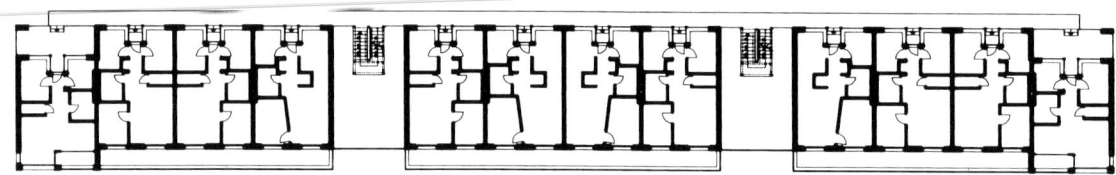

3. Obergeschoss
3rd floor

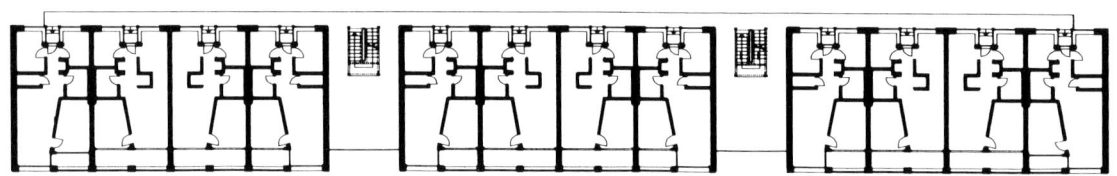

2. Obergeschoss
2nd floor

1. Obergeschoss
1st floor

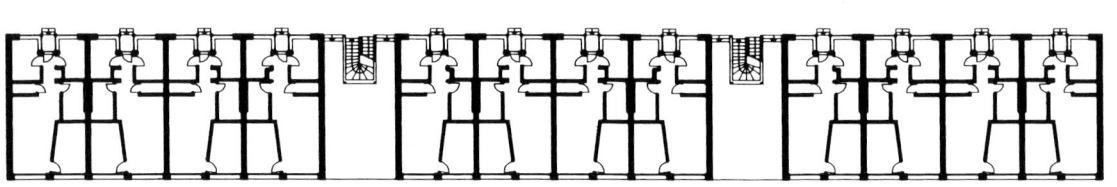

Erdgeschoss
ground floor

WOHNANLAGE IN DESSAU-ZIEBIGK, DEUTSCHLAND
HOUSING DEVELOPMENT IN DESSAU-ZIEBIGK, GERMANY

Reihen- beziehungsweise Doppelhäuser in den Auen der Elbe. Ein Stadtentwicklungsgebiet in den neuen deutschen Bundesländern, äußerste Ökonomie daher vorausgesetzt. Der (vorgegebene) Städtebau war ein Wettbewerbsergebnis und konnte nur geringfügig modifiziert werden. Grundprinzip: „Inseln", die Plätze sind, um die sich die Häuser gruppieren, und eine Wohnzeile, ausgerichtet auf einen historischen Pavillon.

Ein einfacher Entwurf: Von der Straße führt eine Rampe nach unten zum Abstellplatz für das Auto; von dort geht es über eine Treppe in die zweigeschossige Wohnung hinauf. Der Wohnraum liegt etwas über dem Terrain, in den Garten steigt man daher über ein paar Stufen hinunter. Beim (vergleichsweise luxuriösen) Einzelhaustyp signifikant: der gläserne Dachaufbau. Bei den – unter den gegebenen Umständen: marktkonformeren – Doppelhäusern eine zweite Wohnung über die untere geschichtet. Aber auch hier: eine eingeschnittene Terrasse als Freifläche.

Ein rigoroses Materialkonzept: Putz und Holz. Nur die Außenstiegen zur oberen Wohnung in Streckmetall verpackt. Für die axiale Ausrichtung der Wohnzeile Richtung Pavillon nicht unerheblich: der breite Dachüberstand als zusätzliche Außenraumformulierung. Interessant auch die individuelle Nutzbarkeit der Garage, in der räumliches Reservepotential steckt. Außerdem wichtig: die Freiraumgestaltung samt integriertem Rankgerüst und bepflanzter Böschung, die den Blick vom Garten ins „Garagenloch" abschirmt.

Terraced and double houses in the water meadows of the Elbe. An urban development area in the "new" German states. Consequently stringent economy was a prerequisite. The (existing) development was the product of a competition and could be only slightly modified. Basic principle: "islands" forming open spaces around which the houses are grouped and, additionally, a line of houses directed towards a historic pavilion.

A simple design. A ramp leads down from the road to the car parking space, from there one goes up a staircase to the two-storey apartment. The living room is slightly above ground level, so that one goes down a few steps to reach the garden. The glass rooftop element is a significant feature in the (relatively luxurious) single-house type. In the – due to the given circumstances – more market-oriented double houses one apartment is placed above the other. But here there is also an incised terrace providing an outdoor space.

A rigorous material concept: render and wood. Only the external staircase leading to the upper apartment is wrapped in expanded metal. The broad projection of the roof is an additional factor that shapes the external space and is also significant for the axial orientation of the row of houses towards the pavilion. The individual usability of the garage harbours a reserve of spatial potential that is also interesting. Another important aspect is the design of the open spaces with an integrated trellis and a planted slope screening the view from the garden of the "garage hole".

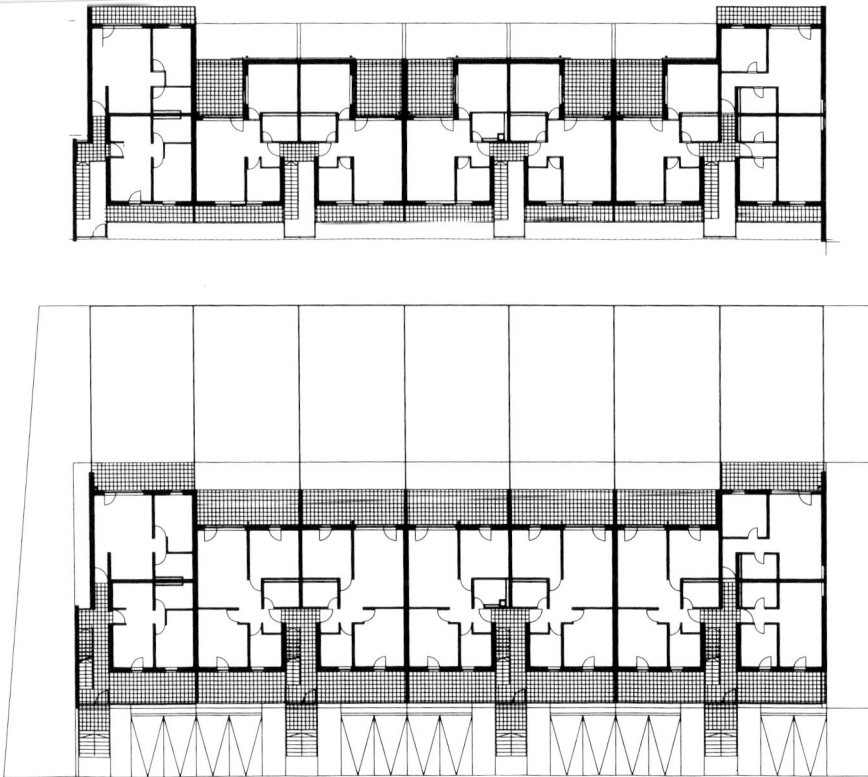

WOHNEN UND ARBEITEN AM HÖCHSTÄDTPLATZ
IN WIEN-BRIGITTENAU
LIVING AND WORKING ON HÖCHSTÄDTPLATZ
IN VIENNA-BRIGITTENAU

Ein Gründerzeitviertel nahe der Donau. Blockraster, lange Straßenfluchten und eigentlich nur eine leere Parzelle – die aber Höchstädtplatz heißt. Ein Stück unverbauter Fläche, zerschnitten von Straßenbahngleisen und Fahrbahnen.

Bezugspunkte des Areals: ein Park im Hintergrund und vorne, an der Ecke, die kleine, achtgeschossige Scheibe des ehemaligen Globus-Verlages, ein Bauwerk aus den fünfziger Jahren, an dessen Planung Margarete Schütte-Lihotzky mitgewirkt hat.

Thema der geforderten Neubebauung entlang der stark befahrenen Dresdner Straße: Arbeiten und Wohnen. Übergeordnete Aufgabenstellung: die städtebauliche Neuordnung und Klärung des Platzes.

Erste Überlegung von H & V: Den Raster der geschlossenen Gründerzeithöfe weiterzuführen, erscheint an dieser Stelle problematisch, weil ruhiges Wohnen in den unteren Geschossen nur Richtung Hof möglich wäre.

Zweite Überlegung: Maßstab und Typologie des Schütte-Lihotzky-Hauses erscheinen hingegen entwickelbar, ein spannender, kontrapunktischer Akzent im Einerlei des alten Blockrasters.

A Gründerzeit district close to the Danube: a block grid pattern with long streets lined by buildings and, in fact, only one empty site – which is called Höchstädtplatz: a piece of undeveloped ground carved up by tram tracks and traffic lanes.

The focal points of the area are a park in the background and, at the front, the small eight-storey slab of the former Globus-Verlag (publishing house) a building dating from the fifties, in the design of which Margarete Schütte-Lihotzky was involved.

The theme of the new development along busy Dresdner Strasse was Working and Living. A primary consideration was the urban reorganisation and clarification of Höchstädtplatz.

H & V's first reflection: to continue the grid made by the enclosed Gründerzeit courtyards appeared problematic: Acceptable living conditions on the lower floors seemed possible only in apartments facing onto the courtyard.

Their second idea: a further development of the scale and typology of the Schütte-Lihotzky building that would provide a more exciting, contrapuntal accent in the monotony of the block grid.

Folgerichtige Konsequenz: die Errichtung eines Sockelgebäudes entlang der Dresdner Straße, in dem Gewerbe- und andere Arbeitsflächen Platz finden; und darauf Wohnhausscheiben, sechs bis zehn Geschosse hoch. Hintergedanken: im Sockelgebäude die Errichtung einer sehr einfachen Grobstruktur, die erst im Zug der Inbesitznahme Schritt für Schritt ausgebaut wird; aber eingeschnittene Lichthöfe, die auch hier für gut tagesbelichtete Situationen sorgen; schließlich: die Möglichkeit der Umnutzung dieses Bereiches – etwa als Hochgarage.

The appropriate result of their reflections: the construction of a plinth building along Dresdner Strasse in which commercial and other work spaces could be housed and on top of it apartment block slabs six to ten storeys high. Some of the ideas behind this concept were: using the plinth building to create an extremely simple basic structure which could be developed, step by step, in the process of occupying it, the provision of incised courtyards which here too allow good natural lighting and, finally, the possibility of using this section quite differently, for instance as a multi-storey car park.

Substantiell für die Qualität dieser Planung ist jedoch das Konzept, eine durchgehende, begrünte Freiflächenlandschaft zu schaffen, in der die Wohnhausscheiben stehen. Auf dem Niveau des dritten Obergeschosses angedacht, sorgt dieser „Stadtpark" für Aufenthaltsqualität und Grünblick und liefert damit wohl das einzige Argument, warum hier jemand wohnen sollte. Wie gesagt, ein Park, in dem Gebäude stehen. Mit einer Blickverbindung hinüber zum alten Park.

Städtebaulich ausschlaggebend war die Strategie, die bestehenden Straßenfluchten zu brechen, zu stören, und damit darauf hinzuweisen, dass und wo etwas anderes passiert: nämlich am Höchstädtplatz. Letzterer eingefasst durch eine Pergola, die die Höhe des Sockelgebäudes weiterführt. Kommunikation zwischen Mauern, ein vermittelndes Element.

Of substantial importance for the quality of this planning is, however, the concept of a continuous planted open landscape in which the apartment slabs stand. Planned at third floor level this "City Park" provides quality living and a view of nature and thus supplies the only argument as to why someone should live here. As said above a park in which buildings stand with a visual connection across to the old park.

In urban planning terms the decisive idea was the strategy of breaking and disrupting the existing street lines and indicating firstly: that something different occurs here, secondly: where it happens, i.e. on Höchstädtplatz. The latter is defined by a pergola that continues the height line of the plinth building. Communication between walls, a mediating element.

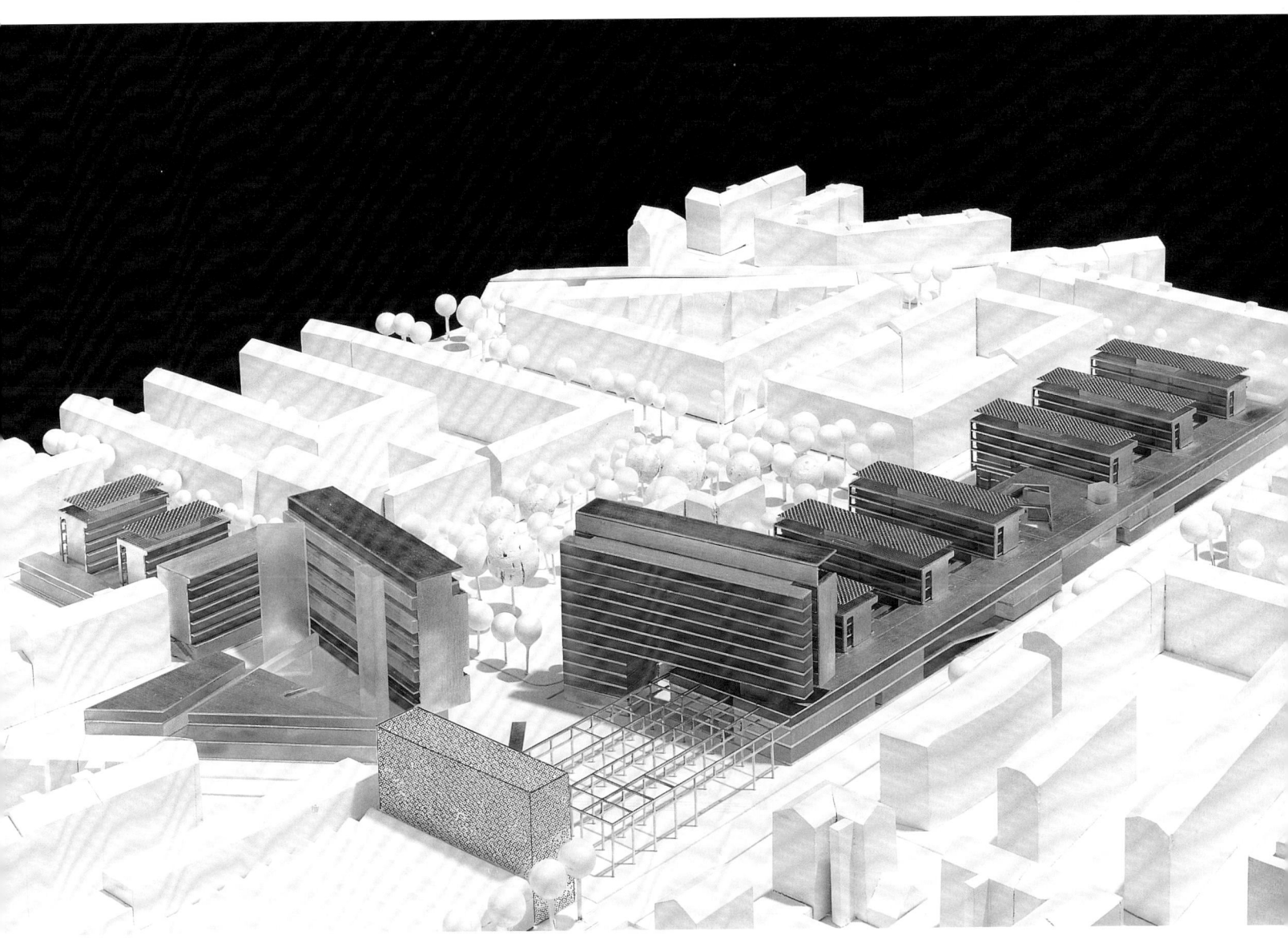

NEUORGANISATION DES BAHNHOFSAREALS ESCH/ALZETTE, LUXEMBURG
REORGANISATION OF THE AREA AROUND ESCH-SUR-ALZETTE RAILWAY STATION, LUXEMBOURG

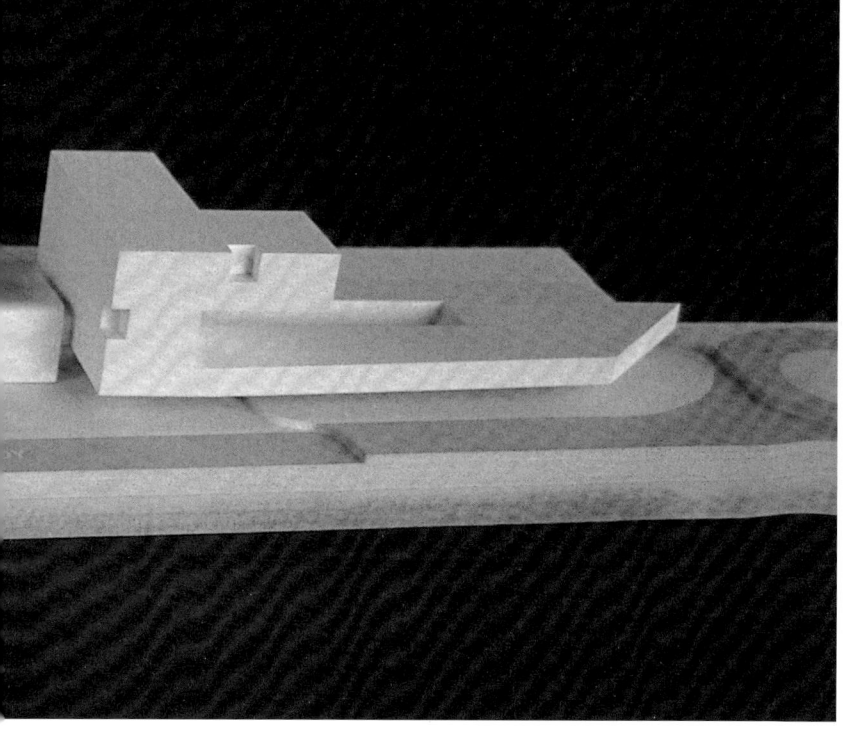

Ein städtebauliches Projekt. Esch/Alzette ist die zweitgrößte Stadt Luxemburgs, Sitz der Stahlindustrie und seit Generationen mehrheitlich bewohnt von Mitbürgern ausländischer (hauptsächlich italienischer) Herkunft. Der Bahnhof – eine schöne Halle – stammt aus den sechziger Jahren, ebenso eine große Bürohaus-Scheibe.

Das Umfeld: Entwicklungsgebiet, sowohl stadtseitig als auch dahinter, Richtung Galgenberg, einem durchgrünten Naherholungsgebiet.

Das Konzept: städtische (Freizeit-)Funktionen vor dem Bahnhof, Arbeiten und Wohnen Richtung Galgenberg, der durch eine Brücke über die Gleisanlagen direkt an die Stadt angeschlossen wird. Rechts vor dem Bahnhof und über dem Busbahnhof: gastronomische Einrichtungen, Veranstaltungsräume, eine Bowling-Bahn. Linker Hand: eine große, zweigeschossige, von oben belichtete Einkaufsmall. Nicht nur wichtige Drehscheibe städtischen Konsums, sondern vor allem stadträumlich von Bedeutung. Definition einer neuen Platzkante, parallel zu den Gleisanlagen, offen zum Zentrum. Auf der anderen Seite der Gleise, Richtung Galgenberg: eine dichte Bebauung mit Büros und – in den auskragenden Bauteilen – Wohnungen. Städtebaulicher Trick: Aus der an sich geschlossen konzipierten und nach Süden orientierten Bebauung sind Teile ausgeschnitten und parkähnlich begrünt. Kleine „Wolkenbügel", städtisch in der Grundfigur, aber eingebettet in Freiflächen, als Übergangszone zum Grünraum. Angedachte Materialisierung: Stahl und Glas.

An urban project. Esch-sur-Alzette is Luxembourg's second largest city, for generations the majority of the population has been made up of foreigners, mostly of Italian origin, which accounts for the local open atmosphere.

The railway station, an important factor for freight transport, dates from the sixties and has a fine hall worth preserving. Beside it is a large slender block (the highest building in the area, also from the sixties) containing offices. The surroundings: a development area, both on the city side in front of the railway station and also behind it, in the direction of Galgenberg which is a local "green lung" for the inhabitants.

The concept: urban (leisure) functions in front of the railway station, behind it, in the direction of Galgenberg, working and living – to be connected directly to the city by a bridge over the railway tracks. To the right of the railway station and above the bus station: restaurant facilities, function rooms and a bowling alley, to the left of the train station a large, two-storey, top-lit shopping mall. Not merely an important centre of urban consumption – which in the final analysis also economically benefits the surroundings – but also of primary urban significance. The definition of a new edge to the square that is parallel to the tracks and open towards the centre. On the other side of the railway, towards Galgenberg, is a dense development containing offices and, in the projecting elements, apartments. The urban trick: parts are cut out of the essentially closed, south-facing development and landscaped. Several small "Wolkenbügel", urban in terms of their basic pattern but embedded in open areas, are used here to formulate transitional zones to the leafy area of the Galgenberg. The planned materials are steel and glass.

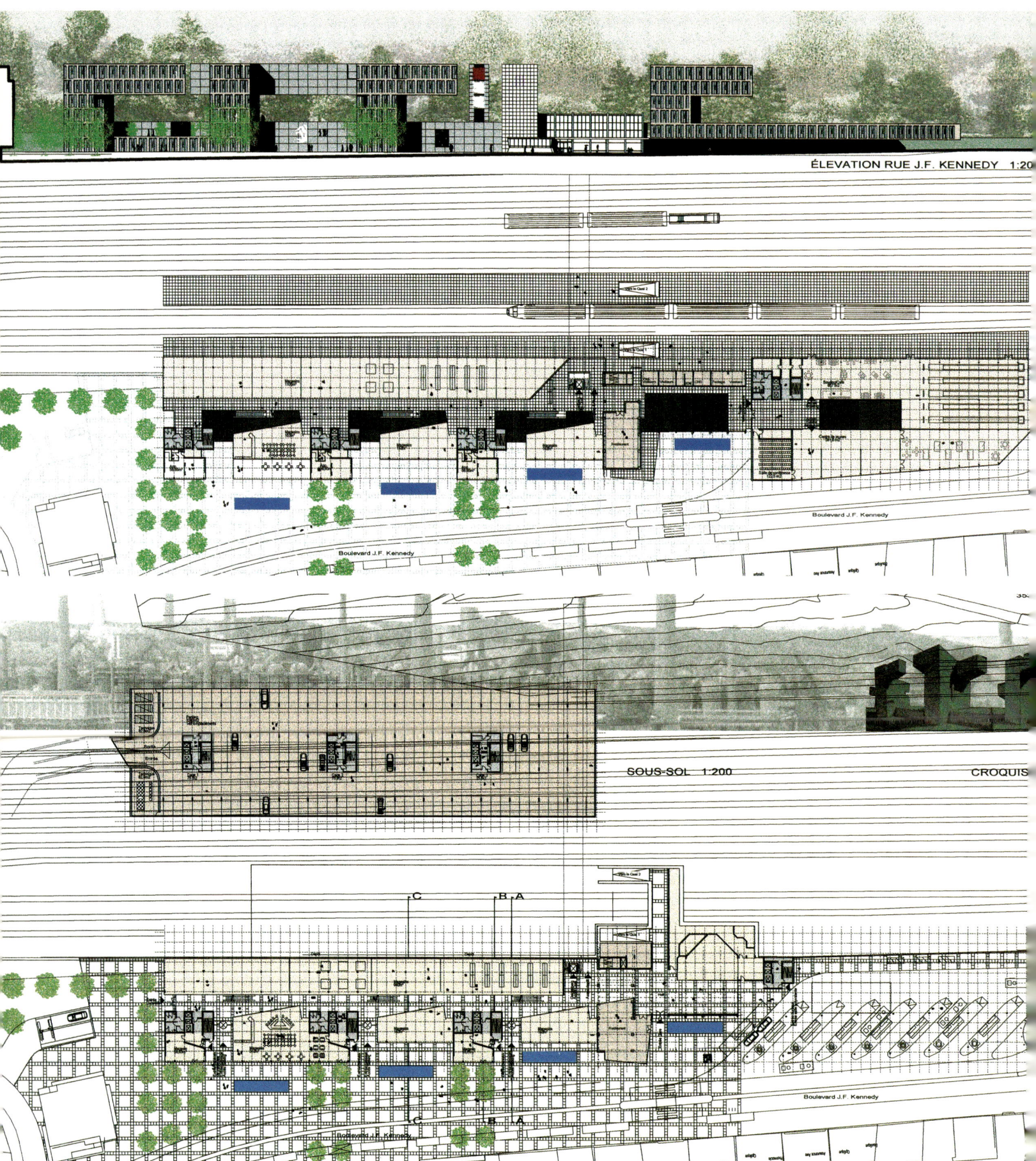

1. Obergeschoss
1st floor

Erdgeschoss
ground floor

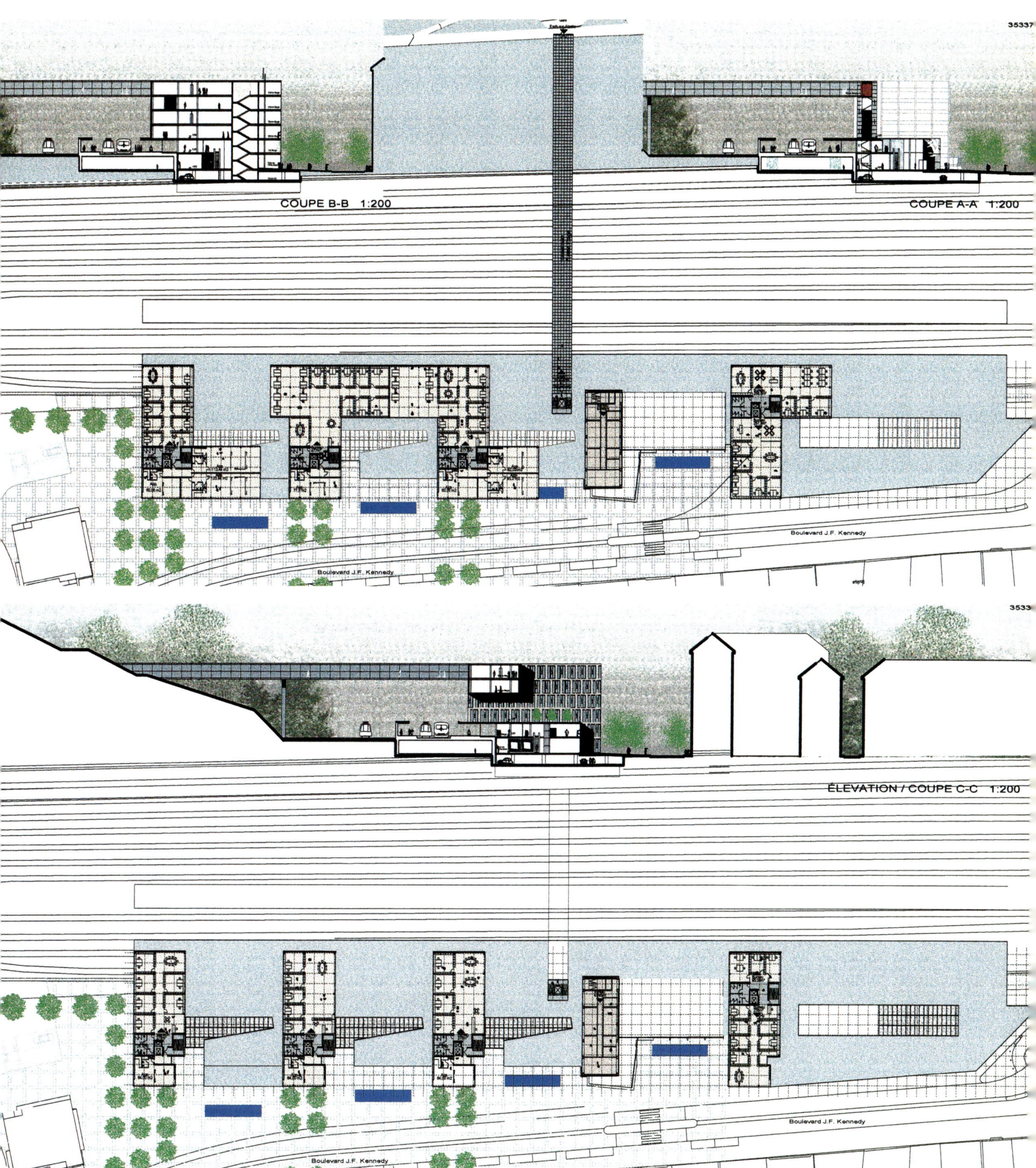

4. + 5. Obergeschoss
4th+5th floor

2. Obergeschoss
2nd floor

SENIORENRESIDENZ UND HOTEL IN KÖLN, DEUTSCHLAND
SENIOR CITIZENS HOME AND HOTEL IN COLOGNE, GERMANY

An inner-city location within view of the cathedral, the railway station is in walking distance, surrounded by banks, administration buildings, the post office. The clients' intention: a home for senior citizens connected to a hotel and to the inner-city infrastructure. A seriousminded contribution to achieving a multi-layered mix in this district.

This is definitely not an island for the elderly, indeed avoiding such was a prerequisite for the design. While the powerful block-perimeter development with its two internal courtyards responds to the development pattern of the surroundings it also differentiates it. On one side is a public courtyard with shops and a restaurant. Behind, in a second courtyard, is a more intimate space to withdraw to. But here too temporary additional uses are integrated, for instance the hall used for various events can expand into this open space.

Concrete measures: a set-back three metres behind the building line, a building skin with two layers which encloses balconies a good two meters deep. The apartments are fully glazed towards the outside but are articulated by means of a "perforated façade", a black, structured concrete panel made of pre-cast elements that is placed in front on the street side. On the courtyard side a frame will allow creepers to cover the façade.

Cuts: an architectural principle which adds its own contribution: the building elements are split, cut open along their full length, between them are generous trapezoidal corridors, lit from above, that invite one to linger. The apartments are adapted to meet the requirements of disabled people and planned in such a way that the two living rooms can be used separately.

Die Höfe intensiv begrünt, im öffentlichen Bereich auch eine Wasserfläche und die Statue des Albertus Magnus. Ein rigoroses Materialkonzept: Schwarzer Beton, die Balkonuntersichten weiß gestrichen, Stahl, Glas; Erschließungsräume – die Nottreppenhäuser in der Seniorenresidenz, die über alle Geschosse durchgehende Halle im Drei-Sterne-Hotel – in blauem Glasbaustein und nach außen sichtbar.

The courtyards are intensively planted. In the public area there is also a pool and a statue of Albertus Magnus. The choice of materials is rigorous: black concrete, balcony soffits painted white, steel and glass. Blue glass block is used in the circulation spaces – the escape staircases in the home for the elderly, the hall extending through all storeys in the three-star hotel – which are visible from outside.

Bauherr | client **Rentaco**
Planung | planning **Hermann & Valentiny et Associés,
   Jöhnssen Ranft Lüke, Köln**
Projektleiter | project manager **Axel Christmann, G. G. Kirchner**
Grundstücksfläche | site area **8.756 m²**
Anzahl Wohneinheiten | number of dwellings **322**
Anzahl der Hotelzimmer | number of hotel rooms **131**
Bruttofläche | total floor area **46.970 m²**
Planungsbeginn | start of planning **9/1996**
Baubeginn | start of construction **9/1998**
Fertigstellung | completion **9/2000**

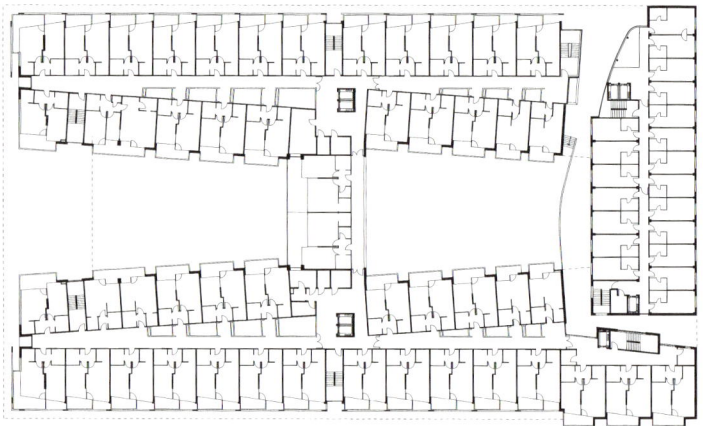

Regelgeschoss
standard floor plan

BAUTEN | BUILDINGS

1980 Restaurant „Leo", Mödling bei | near Wien, A

1981–82 Restaurant „Phoenix" in Luxembourg, L

1981–86 Stadtvilla in der | urban villa on Rauchstrasse, IBA-Berlin, D

1981–92 Rond Point Schuman, Luxembourg, L

1983–85 Haus Hermann mit | with Atelier Hermann & Valentiny, Wien, A

1984 Markusturm bei | near Schengen, L

1984–85 Haus Ruppert, Schengen, L

1984–85 Haus Müller, Wintrange, L

1984–85 Atelier Hermann & Valentiny, Remerschen, L

1984–86 Tunnel St-Esprit, L

1984–87 Zollstation auf der Autobahn | Toll station on the motorway Luxembourg–Trier, L

1985–86 Turm Mont St-Jean bei | near Dudelange, L

1985–87 Haus Reuter, Bech-Kleinmacher, L

1985–93 Diverse Möbelentwürfe und Objekte | Various designs for furniture and objects

1986–88 Feuerwehrzentrale | Central fire brigade station, Itzig, L

1986–92 Mühle Bestgen, Schifflange, L

1987 Pavillon Galgenberg, Esch/Alzette, L

1987–88 Haus Aistleitner, Wien, A

1987–90 Umbau einer Schuhfabrik | Conversion of a shoe factory, Kayl, L

1987–91 Schloss Collart, Bettembourg, L

1988–89 Tutesall Luxembourg (Umbau des alten Männergefängnisses von Luxembourg | Conversion of the old male prison), L

1988–89 Haus Maglica, Remich, L

1988–89 Haus Bortuzzo, Bereldange, L

1988–89 Haus Valentiny-Zucca, Aspelt, L

1988–90 Wohnbau | Housing development, Erlachgasse, Wien, A

1989–90 Haus Hoffmann, Boulaide, L

1989–90 Frisiersalon | Hair stylists salon, Wien, A

1989–91 Haus Brandstätter, Wien, A

1990–92 Haus in Brunn/Gebirge, A

1991–92 Wohnungen für Bedürftige | Apartments for low income groups, Grevenmacher, L

1991–94 Gesamtschule | Comprehensive school, Schweglerstrasse, Wien, A

1991–94 Sozialer Wohnbau | Local authority housing Grevenmacher, L

1992– Revitalisierung und Erweiterung | Revitalisation and extension to Schloss Mannswörth, Schwechat bei | near Wien, A

1992–93 Anna-Haus, Remerschen, L

1992–95 Hotel- und Dienstleistungskomplex | Hotel and service industry complex, Halle an der Saale, D; Auszeichnung: 1. Preis | 1st prize, Architekturpreis des Landes | Architecture prize of the State of Sachsen-Anhalt 1995

1993–95 Luxemburger Botschaft | Embasssy of Luxembourg in Wien, A; Auszeichnung: 1. Preis | 1st prize, Architekturpreis der | Architecture prize of the „Fondation l'Architecture et de l'Ingénierie Luxembourg"

1993–95 Haus am Josefssteig, Klosterneuburg, A

1993–95 Zubau und Platzgestaltung | Extension and design of open space, Städtisches Theater in Luxembourg, L

1993–95 Wohntürme | Housing towers, Halle an der Saale, D

1993–95 Büro-, Wohn- und Geschäftshaus | Office, apartment and commercial building, Schweglerstrasse, Wien, A

1993–95 Feuerwehrhaus | Fire brigade station, Schengen, L

1993–96 Gemeindehaus | Town council building Bech-Kleinmacher, L; Luxemburger Architekturpreis für die beste Realisierung aus Beton | Luxembourg architecture prize for the best concrete building

1993–97 Wohnanlage | Housing development, Dudelange, L

1993–98 Sporthalle für | Sports hall for Lyceum, Diekirch, L

1993–2005 Umbau | Conversion Lyceum, Diekirch, L

1993–95 Siedlungsprojekt | Housing project Dessau-Ziebigk, D; Platz 1 | 1st place

1995–97 2 Wohnblöcke | 2 Apartment blocks, Mustereinzel- und -doppelhaus | Model single and double house; Platz 3 | 3rd place

1994–95 Weinkellerei | Winery Moos-Vesque, Vallée de la Moselle, L

1994–96 Wohnanlage | Housing development, Berlin-Kirchsteigfeld, Potsdam, D

1994–98 Wohnanlage | Housing development Avalon, Luxembourg-Kirchberg, L

1995–96 Galerie Clairefontaine, Luxembourg, L

1995–96 Geschäftslokal | Shop Thun-Hohenstein, Wien, A

1995–97 Wohnanlage | Housing development, Berlin-Karow, Block 25/30/31, D

1995–98 Kindertagesstätte | Children's day care centre, Bettembourg, L

1995–99 Vestiairen und Bistro für Sportanlage | Changing rooms and bistro for a sports complex, Remerschen, L

1996–97 Haus mit den zwei Gesichtern | House with two faces, Klosterneuburg, A

1996–97 Haus Ierace, Sanem, L

1996–97 Realisierung „Wohnen und Arbeiten" | Construction "Living and Working", Wien, A

1996–2000 Realisierung Reihenhäuser Telefonweg | Construction Telefonweg terrace houses, Wien, A

1996–2000 Seniorenresidenz | Senior citizens residence / Hotel „Am Dom", Köln, D

1997 Einfamilienhaus | Single family house Dr. Karlas-Pichler, Wien, A

1997– Umbau Einfamilienhaus | Redesign of a single family house Maderbacher/Foidl, Baden bei Wien, A

1997–99 Lager, Büro, Wohnung und Ordination | Storeroom, office apartment and practice Lawi, Wien, A

1997–99 Wohnbauten | Housing blocks Dernjacgasse / Perfektastrasse, Wien, A

1997–99 Haus Vandenberg, Remich, L

1997–99 Einfamilienhaus | Single family house in Wien, A

1997–2001 Umbau ehemalige Brotfabrik, Wohnen und Arbeiten, Restaurant | Conversion of a former bakery, living and working, restaurant Wien, A

1997–2000 Stadtteilzentrum | Urban district centre Halle-Neustadt, D

1997–2000 Seniorenresidenz | Senior citizens residence „An der Grossen Bleiche", Mainz, D

1998–99 Aufstockung Gemeindehaus | Addition of a floor to the local council building, Dalheim, L

1998–99 Umbau Bürohaus ehemalige Lederfabrik in Büro H & V | Conversion of a former leather factory into an office for H & V, Wien, A

1998–2000 Verwaltungsgebäude | Administration building „Ciments S.A.", Esch/Alzette, L

1998–2000 Verwaltungsgebäude | Administration building „Materiaux S.A.", Luxembourg, L

1999–2000 Haus Hirtt, Wellenstein, L

1999–2000 Doppelhaus Klein-Kurt, Kopstal, L

1999–2003 Kindergarten, Schüttrange, L

1999– Geschäftshaus | Retail building Favoritenstrasse, Wien, A

1999–2000 23Wipro-Café Wien, A

1999– Industrieanlage-Werk | Industrial estate Möllersdorf bei | near Wien, A

1999– Zu- und Neubau eines Wohnhauses | New apartment building and extension, Pragerstrasse, Wien, A

1999– Wohnhaus | Apartment building, Anton-Bosch-Gasse, Wien, A

2000– Kunstgalerie Rackey, Bad-Honnef, D

2000– Restaurant Wasserkühler, Saarbrücken, D

2000– Nutzung Weltkulturerbe Völklingen, D

2000– Schulkomplex | School complex, Remerschen, L

2000– Schwimmbad | Indoor swimming pool, Luxembourg-Bonnevoie, L

2000– Neubau von Bürogebäuden für die | New office building for Commerzbank am Kirchberg, L

2000– Neugestaltung | New design for the Theaterplatz, Luxembourg, L

2000– Wohnbau | Apartment block Avalon Haus 13, Luxembourg-Kirchberg, L

2000– Senioren-Pflegeheim mit Tagesstätte | Old persons nursing home with day care centre, Luxembourg-Kirchberg, L

2000– Atelier und Wohnen | Studio and Housing in Lindabrunn, A

2000– EURO RSCG – Büro in der Brotfabrik | Office in the bakery, Wien, A

PROJEKTE | PROJECTS

1991–94 Dorferneuerungsprojekt | Village renewal project, Bascharage, L

1992 Revitalisierung und Erweiterung | Revitalisation and extension Schloss Mannswörth, A

1996 Gewerbe | Commercial Nauseagasse, Wien, A

Gewerbe | Commercial Arndtstrasse, Wien, A

Handelskai-Studie | Study Wien, A

1996–99 Haus Rothengatter, Rüsselsheim, D

1997–99 Lager, Büro, Wohnung und Ordination | Storeroom, office, apartment, practice, Wien, A

1998 Einfamilienhaussiedlung | Housing estate, Purkersdorf bei Wien, A

1999 Liftstation | Ski lift station, Lackenhof, A

1999 Bebauungsplan | Development plan, Kopstal – Op der Schanz, L

Revitalisierung Biedermeierhaus | Revitalisation of a Biedermeier house, Mollardgasse, Wien, A

Studie | Study, Linienamtsgasse Wien, A

Büro- und Wohnhaus | Office and apartment building in Bratislava, SL

Bewerbungsverfahren Büro- und Kaufhaus | Application for commision for an office and department store building, Langenhagen, D; 1. Rang | 1st place

Seit 1999 Bebauungsplan | Development plan Luxembourg-Kirchberg, L

Nutzungskonzept Kraftwerk | Concept for the use of a power station, Wehrden, D

Büro und Wohnen | Office and residential development, Modecenterstrasse/Guglgasse, Wien, A

Gleisdreieck, Wien, A

2000 Einfamilienhaus | Single family house, Giesshübel, A

WETTBEWERBE | COMPETITIONS

1979 „A House for K. F. Schinkel", Japan Architect; honorable mention

„Eigenheim – nicht Einzelheim" Wien | „A house of one's own – not a house on its own", Vienna; 1. Preis | 1st prize

1980 Rauchstrasse Berlin, D, 2. Preis | 2nd prize; IBA

1981 Feuerwehrhaus in Mödling bei Wien | Fire brigade station in Mödling, near Vienna, A; 2. Preis | 2nd prize

1984 Schulzentrum in Wien | School centre in Vienna, A; Ankauf | mention

Aussichtsturm | observation tower in Dudelange, L; 1. Preis | 1st prize

Anhalterbahnhof Berlin, D

1985 Handelsakademie in Wien | Commercial College, Vienna, A

Wohnungsbau und Platzgestaltung in Wien | Housing and open space, Vienna, A

Umgestaltung des Schlosses Collart | Redesign of Schloss Collart in Bettemburg, L; 1. Preis | 1st prize

1986 Capital area in St. Paul, Minnesota, USA

1987 Feuerwehr | Fire brigade station, Salzburg, A

1988 Wohnanlage | Housing development in Linz, A; Ankauf | mention

Auszeichnung (Zollstation Autobahn Luxembourg–Trier) für die schönste Stahlkonstruktion | Award for the finest steel structure (Toll station on the Luxembourg–Trier motorway): CBLIA Staalprijs – Bruxelles, B

1989 Kuranlage | Spa resort Bad Tatzmannsdorf, A

Österreichischer Pavillon für die Weltausstellung | Austrian EXPO pavilion in Sevilla

1990 Luxemburger Pavillon für die Weltausstellung | Luxembourg Pavilion for the EXPO in Sevilla; 2. Preis | 2nd prize

Wohnbau | Apartment block in Rémerwée, L; 1. Preis | 1st prize

Wohn- und Geschäftszentrum | Housing and commercial development in Saarbrücken, D

Wohnanlage | Housing development auf dem Kirchberg, Luxembourg, L; 1. Preis | 1st prize

1991 Gestaltung der Fußgängerzone vor dem Großherzöglichen Palais | Design of the pedestrian zone in front of the Grand Ducal Palace in Luxembourg, L; 1. Preis | 1st prize
„Centre Mondial de la Paix" in Verdun, F; 2. Preis | 2nd prize
Wohnhausanlage | Housing development in Wien, A; Ankauf | mention
Krematorium | Crematorium in Hamm, L; 2. Preis | 2nd prize
Hotel & Dienstleistungskomplex | Hotel and service industry complex Dessau, D; 5. Preis | 5th prize

1992 Kinderhaus | Childrens' House in Trier, D; Ankauf | mention
Wohn- und Geschäftshaus | Housing and commercial building, Luxembourg, L
Städtebaulicher Ideenwettbewerb | Urban ideas competition, Folsterhöhe, Saarbrücken, D: 5. Preis | 5th prize
Städtebaulicher Ideenwettbewerb | Urban ideas competition Cents, L
Internationaler Ideenwettbewerb | International ideas competition Hauptstadt Berlin-Spreebogen, D
Geladener Ideenwettbewerb | Invited entry ideas competition Expo 2000, Hannover, D

1993 Geladener Wettbewerb | Invited entry competition Dortmunder Union Brauerei, D
Geladener Wettbewerb | Invited entry competition Hindenburgplatz, Münster, D
Städtebaulicher Ideenwettbewerb Stadterweiterung | Ideas competition for urban expansion, Süssenbrunn, Wien, A

1994 Geladener Städtebaulicher Ideenwettbewerb „Wohnen und Arbeiten" | Invited entry competition „Living and Working", Wien, A
Geladen zum Internationalen Wettbewerb | International invited entry competition Museum Simeonstift in Trier, D
Staatspreis im Bereich Entwurf und Gestaltung | State prize in the field of planning and design, 1994, D

1995 Realisierungswettbewerb zur Errichtung eines Abgeordneten- und Ministerialdienstgebäudes | Competion for the erection of a building for parliamentarians and civil servants, Mainz, D
Luxemburger Architekturpreis für öffentliche Gebäude | Luxembourg architecture prize for public buildings
Architekturpreis | Architecture prize Sachsen-Anhalt, D
Bauträgerwettbewerb | Developers competition Kagran/West, Wien, A

1996 Sozialer Wohnbau – ehem. Schmidtstahlwerke | Local authority housing – former Schmidt Steel Works, Wien-Favoriten, A: 2. Preis | 2nd prize
Bauträgerwettbewerb | Developers competition, Gasometer Wien-Simmering, A
Schule | School Prandaugasse, Wien, A
Pflegeheim | nursing home in Wasserbillig, L
Realisierungswettbewerb Regierungsstandort | Government buildings competition Heinrich-Mann-Allee, Potsdam, D
Internationaler Wettbewerb Österreichische Botschaft | International competition for the Austrian Embassy in Berlin, D
Bauträgerwettbewerb | Developers competition, Franz-Jonas-Platz, Wien, A
Bauträgerwettbewerb Autofreies Wohnen | Developers competition, Living without the Car, Wien, A
Bauträgerwettbewerb | Developers competition Perfektastrasse, Wien, A 1. Preis | 1st prize
Fassadenplanung | Façade design Ekazent, Halle-Neustadt, D; 1. Preis | 1st prize

1997 Geladener Wettbewerb Philharmonie | Invited entry competition Philharmonic Building, Luxembourg-Kirchberg, L; 5. Preis | 5th prize
Multifunktionelle Halle | Multi-purpose hall, Linz, A
Städtebaulicher Ideenwettbewerb ehem. Kasernengelände | Urban planning ideas competition for the former barracks, Münster, D
Musée National d'Histoire et d'Art, Luxembourg, L; 3. Preis | 3rd prize
Verwaltungsgebäude | Administration building für die S.E.S., Betzdorf, L
Wiederaufbau von | Reconstruction of Schloss Bensberg in Köln, D
Wohnungen | Apartments in Köln, D
Musiktheater | Music theatre Linz, A
Geladener Wettbewerb | Invited entry competition Dr. Vogler, Zell/See, A

1998 Realisierungswettbewerb Neubau Verwaltungsgebäude für die | Competition for a new administration building for the Ciments S.A. in Esch/Alzette, L
Ideenwettbewerb Sozialer Wohnbau | Ideas competition for local authority housing, Rösslergasse, Wien, A
Ideenwettbewerb Stadt 2000 | Ideas competition City 2000, KDAG-Gründe, Wien, A; Ankauf | mention
SCS Cableliner, NÖ, A
Luxemburger Architekturpreis für die beste Realisierung aus Beton | Luxembourg architecture prize for the best concrete building

1999 Geladener Städtebaulicher Realisierungswettbewerb | Invited entry urban planning competition Hessentor, Neuss, D
Gutachten – Testprojekt | Expert report – test project KDAG Stadt 2000 – Wien, A
Studie | Study Linienamtsgasse, Wien, A
Studie | Study Modecenterstrasse, Wien, A
Expertenverfahren | Expert report Höchstädtplatz „Castor und Pollux", Wien, A
Schwimmbad | Indoor swimming pool in Luxembourg-Bonnevoie, L; 1. Preis | 1st prize

2000 Geladener Wettbewerb Werkstatt und Tagesförderungszentrum für Behinderte | Invited entry competition for a workshop and day centre for the disabled, Neuwied, D
Geladener Wettbewerb Neubau Geschäfts- und Wohngebäude | Invited entry competition for a new housing and commercial development, Ernest-Thun-Strasse, Salzburg, A
Geladener Wettbewerb Umbau und Erweiterung eines Wohnstiftes | Invited entry competition for the redesign and extension of a housing foundation, Soleuvre, L
Mautner-Markhoff/Schlachthausgasse, Wien, A; 2. Rang | 2nd place
Geladener Wettbewerb Werkstatt und Tagesförderungszentrum für Behinderte | Invited entry competition for a workshop and day centre for the disabled, Flammersfeld, D
Gutachten – Überarbeitung Testprojekt | Expert report – reworking of the test project KDAG Stadt 2000, Wien, A
Geladener Wettbewerb städtebauliche Erweiterung des Bahnhofsbereiches | Invited entry urban planning competition for the expansion of the railway station district, Esch/Alzette, L
Wettbewerb | Competition Interspar, Linz, A
Geladener Wettbewerb | Invited entry competition Commerzbank Am Kirchberg, L; 1. Rang | 1st place
Geladener Wettbewerb Wohnheim für Senioren | Invited entry competition for an old persons home, Château Heisdorf, L; 1. Rang | 1st place
Geladenes Expertenverfahren | Invited entry expert report process, Brauerei Liesing, Wien, A; 2. Rang | 2nd place

VERÖFFENTLICHUNGEN | PUBLICATIONS

Neue Achitekturdarstellung, D, 79/80, p.102,
    Parlamentsgebäude in Luxemburg und
    Haus für K. F. Schinkel
The Japan Architect, JP, 2/80, p.22,
    La rénovation du château Collart à
    Bettembourg
Luxemburger Wort, L, 12/80, p.4,
    Architekturwettbewerb in Berlin
Luxemburger Land, L, 8/81, p.8,
    A House for K. F. Schinkel
    (mention honorable)
Luxemburger Land, L, 12/81, p.12,
    Internationale Bau-Ausstellung Berlin
    1984
Luxemburger Wort, L, 2/82, p.5,
    Neuerscheinung, Athos der heilige Berg
Le Républicain Lorrain, F, 4/82, p.5,
    Rond Point Schuman, Luxemburg
Wettbewerbe, A, 5/83, p.15,
    Stadtvillen am Tiergarten Berlin, Haus 7
Luxemburger Wort, L, 3/84, p.4,
    Universität Nancy Ausstellung „Jeunes
    Architectes"
Le Journal de Nancy, F, 3/84,
    Valentiny et Hermann:
    l'architecture illustrée
Lotus international, I, 4/84, p.22,
    Stadtvilla in der Rauchstraße, Berlin
Architektur- & Bauforum, A, 5/84, p.17,
    Stadtvilla in der Rauchstraße, Berlin
Stadt (Berlin), D, 8/84, p.21,
    Stadtvilla in der Rauchstraße, Berlin
Wettbewerbe, A, 10/84, p.42,
    Neubau einer HBLA, HAK und
    Berufsschule, Wien
Weekend a Visen, NL, 11/84,
    Stadtvilla in der Rauchstrasse, Berlin
A&V, E, 2/85, p.68,
    Casa 7 Berlin
Journal, L, 2/85, p.10,
    Ausstellung im städtischen Cercle-Gebäude
Luxemburger Wort, L, 3/85, p.5,
    Ausstellung „Hermann & Valentiny
    Zeichnungen"
Le Républicain Lorrain, L, 3/85 p.4,
    Exposition Hermann et Valentiny au
    cercle municipal
Journal, L, 3/85 p.12,
    Hermann & Valentiny Zeichnungen
Revue, L, 4/85, p.36,
    Luxemburger Architekten krempeln
    europäische Städte um
Art, D, 4/85 p.56,
    Stadtvilla in der Rauchstraße, Berlin
Neue Zeitung Graz, A, 4/85,
    Architekturzeichnungen mit Witz und
    Können: H & V im Forum Stadtpark
Urbanisme, F, 6/85, p.68,
    Le quartier des diplomates à Berlin
Wettbewerbe, A, 6,7/85, p.50,
    Wohnen und Stadterneuerung, Wien 2
Tageblatt, L, 7/85, p.13,
    Architektenwettbewerb um das
    Bettemburger Collart-Schloß

Le Républicain Lorrain, F, 7/85, p.7,
    Concours de l'aménagement du château
    Collart
Luxemburger Wort, L, 7/85,
    Gewinner des nationalen Wettbewerbes
    zur Restaurierung des Collartschlosses
    ermittelt
Bauwelt, D, 8/85, p.1259,
    Zwischen Mies und Memphis – Stadtvilla
    Rauchstraße
Casa, I, 8/85 p.124,
    Otto architetti per un blocco aperto
    (Berlin Stadtvilla)
Le Républicain Lorrain, F, 8/85, p.4,
    La rénovation du château Collart à
    Bettembourg
Habiter, CH, 10/85, p.14,
    Maison unifamiliale
Wettbewerbe, A, 12/85, p.22,
    Haus Hermann Wien
Wettbewerbe, A, 12/85, p.79,
    Stadtvillen am Tiergarten Berlin, Haus 7
AMC, F, 12/85, p.70,
    Berlin, Rauchstraße
Baumeister, D, 1/86, p.28,
    Stadtvilla in der Rauchstraße, Berlin
Bauwelt, D, 3/86, p.324,
    Haus aus dem Haus
Tageblatt, L, 3/86, p.4,
    Ausstellung im städtischen Cercle-Gebäude
Wettbewerbe, A, 4/86 p.28,
    Turm Mont St. Jean in Dudelange
Wettbewerbe, A, 4/86, p.98,
    Neubau eines Bundesschulzentrums in
    Wien 11
Architektur & Wettbewerbe, D, 6/86, p.13,
    Stadtvilla in der Rauchstraße, Berlin
Luxemburger Wort, L, 7/86,
    Leserbrief gegen den Rond Point Schuman
Domus, I, 8/86 p.9,
    Nella Torre, Schengen | The Markusturm
    near Schengen
Bauwelt, D, 8/86, p.1241,
    Den Ort bezeichnen
Journal, L, 8/86, p.2, R.-P. R. Schuman:
    Ein Projekt zum verhindern
Luxemburger Wort, L, 9/86, p.9,
    Leserbrief gegen den Rond Point Schuman
Tageblatt, L, 9/86, p.2,
    Kontroverse um den Rond Point Schuman
Luxemburger Wort, L, 10/86, p.19,
    Leserbrief gegen den Rond Point Schuman
Luxemburger Wort, L, 10/86, p.13,
    Für einen prächtigen Stadteingang an der
    Kirchberger Autobahn
Luxemburger Land, L, 10/86, p.13,
    À propos du Rond Point Schuman
Luxemburger Wort, L, 11/86, p.9,
    Gemeindehaus Bettembourg
Télécran, L, 11/86 p.36,
    Rond Point Schuman, Luxemburg
Revue, L, 11/86, p.14, Bettemburger Schloßherr-
    lichkeit als Gemeindezentrum
Wettbewerbe, A, 1/87, p.16-18,
    Architektenbüro Hermann & Valentiny in
    Remerschen

Wettbewerbe, A, 1/87 p.107,
    Hauptfeuerwache Salzburg
Der Aufbau, A, 2/87, p.105,
    Wettbewerb Chancen für den
    Donauraum Wien
Archiectural Design, GB, 6/87, p.16,
    Agricultural Shed, Itzig
Wettbewerbe, A, 6,7/87, p.40,
    Pavillon auf dem Galgenberg, Esch-Alzette
Luxemburger Land, L, 9/87, p.6,
    Das Point Schumann-Projekt
Architecture and Urbanism, JP, 10/87 p.125,
    House from House, Suburb of Vienna
Luxemburger Wort, L, 12/87,
    Rond Point Schuman, Luxemburg
Architektur- & Bauforum, A, 128/88, p.14-36,
    Hermann & Valentiny:
    Arbeiten 1980–1988
Triple Face, L, 88, p.70,
    Restauration du moulin Bestgen à
    Schifflange und de la fabrique de
    chaussures à Tetange
Entwürfe für Wien, A, 88, p.30,
    Wohnbau Erlachgasse
Le Républicain Lorrain, F, 1/88,
    Rond Point Schuman, Luxemburg
Architecture and Urbanism, JP, 2/88, p.9,
    Tower of Mount St. Jean und Markus
    Tower, Schengen
Petite Crème, L, 6/88, p.29,
    Arc de Triomphe Rond Point Robert
    Schuman
Deutsche Bauzeitung, D, 7/88, p.30,
    Aussichtsturm Mont St. Jean in Dudelange
    und Markusturm in Schengen
Wettbewerbe, A, 7/88, p.16,
    Zollstation Wasserbillig
Luxemburger Land, L, 8/88, p.2,
    Zollstation Wasserbillig
Le Républicain Lorrain, F, 8/88, p.7,
    Moulin Bestgen, Schifflange
Luxemburger Wort, L, 11/88, p.8,
    Feierliche Einweihung des neuen
    Festsaales in Bettembourg
Le Républicain Lorrain, L, 11/88 p.8,
    Nouveau centre culturel à Bettembourg
Trierischer Volksfreund, D, 11/88, p.8,
    Trier als Einkaufsstadt muß erreichbar sein
Luxemburger Wort, L, 11/88,
    Concours 1988 des plus beaux ouvrages
    en acier
Revue, L, 12/88, p.14,
    Gemeindehaus Bettembourg
Baumeister, D, 1/89, p.66,
    Zollstation Wasserbillig
Wettbewerbe, A, 1/89, p.118,
    Wohnbebauung Linz-Ebelsberg / Ennsfeld
    OÖ
Le Républicain Lorrain, F, 3/89, p.4,
    Rond Point Schuman, Luxemburg
Luxemburger Wort, L, 5/89, p.5,
    Wer baut am europäischen Haus?
Art, D, 6/89, p.46,
    Gemeindehaus Bettembourg
Luxemburger Wort, L, 9/89, p.8,
    Neugestaltung an der Place de l'Etoile,
    Luxemburg

Tageblatt, L, 9/89, p. 9,
    Neugestaltung an der Place de l'Etoile,
    Luxemburg
Wettbewerbe, A, 9,10/89, p. 72,
    Revitalisierung Gutshof Collart,
    Bettembourg
Baumeister, D, 2/90, p. 29,
    Tutesall in Luxemburg
Bauwelt, D, 3/90, p. 488,
    Luxemburg: Umbau eines Arbeitssaales
Baumeister, D, 7/90, p. 33,
    Grenzübergang Wasserbillig
Revue, L, 1991, p. 49,
    Architekturbiennale in Venedig
Luxemburger Wort, L, 3/91, p. 5,
    Eine sinnliche und poetische Architektur
Luxembuger Land, L, 3/91 p. 13,
    L'axe Vienne – Luxembourg
Tageblatt, L, 3/91, p. 10,
    Raumpoesien von
    Hermann und Valentiny
Journal, L, 3/91, p. 14,
    Die Türme der zwei Architekten
Salzburger Nachrichten, A, 5/91,
    Der neue Gestaltungsbeirat stellt sich vor
Falter, A, 8/91, p. 25,
    Architektur zwischen den Zeiten,
    Erlachgasse Wien 10
Luxemburger Wort, L, 9/91, p. 4,
    Les architectes Hermann et Valentiny
    à la Biennale à Venise
Luxemburger Wort, L, 10/91, p. 6,
    Hermann & Valentiny in Venedig
City Luxembourg, L, 10/91, p. 26,
    Le Luxembourg en vedette à Venise
Télécran, L, 10/91, p. 10,
    H & V in Venedig
Voilà Luxembourg, L, 11/91, p. 102,
    Biennale d'architecture à Venise
Cobowr, NL, 11/91,
    Stadtvilla in der Rauchstrasse, Berlin
Luxemburger Wort, L, 1/92,
    Baustelle für 32 Sozialwohnungen
    eröffnet
Le Républicain Lorrain, F, 1/92, p. 3,
    32 nouveaux appartements à
    Grevenmacher
Výtvarný Zivot, Pol, 1/92, p. 52,
    Tutesall in Luxemburg und Turm Mont
    St. Jean in Dudelange
Wettbewerbe, A, 1,2/92, p. 62,
    Wohnbau Erlachgasse Wien 10
Abitare, I, 3/92, p. 120,
    Exposition Hermann et Valentiny à la
    gallerie Clairefontaine
Nedel'ny Telegraf, Bras., 8/92, p. 4,
    Architekturvisionen
L'industria delle costruzioni, I, 8/92, p. 82,
    Neuerscheinung H & V bei Karl Krämer
L'industria delle costruzioni, I, 11/92, p. 56,
    Arbeiten von H & V
Perspektiven, A, 5/93, p. 26,
    Zubau einer Volks- und Hauptschule,
    Schweglerstraße, Wien 15
Brau und Brunnen, D, 10/93, p. 40,
    Das Dortmunder U

Wettbewerbe, A, 12/93, p. 52,
    Volks- & Hauptschule
    Schwegelerstraße, Wien
Baumeister, D, 4/94, p. 53,
    Anna-Haus in Remerschen
Architekturzentrum Wien, Workshop-Bericht, A,
    4/94, Pragerstraße
Trierischer Volksfreund, L, 7/94, p. 9,
    Grenzübergang Wasserbillig wird in
    Tankstelle umgebaut
Bild, D, 8/94, p. 3,
    5 moderne Neubauhäuser in Neu-Halle
Mitteldeutscher Express, D, 8/94, p. 14,
    Büro & Hotelkomplex in Halle-Neustadt
Mitteldeutsche Zeitung, D, 8/94, p. 10,
    Steigenberger Esprix Hotel in
    Halle-Neustadt
Bild, D, 8/94 p. 3,
    Steigenberger eröffnet im Februar 95
Mitteldeutsche Zeitung, D, 8/94, p. 13,
    5 moderne Neubauhäuser in Neu-Halle
Wettbewerbe aktuell, A, 9,10/94, p. 56,
    Steinergasse, Wien 23
Mitteldeutsche Zeitung, D, 10/94, p. 20,
    Steigenberger Esprix Hotel in
    Halle-Neustadt
Revue, L, 12/94, p. 60,
    Luxemburger Architekturpreis
    erste Auflage
Häuser, D, 1/95, p. 38,
    und so was nennt sich Siedlungshaus
Mitteldeutscher Express, D, 2/95,
    Steigenberger Esprix Hotel in
    Halle-Neustadt Eröffnung
Mitteldeutsche Zeitung, D, 2/95, p. 15,
    Steigenberger Esprix Hotel in
    Halle-Neustadt
Bild, D, 2/95,
    Steigenberger Esprix Hotel in
    Halle-Neustadt Eröffnung
Mitteldeutsche Zeitung, D, 4/95, p. 13,
    Steigenberger Esprix Hotel in
    Halle-Neustadt Eröffnung
Häuser, D, 4/95, p. 88,
    Anna-Haus in Remerschen
Luxemburger Wort, L, 9/95, p. 18,
    Hermann et Valentiny exposent à la
    galerie Clairefontaine
Luxemburger Land, L, 9/95, p. 16,
    Hermann et Valentiny exposent à la
    galerie Clairefontaine
Le Républicain Lorrain, F, 10/95, p. 4,
    Hermann et Valentiny exposent à la
    galerie Clairefontaine
Revue, L, 10/95, p. 86,
    Architektenduo zwischen Wien und
    Luxemburg
Architektur aktuell, A, 11,12/95, p. 11,
    Luxemburgischer Architekturpreis
    an H&V vergeben
Callwey-Verlag, D, 11,12/95 p. 10,
    Buchvorstellung: Wolfgang Bachmann:
    Hermann & Valentiny

Télécran, L, 12/95, p. 16,
    Steigenberger Esprix Hotel in
    Halle-Neustadt
Mitteldeutsche Zeitung, D, 12/95, p. 10,
    Steigenberger Esprix Hotel in
    Halle-Neustadt
BIO OAI, L, 12/95, p. 7,
    Ambassade Luxembourgeoise à Vienne
Journal, L, 12/95, p. 11,
    Architekturpreis Sachsen-Anhalt 1995
Luxemburger Wort, L, 12/95,
    Architekturpreis Sachsen-Anhalt 1995
Télécran, L, 12/95, p. 16,
    Hotel in Halle
De Gemeenebuet, L, 1/96, p. 2,
    Gemeindehaus Bech-Kleinmacher
Deutsche Bauzeitschrift, D, 2/96, p. 51,
    Gemeindehaus Bech-Kleinmacher
Baumeister, D, 2/96, p. 8,
    Steigenberger Esprix Hotel in
    Halle-Neustadt
Baumeister, D, 2/96, p. 8,
    Luxemburgische Botschaft in Wien
Baumeister, D, 2/96, p. 18,
    Neuerscheinung H & V bei Callwey
Beton Zement, A, 3/96, p. 36,
    Gemeindehaus Bech-Kleinmacher
Beton Zement Sonderbuch, A, p. 32,
    Klosterneuburg
Architektur, D, 3/96, p. 12,
    Neuerscheinung H & V bei Callwey
Perspektiven, A, 3,4/96, p. 21,
    Die Ästhetik von Ingenieurbauten –
    Die Gasometer in Simmering
Architektur aktuell, A, 4/96, p. 54,
    Körper, Schichten und Material
Frankfurter Allgemeine, D, 4/96, p. 42,
    Luxemburgische Botschaft in Wien
Tageblatt, L, 4/96, p. 24,
    Gemeindehaus Bech-Kleinmacher
BIO OAI, L, 4/96, p. 14,
    Conférence à la Banque de Luxembourg
Luxemburger Land, L, 4/96, p. 11,
    Luxemburgische Botschaft in Wien
Luxemburger Wort, L, 4/96, p. 4,
    Architektur als gestalterischer Prozeß
Architektur Aktuell, A, 4/96, p. 54,
    Hotel Steigenberger-Esprix in Halle und
    Gemeindehaus Bech-Kleinmacher
Deutsche Bauzeitschrift, D, 4/96, p. 85,
    Werkstattbericht Hermann & Valentiny
Tageblatt, L, 4/96, p. 6,
    H&V de l'architecture-aventure
Wettbewerbe, A, 5/96, p. 81,
    Wohnbebauung ehemaliger Schmidstahl-
    werke, Wien 10
Der Standard, A, 5/96, p. 7,
    Gasometerprojekt in Wien-Simmering
Die Presse, A, 5/96,
    Gasometerprojekt in Wien-Simmering
Architektur Aktuell, A, 6/96, p. 106,
    Porzellangeschäft Thun-Hohenstein
Architektur, D, 6/96, p. 92,
    Gasometerprojekt in Wien-Simmering
AIT, D, 6/96, p. 46,
    Hotel Steigenberger-Esprix in Halle

Profil, A, 6/96, p. 93,
  Seltsame Gehäuse
Die Presse, A, 7/96, p. 9,
  Was bleibt wenn nichts bleibt –
  Gasometerprojekt in Wien-Simmering
BIO OAI, L, 7/96, p. 15,
  Gasometerprojekt in Wien-Simmering
Bundesbaublatt, D, 10/96, p. 770,
  Steigenberger Esprix Hotel in
  Halle-Neustadt
Wettbewerbe, A, 10,11/96, p. 103,
  Franz Jonasplatz, Wien 21
Luxemburger Wort, L, 1/97,
  Mies van der Rohe Pavillon Award
Revue, L, 1/97, p. 34,
  Galerie Clairefontaine
Die Zeit, D, 4/97, p. 52,
  Steigenberger Esprix Hotel in
  Halle-Neustadt
Kurier, A, 5/97, p. 4,
  Nach der Jury muß Ökohaus auch
  Bewohner überzeugen
Mitteldeutsche Zeitung, D, 6/97,
  Die moderne Architektur im Blickpunkt
Anhaltiner Sonntag, D, 6/97,
  Die moderne Architektur im Blickpunkt
Architektur, D, 6/97, p. 28,
  Wettbewerb für die luxemburgische
  Staatsphilharmonie
Trierischer Volksfreund, D, 7/97, p. 10,
  Neugestaltung des Rindertanzplatzes
Trier Rathaus Zeitung, D, 7/97, p. 3,
  Neugestaltung des Rindertanzplatzes
Wettbewerbe, A, 7,8/97, p. 47/77,
  Sechs kleine Neubauplätze Parzelle C
Luxemburger Wort, L, 8/97, p. 4,
  Ubu Roi von François Valentiny
  in Bonnevoie
Tageblatt, L, 8/97, p. 11,
  Ubu Roi von François Valentiny
  in Bonnevoie
Luxemburger Wort, L, 10/97, p. 6,
  Ubu Roi von François Valentiny
  in Bonnevoie
De Feierkrop, L, 10/97, p. 2,
  Kritik zum Projekt
  „Fisch in der Mosel an der Hettermillen"
NÖ Nachrichten, A, 11/97, p. 27,
  Grossauer Villenbau erregt die Gemüter
Architektur aktuell, A, 12/97, p. 108,
  Wohnen mit Ausblick
Deutsche Bauzeitschrift, D, 12/97, p. 41,
  Einfamilienhaus in Klosterneuburg
Télécran, L, 12/97, p. 32,
  Portrait François Valentiny
Beton Zement, D, 97, p. 32,
  Haus am Seitweg, Klosterneuburg
Spiegel, D, 1/98,
  Wohnanlage für Senioren auf
  historischem Grund, Köln
Licht & Architektur, D, 1/98, p. 25,
  Galerie Clairefontaine, Luxemburg
Mitteldeutsche Zeitung, D, 2/98,
  Multiplex-Kino in Halle-Neustadt
Kölner Stadt-Anzeiger, D, 2/98, p. 15,
  Wohnanlage für Senioren auf
  historischem Grund, Köln

Architektur Aktuell, A, 4/98, p. 82,
  Wohnbauten Dudelange,
  Galerie Clairefontaine, Haus Ierace
AMC le moniteur architecture, F, 5/98, p. 82/83,
  Maison avec vue – Klosterneuburg,
  Autriche
Verlag für Bauwesen, D, 98, p. 58-67,
  Holz Variationen/Mischkonstruktionen in
  Holz, Stein, Glas, Stahl
Die Presse, A, 5/98, p. 9,
  Umbau eines Einfamilienhauses
  in Salzburg
Luxemburger Wort, L, 10/98,
  Mention Béton für Hermann & Valentiny
Deutsche Bauzeitschrift, D, 10/98, p. 81,
  Büroanbau in Remerschen
Revue, L, 10/98, p. 52,
  Prix luxembourgeois
  d'architecture 98 (mention béton)
Licht & Architektur, D, 2/99, p. 43,
  Sporthalle Diekirch
Zement Beton, A, 2/99, p. 25,
  Haus mit zwei Gesichtern
Wettbewerbe, A, 1,2,3/99, p. 144,
  Stadt 2000, KDAG-Gründe Wien 12
Cement, NL, 3/99, p. 47,
  Gemeindehaus Bech-Kleinmacher
Architecture & Bâtiments, L, 4/99, p. 30,
  Sporthalle Diekirch
Baumeister, D, 7/99,
  Büro Hermann & Valentiny Remerschen
Baumeister, D, 8/99,
  Spezialheft Luxemburg: Sporthalle Lyceum
  Diekirch
Wettbewerbe, A, 9,10/99, p. 59,
  Höchstädtplatz Wien 20
News, A, 10/99, p. 128,
  Lofts in der Brotfabrik
De Feierkrop, L, 10/99, p. 2,
  Stararchitekt Fränz Valentino hat wieder
  zugeschlagen
Luxemburger Wort, L, 10/99, p. 15,
  Einweihung des ausgebauten
  Gemeindehauses in Dalheim
Le Républicain Lorrain, F, 10/99, p. 6,
  Une piscine neuve pour Bonnevoie
Luxemburger Wort, L, 10/99, p. 11,
  Neue Schwimmhalle besticht durch Form
  und Funktionalität
Tageblatt, L, 10/99, p. 20,
  Neues Schwimmbad für Bonneweg
Tageblatt, L, 10/99, p. 33,
  Vergrößertes Gemeindeamt sorgt
  für Diskussion
Journal, L, 10/99, p. 21,
  Erster Preis für die
  Bonneweger Badeanstalt
Luxemburger Wort, L, 10/99,
  Dalheim, höchste Zeit, um unser
  Schweigen zu brechen
Luxemburger Wort, L, 10/99,
  In Dalheim tut sich was
Télécran, L, 10/99, p. 33,
  Rathaus Dalheim – Schön oder nicht
  schön

Die Presse, A, 11/99, p. 11,
  Kindergarten von Hermann & Valentiny
  in Bettembourg
NÖ gestalten, A, 11/99, p. 18,
  Wohnen mit Ausblick
Tageblatt, L, 12/99, p. 20,
  Einweihung des ausgebauten
  Gemeindehauses in Dalheim
BIO OAI, L, 12/99, p. 11,
  Lauréat du concours piscine à Bonnevoie
Luxemburger Wort, L, 12/99, p. 13,
  Einweihung des ausgebauten
  Gemeindehauses in Dalheim
Le Républicain Lorrain, F, 12/99, p. 2,
  Dalheim inaugure sa maison communale
Architecture & bâtiments, L, 3/00, p. 33,
  Lycée Classique Diekirch
Wettbewerbe, A, 4,5,6/00, p. 200,
  Schwimmbad Luxemburg-Bonnevoie
Callwey, D, 4/00, p. 36,
  Häuser am Hang – Janusköpfig
Mitteldeutsche Zeitung, D, 9/2000, p. 14,
  Einkaufen im Schiffsbauch
Die Presse, A, 10/00, Spectrum p. 14,
  Backstein und Streckmetall
Dividende, A, 10/00, p. 38,
  Brotfabrik in Wien wird zu einem Zentrum
  für Kreativität
Revue, L, 10/00, p. 34,
  Wohnstifte Köln und Mainz
Architektur Aktuell, A, 1-2/2001, Titelseite, p. 46
  Im Bauch der Architektur, oder: Wien ein
  Architekturbüro lernte, die Farbe zu lieben
Wettbewerbe, A, 2-3/2001, p. 98
  Brauerei Liesing, Wien 23
Die Presse, A, 4/2001, p. 43
  Die Transformation einer Brotfabrik

BÜCHER | BOOKS

Hubert Hermann & Francy Valentiny,
   Eigenverlag | published by the architects
   1980
Hermann & Valentiny, Monographie,
   Karl Krämer Verlag, Stuttgart 1991
Hermann & Valentiny, Monographie,
   Edition Baumeister, Callwey Verlag,
   München 1995

AUSSTELLUNGEN | EXHIBITIONS

1975 Kleine Galerie, Wien, A

1980 Zentralvereinigung der Architekten Österreichs | Central Association of Architects in Austria
Sommerakademie | Summer Academy in Salzburg, A

1981 Sommerakademie | Summer Academy in Salzburg, A

1982 Ecole d'Architecture de Nancy, F
Ecole d'Architecture de Strasbourg, F

1985 Cercle municipal de Luxembourg, L
Forum Stadtpark Graz, A
IBA-Ausstellung | IBA exhibition, Gropiusbau, Berlin, D
Architekturmuseum Frankfurt, D

1986 Kulturtage in Karlsruhe, D
Max Protech-Gallery, New York, USA

1989 Architektenkammer | Chamber of Architects, Wien, A
Cercle municipal de Luxembourg, L

1990 Sommerakademie | Summer Academy in Luxembourg, L
Galerie Clairefontaine in Luxembourg, L

1991 Teilnahme als Vertreter Luxembourgs an der Architekturbiennale in Venedig | Representatives of Luxembourg at the Venice Architecture Biennale, I
Galerie Clairefontaine in Luxembourg, L

1994 Bilder und Skulpturen | Paintings and sculptures, Galerie Luger, Wien, A
Ausstellung „Raumpoesien" – Initiative Architektur | Exhibition "Spatial Poetry" – Initiative Architecture, Salzburg, A

1995 Galerie Clairefontaine in Luxembourg, L
Teilnahme an der Triennale | Participants in the Triennale, Milano, I

1996 Banque du Luxembourg, L
Ecole d'Architecture de Nancy, F

1998 Sammelausstellung | Group exhibition
Galerie Clairefontaine in Luxembourg, L

2001 Sonderausstellung „Architektur in Luxemburg" im „Ausstellungszentrum im Ringturm", Wien | Special exhibition "Architecture in Luxembourg" in "Ausstellungszentrum im Ringturm", Vienna

VORTRÄGE | LECTURES

Internationale Sommerakademie Salzburg, Universität für angewandte Kunst, Wien; Ecole d'Architecture, St-Luc Gent; Ecole d'Architecture St-Luc, Brugge, Liège; Ecole d'Architecture de Nancy, Ordre des Architectes de Luxembourg; Technische Hochschule Darmstadt; Institut für Kunstgeschichte Tübingen; Gastvorlesungen | visiting lecturers in Portland, Seattle, Wash.; Technische Universität Graz; Ceske vysoke uceni technicke v Praze; Fondation de l'Architecture et de l'Ingénierie, Luxembourg; Hochschule Bochum; Hochschule Wuppertal; Architektenkammer Sachsen-Anhalt Magdeburg; Hochschule für Technik, Wirtschaft und Kultur, Leipzig; FH-München; FH-Erfurt; Wissen-Aktuell in Wien.

SEMINARE | SEMINARS

Ecole d'Architecture de Nancy; Fachhochschule Trier; Ceske vysoke uceni technicke v Praze; Sommerakademie | Summer Academy Luxemburg; Gastprofessur an der Hochschule für Technik,Wirtschaft und Kultur | Visiting professors on Hochschule für Technik, Wirtschaft und Kultur, Leipzig; Workshop Regensburg; Workshop Donaukanal – Strategie zur Belebung des Donaukanals | Strategy for the revitalisation of the Danube Canal.

BIOGRAFIEN | BIOGRAPHIES

Mag. arch. Hubert Hermann
1955 geboren in Wiener Neustadt, Österreich
Architekturstudium an der Universität für angewandte Kunst in Wien bei Prof. Wilhelm Holzbauer
Förderungspreis des Bundesministeriums für Wissenschaft und Forschung, Wien
Seit 1980 Partner von François Valentiny
1984–85 Assistent an der Universität für angewandte Kunst in Wien
1987–92 Gastdozent an der Fachhochschule, Abteilung Architektur, in Trier

Mag. arch. Hubert Hermann
1955 born in Wiener Neustadt, Austria
studied architecture at the University of Applied Arts in Vienna under Prof. Wilhelm Holzbauer
awarded a scholarship by the Federal Ministry for Science and Research, Vienna
since 1980 in partnership with François Valentiny
1984–85 assistant at the University of Applied Arts in Vienna
1987–92 visiting lecturer at the University of Applied Sciences, Department of Architecture, Trier

Mag. arch. François J. V. Valentiny
1953 geboren in Remerschen, Luxemburg
Architekturstudium an der Ecole d'Architecture de Nancy und an der Universität für angewandte Kunst in Wien bei Prof. Wilhelm Holzbauer
Förderungspreis des Bundesministeriums für Wissenschaft und Forschung, Wien
Seit 1980 Partner von Hubert Hermann
1980–81 Assistent an der Internationalen Sommerakademie Salzburg
1987–92 Gastdozent an der Fachhochschule, Abteilung Architektur in Trier
1991 bis 1994 Mitglied des Gestaltungsbeirates der Stadt Salzburg
Seit 1997 Mitglied des Architektur- und Städtebeirates der Stadt Trier
Seit 2000 Gastprofessor an der Hochschule für Technik, Wirtschaft und Kultur in Leipzig
Seit 2000 Mitglied im Beirat des Deutschen Architektur Museums in Frankfurt

Mag. arch. François J. V. Valentiny
1953 born in Remerschen, Luxembourg
studied architecture at the Ecole d'Architecture de Nancy and at the University of Applied Arts in Vienna under Prof. Wilhelm Holzbauer
awarded a scholarship by the Federal Ministry for Science and Research, Vienna
since 1980 in partnership with Hubert Hermann
1980–81 assistant at the International Summer Academy Salzburg
1987–92 visiting lecturer at the University of Applied Sciences, Department of Architecture, Trier
1991–94 member of the design advisory committee of the city of Salzburg
since 1997 member of the architecture and city advisory committee of the city of Trier
since 2000 professorship at the University of Technology, Economics and Cultural Affairs in Leipzig
Since 2000 member of the advisory board of the German Architecture Museum in Frankfurt

PARTNER SEIT | SINCE 1997
Dipl. Ing. Arch. Axel Christmann
1963 geboren in Trier, Deutschland
Studium der Germanistik und Philosophie an der Universität Trier
Architekturstudium an der Fachhochschule des Landes Rheinland-Pfalz / Trier

1963 born in Trier, Germany
studied German and philosophy at the University of Trier studied architecture at the University of Applied Sciences of the State of Rhineland-Palatinate in Trier

PARTNER SEIT | SINCE 1997
Dipl. Ing. Arch., Dipl. Des. Thomas Letz
1958 geboren in Frankfurt/Main, Deutschland
Innenarchitektur- und Architekturstudium an der Fachhochschule des Landes Rheinland-Pfalz / Trier

1958 born in Frankfurt/Main, Germany
studied interior design and architecture at the University of Applied Sciences of the State of Rhineland-Palatinate in Trier

PARTNER SEIT | SINCE 2000
Dipl. Ing. Werner Feltes
1970 geboren in Trier, Deutschland
Architekturstudium an der Fachhochschule des Landes Rheinland-Pfalz / Trier

1970 born in Trier, Germany
studied architecture at the University of Applied Sciences of the State of Rhineland-Palatinate in Trier

PARTNERIN SEIT | PARTNER SINCE 2001
mgr inz. arch. Marijana Popovic
1963 geboren in Valjevo, Jugoslawien
Architekturstudium Polytechnikum Warschau

1963 born in Valjevo, Yugoslavia
studied architecture at the Warsaw Polytechnic

MITARBEITER DER BÜROS HERMANN & VALENTINY IN WIEN UND LUXEMBURG | ASSISTANTS IN THE HERMANN & VALENTINY OFFICES IN VIENNA AND LUXEMBOURG

Dipl. Ing. Oliver Arenz
Dipl. Ing. Sabine Ehrich
Dipl. Ing. Vera Schülke
Dipl. Ing. Daniela Flor
Dipl. Des. GG Kirchner
Dipl. Ing. Katja Norwig
Dipl. Ing. Thuy Phati
Dipl. Ing. Vera Schülke
Dipl. Ing. Manuela Vanck
Dipl. Ing. Manfred Wagner

Josef Benzmüller
Claude Giger
Nicole Harmsma
Paul Majerus
Marie France Matz
Ana Dos Santos
Sylvia Traxler

Kourosh AFHAMI – Suzanne AIGNER – Klaus APPELT – Michael AUGUSTIN – Stefan Bach – Carmen BARTHELMY – Claudia BASTUCK – Stefan BECKER – Anne Marie BLUM – Ralf BOCK – Bébé BRANSS – Anne BUCHLER – Marco CANU – Patrick CAPESIUS – Thomas CARENTZ – Anna-Rita CEDRONI – Johakim CLEMENS – Jeanne COLLING – Grethe CONNERTH – Ralf COUSSÉ – Friedrich DANGELMAIER – Cihan DANISMAN – Friederike DÜREN – Angelika EDALATI – Alfred EICHBERGER – Elke ESCHERICH – Gundula FELLER – Jörg FISCHER – Peter FRANK – Sonja FRIEDERICH – Sonja GENGLER – Sharon GERSPACH – Liette GÖRGEN – Anke GOLL – Klaas GORIS – Karl-Heinz GRELL – Conny GROSSER – Susanne GRÜNER – Paul GRUNDEI – Marc GUBBINI – Frank HARTMANN – Danielle HAUPERT – Edgar HAUSER – Dirk HAUSMANN – Mario HEIN – Diane HEIREND – Tom HEMMEN – Alexandra HEYDT – Alexa HOFFMANN – Ulf HOLLER – Alain JACQUEMART – Monika JOST – Iris KAINZ – Rainer KASIK – Beate KATHÖFER – Marie KETTER – Karin KIST – Ira KLÖPPNER – Thorsten KNEDEL – Claudia KÖNIG – Alexander KÖRÖSZI – Michael KRIETSCH – Martin LEHNEN – Jörg LENSCHOW – Christoph LINSCHEIDT – Katia LUBIBOGOFF – Marie Hélène LUCAS – Caroline LUZI – Susanna MAUSS – Sonja MEUTES – Colum MULHERN – Christine MULLER – Petra OLY-SCHILLING – Johann OSTERRIEDER – Renella PALMER – Michel PETIT – Georg RALL – Françoise RAMAIOLI – Mario REINERT – Sabine REISER – Reinhold RENN – Birgit RUBACH – Maurizio SABINI – Christiane SACHSE – Guy SCHILTZ – Robert SCHMIDT – Andreas SCHMITZER – Jens SCHULZ – Jonina SIGURDARDOTTIR – Sergio SOTO – Maria SPADA – Laura SPINADEL – Marc-Olivier STELLWAG – Thorsten STRAUSS – Bob STROTZ – Regina SZUCSITS – Ilektra THEODOSIOU – Monika TRESSEL – Fernand VALENTINY – Alain VAN AERDE – Armin WALD – Manfred WEBER – Michael WENZL – Reinhard WIMMER – Simone WINKLER – Frank WOLFERS – Kurt ZWEIFEL

Fotonachweis | photo credits

G. G. Kirchner: 12, 14, 15, 17, 18 (2x), 19, 21, 26, 27, 29, 30 (2x), 31, 40, 41, 54, 55 (2x), 62, 63 (2x), 64-67, 88, 91, 118, 119, 121-125, 127, 128, 130, 136, 137, 139-143, 144 (2x), 145-155, 160, 161 (2x), 162-165, 167-171, 174-177, 179-187, 190, 191, 194 (3x), 195, 196, 198-201, 203, 205, 206 (2x), 207-209, 211, 216, 220-225, 226 (4x), 227, 228/229

Monique Heintz: 13, 36 (2x), 37-39, 47, 68 (3x), 72, 73, 78 (3x), 79, 82, 83, 84 (2x), 85, 87 (2x), 92, 94 (2x), 95, 97, 105 (2x), 106-109, 132, 133, 135 (2x), 156-158, 214, 215

Anna Blau: 32, 33, 35, 69, 71, 74, 76, 77, 81

Monika Nikolic: 42-46, 48/49, 50, 51 (2x), 52/53, 100-102, 103 (2x)

H & V: 10, 16, 110, 112, 237 (4x), 238 (16x), 239, 240

Monika Klinger: 237

Stefan Thurmann: 93, 96, 99